T0160643

To all who love the value of a
home-cooked family meal.

my Indian Kitchen

PREPARING DELICIOUS INDIAN MEALS WITHOUT FEAR OR FUSS

Hari Nayak

Photography by Jack Turkel

TUTTLE Publishing
Tokyo | Rutland, Vermont | Singapore

Published by Tuttle Publishing, an imprint of Periplus Editions (HK) Ltd

www.tuttlepublishing.com

ISBN 978-0-8048-4089-7

Distributed by

North America, Latin America & Europe
Tuttle Publishing
364 Innovation Drive
North Clarendon, VT 05759-9436 U.S.A.
Tel: 1 (802) 773-8930
Fax: 1 (802) 773-6993
info@tuttlepublishing.com
www.tuttlepublishing.com

Japan
Yaekari Building, 3rd Floor
5-4-12 Osaki; Shinagawa-ku
Tokyo 141-0032
Tel: (81) 3 5437-0171
Fax: (81) 3 5437-0755
sales@tuttle.co.jp
www.tuttle.co.jp

Asia Pacific
Berkeley Books Pte. Ltd.
61 Tai Seng Avenue, #02-12
Singapore 534167
Tel: (65) 6280-1330
Fax: (65) 6280-6290
inquiries@periplus.com.sg
www.periplus.com

15 14 13 12 11   1106CP
10 9 8 7 6 5 4 3 2

Printed in Singapore

Contents

Memories From My Indian Kitchen 8
Indian Food is More Than Just Curry 10
Pairing Wines with Indian Food 14
A Few Simple Techniques 16
Some Helpful Tools 20
Introduction to Indian Ingredients 22

Chapter 1
30 Indian Spice Mixes

Indian Five Spice Mix 31
Ginger-Garlic Paste 32
Red Masala Paste 32
Indian Grilling and Roasting Rub 33
Aromatic Spice Mix 33
Vindaloo Curry Paste 34
Dhaba Spice 34
Green Chili Masala 35
Home-Style Garam Masala 35
Chaat Masala 35

Chapter 2
36 Chutneys and Accompaniments

Plum-Tomato Chutney with Mustard
   Seeds 38
Garlic and Peanut Chutney 39
Mint Chutney 39
South Indian Coconut Chutney 40
Sweet Mango Chutney 41
Spicy Apricot Chutney 42
Cucumber and Onion Chaat 42
Spiced Garlic 43
Avocado and Roasted Cumin Raita 44
Cucumber and Yogurt Raita 45
Pineapple and Beet Raita 46
Carrot Yogurt Slaw 46
Green Mango Pickle 47

Chapter 3
48 Appetizers

Shrimp Bruschetta 50
Crispy Masala Fish Fingers 51
Crunchy Potato and Corn Croquettes 52
Spicy Paneer Cheese Kebabs 52
Spiced Meatballs 53
Smoky Eggplant Dip 54
Masala Pappadums 55
Pomegranate and Mint Potato Salad 56
Shrimp and Apple Salad 57
Samosas Three Ways 58
Split Pea Fritters 60
Potato and Onion Fritters 61
Moong Dal and Cucumber Salad 62
Fruit Chaat 63

Chapter 4
64 Soups and Dals

Broccoli Soup with Walnuts 66
Spinach Soup 67
Fiery South Indian Tomato Soup 67
Indian-Style Lentil Soup 68
Northern Chickpea Curry 69
Spicy Urad Beans 70
Yellow Mung Beans with Spinach 71
Black-Eyed Peas with Mushrooms 72
Spicy Mixed Beans and Lentils 73
Delicious Everyday Dal 74
Red Kidney Bean Curry 75

Chapter 5
76 Vegetables and Cheese Dishes

Hyderabadi Mixed Vegetables 78
Street-Style Grilled Corn on the Cob 79
Stir-fried Vegetables with Yogurt 80
Bengali Potatoes with Spices 81
Spicy Coconut Green Beans 82
Paneer Cheese 83
Smoky Fire-Roasted Eggplant 84

Pumpkin with Coconut 84
Mushrooms and Corn in a Spicy Curry 85
Cauliflower with Ginger and Cumin 86
Stir-Fried Okra 87
Puréed Spinach with Cheese Balls 88
Zucchini with Lentils and Roasted Garlic 89
Stir-Fried Paneer Cheese with Bell Peppers 90
Mangalore Spiced Potatoes 91

Chapter 6
92 *Fish and Seafood*

Fish Tikka 94
Salmon Kebabs 95
Masala-Baked Red Snapper 96
Masala-Crusted Tilapia 97
Malabar Crab Curry 98
Tandoori Skewered Shrimp 99
Stir-Fried Telicherry Mussels 100
Spicy Scallops with Grilled Pineapple Chutney 101
Goan-Style Squid 102
Chili Shrimp with Curry Leaves and
    Coconut 103
Stir-Fried Shrimp 103
Five Spice Blackened Salmon 104
Mangalore Fish Curry 105

Chapter 7
106 *Poultry and Meat*

Pepper Chicken 108
Lemon and Saffron Chicken Kebabs 108
Chicken Curry in a Hurry 109
Coconut Chicken Curry 110
Chicken Tikka Masala 111
Tandoori Chicken 112
Madras Chicken 114
Traditional Lamb Curry 115
Kerala Coconut Beef 116
Spicy Lamb Burgers 117
Marinated Roast Leg of Lamb 118
Spicy and Fragrant Lamb Curry 119
Pork Tenderloin with Mango Salad 119
Pork Vindaloo 120
Masala Lamb Chops 121

Chapter 8
122 *Bread and Rice*

Plain Basmati Rice 124
Coconut Shrimp Biriyani 125
Fragrant Lamb Biriyani 126
Black-Eyed Peas and Rice 127
Saffron Chicken Biriyani 128
Lemon Rice with Peanuts 129
Indian Fried Rice 130
Tamarind Rice 131
Basmati Rice with Whole Spices 132
Mint Rice with Potatoes and Toasted
    Cumin 133
Baked Garlic Naan 134
Whole-Wheat Griddle Breads 136
Fried Puffed Bread 138
Flaky Paratha Breads Stuffed with
    Potatoes 139

Chapter 9
140 *Desserts and Drinks*

Watermelon Mint Ice 142
Sweet Mangoes in a Creamy Custard 143
Sweetened Yogurt with Saffron and
    Pistachios 144
Pistachio Mango Ice Cream 145
Pistachio Biscotti 146
Chai Crème Brûlée 147
Almond Butter Cookies 148
Creamy Rice Pudding 149
Mumbai Fruit Punch 150
Mint Lime Cooler 151
Sweet Mango Yogurt Lassi 152
Ginger Cardamom Chai 153
Indian Lemonade 154

Shopping Guide 155
Acknowledgments 156
Index 157

Memories From My

You know what is truly universal? No matter where you go, what you do, who you meet, or what you eat—you can never forget your roots and the soil on which you grew up! While writing this book, I cannot help but get nostalgic about all the yester-years and all the people in my life who—sometimes even unconsciously—have been instrumental in making me who I am by helping to develop my strong sense of smells, tastes, likes and dislikes, which guides every decision I make at the kitchen counter today!

I grew up in Udupi, a small town nestled amidst the lush green of the southwestern coastal region of India. I can never forget the sounds, sights, tastes and aromas of our typical South Indian household: the spicy chutneys and rice flour being ground at wee hours of the morning by my grandmom, steaming hot *idli* and *dosa* served instantaneously at breakfast, the tinkering sound of spices tempering in a *kadhai*, which would later be part of a hot bowl of *sambar*, and the sound of women in the household—their chatter, the sound of their bangles, trinkets and the murmur of their never ending gossip! Lunch and dinners were always elaborate. One of our favorites was a slow-cooked coconut chicken curry accompanied by piping hot dosas and white bread. The early evening snack time usually consisted of hot cups of cardamom-spiced chai with platefuls of warm *samosa* and a variety of snacks. Lucky for us, every town in India has their unique offering in street food as well. If Delhi boasts of its delectable 'chaats', Mumbai has its *vada-pao* and Kolkata has its famous *kaati* rolls. Some of my memorable childhood evenings have been well-spent on short-eats around the

Indian Kitchen!

street corners of Udupi as well as. Mom would give me a rupee or two, and I would dash out to buy snacks from the road-side!

And then there was the rainy season, and the accompanying sounds of the flirty breeze playing with the leaves of the mango tree in our backyard, the rustic smell of wet earth, and the thud of mangoes falling to the ground. We kids often dashed out to pick them up before the sky broke loose! This priceless robbery of ours would mean that soon a spicy green mango chutney would be on our dining table! Rains meant hot fritters served with chai, and how we loved that! But this was not all! The day would not be complete without a late dinner—one of my favorites being *masala* fried fish with a bowl of steamed rice and vegetables loaded with fresh shredded coconut, mustard seeds and curry leaves. Dinnertime was important for our family—everyone had to be at the table. All of our meals were served family style and never rushed, even if it meant missing our favorite shows on television. (There was no concept of TV dinners.) I still follow that tradition today. There's simply no better way to truly and fully enjoy a meal than to share it with the people you love.

Throughout my childhood I felt very comfortable in and around the kitchen, and I am fortunate that cooking, something I've loved ever since I was a kid, has become my profession. After studying restaurant and hotel management in India, I traveled to the United States to enroll in the famous Culinary Institute of America. During a career that has spanned more than fifteen years, I have had the good fortune to cook for people in India, Europe,

Asia, and now, North America, and to experiment with the cuisines of the world. Along the way, I never stopped exploring the many facets of my own native cooking—be it traditional, regional or contemporary. I kept returning to India, traveling extensively, and eating my way around the diverse regions of the country, all in the name of research. Needless to say, I have developed my own style of cooking Indian dishes, one adapted to contemporary lifestyles and tastes, yet it is the vivid memories from my youth and my home that guide every Indian meal I cook and every ingredient I select. What started as the simple task of cooking masala omelets and making chai for my family on special occasions, or sneaking behind the large *kadai* of the roadside vendor to figure out what makes his fritters so delectable, has become a life's work of feeding countless people—all of whom have different levels of familiarity with Indian cuisine. Cooking for others is my greatest pleasure (and I take special pleasure in introducing Indian cuisine to the uninitiated), but nothing gives me more satisfaction than cooking for the people I love. I am sure the same is true for you—and I hope that you take joy in preparing the recipes in this book for your friends and family.

Hands-down, the recipes this book carries are my favorites. They have evolved over years of work with various Indian spices and the refinement of recipes, some of which owe their origins to my mother and grandmother. If the passion I have for Indian food finds a place in your heart (via your stomach), and also on your dining table, then this book will have served its purpose! And, I thank you for being a part of *My Indian Kitchen*.

Indian Food is Much More Than Just Curry!

The world has fallen in love with Indian food in recent years, and it's little wonder. Indian cuisine is a rich mosaic of exotic spices—everything about it awakens the senses. Combining a heady mixture of subtly blended spices, rich flavors, and enticing aromas, Indian dishes have a lot to offer the cook in the way of tastes, smells, textures and colors. Indian cuisine has long been a staple part of the diet in the United Kingdom—Chicken Tika Masala has now replaced Fish and Chips as *the* national dish there—and in other western countries with substantial Indian populations. It is also creating waves in North America, where it has "arrived" with a bang on the haute cuisine scene and in everyday homes. There is increased availability of Indian ingredients, spices and produce (think of mangoes—they are no longer the exotic fruit they once were), which has changed the cooking styles in non-Indian homes radically in recent years. Many Indian ingredients can be easily purchased at supermarkets or online, and many have become indispensable pantry staples. Slowly and surely, people are recognizing that Indian food is not just about the "curry"—it is a lot more varied and complex in taste, texture and splendor.

When preparing a meal, Indian cooks are guided by the simple principle of including all the different tastes in one meal—sweet, sour, salty, hot and pungent. The different parts of a meal, therefore, include dishes that comprise all these different tastes.

In addition to taste, when it comes to meal-time planning, many Indians are also guided by their religious or cultural practices. Hinduism, practiced by the majority of the Indian population, requires that its adherents follow a mainly vegetarian diet. However, the food habits of Hindus vary according to their community and according to regional traditions. For example, many Hindus living in coastal areas are fish and seafood eaters, and some Hindus even eat meat. On the other hand, there are many religions other than Hinduism in India, some of which may allow the eating of meat but have other restrictions, such as the Muslims, who eschew pork.

Typically, most Indian meals are casual, informal affairs. If unexpected guests turn up, they are welcomed with open arms. Adding to the casual feel, Indian meals consist of several dishes (sometimes even dessert) served all at once—family style. Multiple dishes are brought to the table, from which each person takes his or her share. For everyday meals there is usually a main dish, which is quite elaborately prepared. The accompanying dishes are chosen to go with the main dish—a menu is planned so that each dish complements the other and the flavors will match. Rice and bread are indispensable staples in a typical Indian meal.

Like many Indians, I truly enjoy eating food with my hands and combining the various curries, which makes each bite unique. As author Maya Tiwari (*A Life of Balance*) has noted, "While in the West eating with the hands usually conjures up pictures of a child smeared from head to foot with food, in India, using hands as utensils is a highly refined art." Whether I form my fingertips into a "petal" that cradles scoops of rice and *dal* or use four fingers as a "spoon" and my thumb to slide the blends of sauces, chutneys, meats and vegetables into my mouth, it is a truly satisfying way to eat. Whereas I find eating with my hand (only one is used) to be a sensuous indulgence, I realize it is not for everyone. If you want to give it a try, remember to thoroughly wash your hands before eating.

Most traditional Indian meals involve elaborate preparation, but in our busy lives most of us do not have the luxury to prepare time-consuming meals. So, I have kept the recipes in this book simple yet delicious while preserving their authenticity.

You can easily make the recipes in this book for yourself or for your friends and family. Most of them are quick and don't require any special cooking equipment or techniques. The only thing you will need is a sense of adventure to explore a variety of flavors and aromas and a hearty appetite to savor the authentic foods of India.

Over time you will learn how different spices and herbs interact with each other, as well as other ingredients, creating unique scents and flavors. This knowledge is the key to unlocking the "hidden" magic of Indian cuisine.

I urge you to experiment with the spices and their flavors while trying out these recipes—in this way you'll gain an understanding of how spices mix and mingle with ingredients and how they appeal to your taste buds. Cooking is all about experimenting with what appeals to the senses—to *your* senses—and I exhort you to indulge in this process to your heart's content. Be daring and adventurous, and before long you'll be tantalizing your palate with the subtle flavors of Indian cuisine.

Indian Meals—Indian Style or Your Style

A typical everyday Indian meal always includes a saucy or "wet" dish (either a protein or vegetables), a sautéed or "dry" vegetable dish, bread and/or rice, and plain yogurt or *raita*. An array of pickles, chutneys and salad are standard accompaniments. Vegetables play a very important part in everyday meals, even if the meal is primarily non-vegetarian. Indian meals for entertaining and company tend to be more elaborate than everyday meals, and will include more than one main dish. Special appetizers, drinks and desserts are served. Elaborate rice dishes like *biriyani* and *pulao* will be made, and more complex condiments and other accompaniments are served to complete the meal.

When preparing an Indian meal, whether on a week night after work or for a Saturday evening dinner party, you can cook and serve several dishes all at once, Indian style, or you can divide them up into different courses, just like a western meal, and serve them accordingly. The recipes in this book, therefore, have been divided into different chapters that correlate to typical western courses or components or a meal.

To get you started, here (see right) are some menu suggestions for everyday and more elaborate meals, suitable for entertaining, as well as a non-traditional Indian meal. The recipes in the latter menu are my own easy-to-prepare Indian-inspired inventions, created with the modern cook in mind. Each of these menus creates a complete Indian meal and balances elements of taste and texture. You can make the recipes from *My Indian Kitchen* as they appear in the book or you can be innovative and adventurous to create dishes of your own.

PLANNING YOUR INDIAN MEAL

Simple, Everyday Vegetarian Menu
Delicious Everyday Dal (page 74)
Stir-Fried Okra (page 87)
Whole-Wheat Griddle Breads (page 136)
Plain Basmati Rice or Basmati Rice with Whole Spices
(pages 124, 132)
Green Mango Pickle (page 47)

Simple, Everyday Non-Vegetarian Menu
Chicken Curry in a Hurry (page 109)
Cauliflower with Ginger and Cumin (page 86)
Whole-Wheat Griddle Breads (page 136)
Plain Basmati Rice or Basmati Rice with Whole Spices
(pages 124, 132)
Green Mango Pickle (page 47)

Vegetarian Party Menu
Sweet Mango Yogurt Lassi (page 152)
Mung Dal and Cucumber Salad (page 62)
Crunchy Potato and Corn Croquettes (page 52)
Puréed Spinach with Cheese Balls (page 88)
Stir-Fried Vegetables with Yogurt (page 80)
Northern Chickpea Curry (page 69)
Fried Puffed Bread (page 138)
Black-Eyed Peas and Rice (page 127)
Pineapple and Beet Raita (page 46)
Masala Pappadums (page 55)
Cardamom Apple Kheer (page 149)

Non-Vegetarian Party Menu
Mumbai Fruit Punch (page 150)
Pomegranate and Mint Potato Salad (page 56)
Samosas, Kheema-Filled (page 58)
Masala Lamb Chops (page 121)
Smoky Fire-Roasted Eggplant (page 84)
Mushrooms and Corn in a Spicy Curry (page 85)
Saffron Chicken Biriyani (page 128)
Whole-Wheat Griddle Breads (page 136)
Cucumber and Yogurt Raita (page 45)
Masala Pappadums (page 55)
Pistachio Mango Ice Cream (page 145)

Non-traditional Indian Meal
Raspberry Lemonade (page 154)
Shrimp Bruschetta (page 50)
Pork Tenderloin with Mango Salad (page 119)
Five Spice Blackened Salmon (page 104)
Black-Eyed Peas with Mushrooms (page 72)
Mint Rice with Potatoes and Toasted Cumin (page 133)
Avocado and Roasted Cumin Raita (page 44)
Chai Crème Brûlée (page 147)

Pairing Wines with Indian Food

Traditionally the enjoyment of wine is not part of the Indian lifestyle. When I was growing up in India, the preferred alcoholic drinks were scotch or beer. Drinking was a pre-dinner activity, though drinks were usually paired with freshly made snacks such as spicy kebabs and papadams. To this day, I still prefer a chilled glass of beer when choosing an alcoholic beverage to pair with an Indian meal. Many Indian restaurants will carry beer on their menu, including Indian beers (especially Kingfisher). The best beers to pair with Indian food are relatively light beers—that is, pilsners, lagers and ales. Dark or strongly flavored beers such as stouts, porters and bocks should be avoided.

For wine lovers, pairing wine with Indian food is complicated and challenging, as there are a lot of competing spices and seasonings to contend with. The complex layering of spices and chili heat in Indian dishes makes it tricky. The traditional method of pairing lighter food with whites and heavier foods with reds does not necessarily hold true in Indian cuisine—for example a heavy dish such as creamy lamb curry or beef korma will pair well with whites and a flavorful seafood dish can go well with reds.

The important rule to remember is that there is no rule!!

After consulting several wine experts and master sommeliers, I've come up some general tips to help you make good wine selections:

 The lesser the alcohol level the better because alcohol tends to intensify the heat in a dish. For a white, try something like a Gazelle Vinho Verde from Portugal, which has only 9 percent alcohol, or just about any sauvignon blanc from France's Sancerre region. Those wines usually have alcohol levels no higher than 13 percent. For a red, try the

Heron pinot noir, from the Languedoc region of France, which has an alcohol level in the 13 percent range.

❧ Reds with less oaky and more intense fruit flavors works well with the complex tastes of the cuisine.

❧ Whites with light acidity and mild fruity textures will balance the richness of the Indian dishes.

❧ The refreshing bubbles and palate-cleansing acidity of sparkling wines would also work with Indian dishes that have heavy sauces.

❧ A dry rose, which has some of the complexity as a red as well as the acidity of a lighter white, can also be paired next to a lot of Indian dishes.

Here are some specific suggestions—but they are suggestions only. Following the basic tips above, other wines may be chosen.

Gewürztraminer: Since "gewürztraminer" literally means "spicy grape" in German, this wine can pair perfectly with the spices and seasonings in Indian cuisine, especially ginger and cardamom. And since many bottles have a bit of residual sugar, gewürztraminer will tame the heat in curries and other spicy dishes.

Riesling: With aromas and flavors of crisp apple and peach, good acidity, and often a hint of sweetness, Riesling is a match made in heaven for Indian cuisine. Try a glass or a bottle the next time you have a curry dish made with fruit like peaches or apricots. And, as with gewürztraminer, the touch of sugar in the wine will counter the heat in chili peppers and other spices.

Sauvignon Blanc: Sauvignon Blanc's enticing flavors of lime, grapefruit, gooseberries and herbs make it a food-friendly choice for any cuisine, as the bracing acidity wakes up your taste buds and makes you want to go back for another bite of whatever you are eating. Try it with dishes that include tomatoes, lemons or limes, which will match the wine's acidity. With coconut milk–based curries and other rich dishes, sauvignon blanc will cut some of the richness and taste extremely refreshing.

Rosé: Not to be confused with white zinfandel, rosé wine is completely dry. It has some of the complexity and weight of a red wine (think red berries and spice), as well as the acidity of a lighter white. Rosés can hold their own next to a lot of Indian dishes, including those made with lamb. Since rosé tends to be drier I suggest not pairing it with some of the spicier Indian dishes like *vindaloo* or *murg kali mirch* since it doesn't have the sugar content that helps counter chili heat

Sparkling wine: Often underrated as a food wine, and saved for special occasions, Champagne and other sparkling wines can be enjoyed with many different kinds of food. The refreshing bubbles and palate-cleansing acidity would especially work with Indian dishes that have heavy sauces. When choosing champagne to accompany Indian dishes with a lot of chili heat, choose a sweeter champagne as its higher sugar content works well with spicy foods. Also, a chilled glass of Prosecco, with its sweet, rich and complex flavor, works very well.

Pinot Noir: Crave a bottle of red wine with your Indian food? Pinot noir is a smart choice, as it offers lots of fruit (cherries, raspberries, cranberries,) but typically has silkier, smoother tannins than more full-bodied red wines such as cabernet sauvignon or merlot, so it won't dry out your mouth or fuel the fire of a spicy dish you are enjoying. If you are serving a variety of Indian dishes at your next dinner party pinot noir is a great selection. It can pair with everything from tandoori chicken, to *khadai* stir-fried shrimp and *palak paneer kofta*.

A Few Simple Techniques

The heart and soul of Indian cooking is to be able to master the unique and imaginative use of spices, seasonings and flavorings and learning the nitty-gritty of Indian cooking techniques. You will already be familiar with many of the Indian cooking techniques from your own everyday cooking. The main techniques are steaming (*dum*), tempering (*tarhka*), roasting (*bhunnana*), frying (*talna*) and sautéing (*bhunao*). Other common techniques are roasting and grinding of spices, browning onions, garlic and meats and handling sauces. Each of these "methods" or a combination of two or three or even all may be necessary to prepare an Indian dish. They are not hard to master, but is important to understand the basic principles of each.

SAUCE TIPS Unlike in western cooking, flour is almost never used to thicken Indian sauces. The dark thick sauces in Indian cooking are achieved by a proper balance of the ingredients and the use of the correct cooking techniques. For example, the body of the Indian sauces very often comes from onions, garlic, ginger and tomatoes, which may be chopped, creating a textured sauce, or made into a paste in a food processor or a blender. Once a paste has been made, it is then cooked or browned in oil. The sauce is allowed to cook further until it is reduced and has become thick. Sometimes cream, yogurt, coconut or nut pastes, such as almonds and cashews, are added to Indian sauces, which give a creamy texture.

ROASTING AND GRINDING OF SPICES Roasting is the key to bringing out the flavor of spices. Roasting spices removes the raw smell that untreated spices tend to have and intensifies their flavors by heating up the essential oils. All you need is a small, heavy bottomed skillet (cast iron works great). No oil is used when roasting spices. Whole spices are put in a dry skillet and roasted over medium heat until the spices turn a shade or two darker and become aromatic. The spices are then immediately removed from the hot skillet to avoid over-roasting.

In my kitchen I generally buy the spices whole and then grind them myself as I need them. Because spices retain their flavor and aroma much longer in their whole form than when ground, grinding roasted spices in small batches is the ideal way to use spices, and gives the greatest possible flavor to dishes. Traditionally, in Indian kitchens the grinding of spices is done on heavy grinding stones or with a mortar and pestle. To save time, I grind spices using a spice grinder, though a coffee grinder works equally well.

SAUTÉING (BHUNAO) Unlike classic French sautéing, Indian sautéing, or *bhunao*, is a combination of sautéing, stir-frying and light stewing or braising. It is the process of cooking over medium to high heat, adding small quantities of liquid, such as water or tomato purée, and stirring constantly to prevent the ingredients from sticking. Almost every Indian recipe needs bhunao at some stage, and some at more than one stage. Generally ingredients like onions, ginger, garlic, tomatoes and spices require bhunao. The purpose of this technique is to extract the flavor of each of the ingredients in combination with spices as well as to ensure that the *masala* is fully cooked before adding the main ingredient. Sometimes the main ingredient, such as poultry, meats or vegetables, may also require bhunao. The process of making masala is complete only when the fat leaves the masala, which is very critical in Indian cooking. Traditionally a *kadhai* is used for this technique. I find that if I use a heavy-bottomed saucepan or another deep-sided pan, such as a braiser or Dutch oven, works just as well. Recipes like Puréed Spinach with Cheese Balls (page 88), Hyderabadi Mixed Vegetables (page 78), Traditional Lamb Curry (page 115) and Chicken Tikka Masala (page 111) are good examples of this technique.

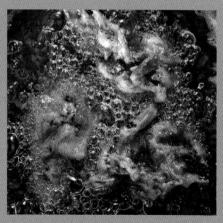

DEEP-FRYING (TALNA) *Talna* refers to deep-frying, Indian style. Generally, for deep-frying, Indian cooks use a *khadai*—a deep pan with a rounded bottom similar to a wok. Unlike a deep fat fryer, the size and shape of the kadhai does not allow large quantities of food to be fried at one time, which results in even frying. When deep-frying, oil should be heated to between 325° and 350°F (160° and 180°C). This is crucial—if the oil is too hot, the outside of the food will brown very quickly, leaving the insides uncooked; and, if the oil is not hot enough the foods will absorb oil and become greasy. When frying, do not over crowd the pan; fry the food in batches, if necessary. Use a slotted spatula or spoon when removing fried food from the oil, and hold each piece against the edge of the pan for a few seconds. This allows excess oil to drain back into the pan. Place fried foods on a tray lined with paper towels to drain. To re-use the oil, turn off the heat under the oil as soon as you're finished frying and let it cool completely. Using a fine-mesh strainer, strain the oil into an airtight container. Store the oil at room temperature until next use.

ROASTING (BHUNNANA) Traditionally, in Indian cooking roasting is done in a charcoal-fired tandoor (clay oven), which gives a unique flavor to roasted meats, breads and vegetables. The juices of the meats drip on the charcoal which sizzles and the smoke that is created gives the food its unique flavor. For home cooking, an open charcoal grill is good substitute for cooking meat kebabs, vegetables and paneer, though the flavor is milder than that achieved in a tandoor. An oven can be used to make breads and to also roast marinated meats and vegetables. A few of the recipes that use the roasting technique are Tandoori Chicken (page 112), Masala-Baked Red Snapper (page 96) and Marinated Roast Leg of Lamb (page 118).

TEMPERING (TARHKA) This technique is very unique to Indian cooking. Oil is heated until it is very hot. A mixture of whole spices with or without chopped garlic and ginger is added to the oil. Hot oil has an extraordinary ability to extract and retain the essence, aroma and flavor of spices and herbs. This process is performed either at the beginning of cooking a dish or after. If done after a dish is cooked, the prepared tempering is poured sizzling hot over the dish to add a burst of flavor (this sometimes done when preparing dals). The seasonings that are most commonly used for tempering include cumin seeds, black mustard seeds, fennel seeds, dried red chilies, cloves, cinnamon, cardamom, bay leaves as well as chopped up ginger, garlic and fresh or dried curry leaves. The ingredients are usually added in rapid succession, rarely together. The purpose of adding tempering ingredients sequentially is to ensure that each ingredient is fully cooked, and thus its flavor fully extracted into the oil, before the next ingredient is added. This method also allow for longer-cooking ingredients or spices to be added first, and shorter-cooking ingredients or spices last, which would otherwise have a tendency to burn if added earlier. The crackling of the spices or a change in their color indicates that the process is complete, unless fresh herbs and vegetables are also being used. A few of the many recipes that use this technique in this book are Carrot Yogurt Slaw (page 46), South Indian Coconut Chutney (page 40), Fiery South Indian Tomato Soup (page 67), Spicy Urad Beans (page 70) and Tamarind Rice (page 131).

BROWNING Most Indian recipes require browning of onions fried over medium-high heat. Evenly browned onions are more flavorful and give sauces a desired rich, deep reddish-brown color. The same goes for garlic—the flavor of garlic is quite amazing if it is fried in oil until it turns golden brown in color. For the best flavor and color, meat is also browned. Browning also sears the meat, which makes it juicy. I like to brown marinated meat before combining it with other ingredients. If I am cooking larger quantity, I brown a few pieces of meat at a time in hot oil and set them aside. I then add the browned meat and all the cooking juices back into the pan with the other ingredients and let it finish cooking in the sauce.

STEAMING (DUM) *Dum* cooking has been described as the "maturing of a dish" as in this technique the food is very slowly cooked in its own steam. Traditionally, the lid was sealed to the cooking vessel with a flour-and-water paste to make sure moisture is trapped within. The vessel was slightly buried in hot coals and, to ensure the food is evenly surrounded by heat, some hot coals were placed on top of the lid. Today the modern oven is used to perform the function of providing even heat. The dish is first cooked on a stove top and then well sealed and placed in the oven to continue to cook in its own steam. The advantage of dum cooking is that since the vapors cannot escape, the food retains all its delicate flavor and aroma. One of the most common and popular dishes prepared using this technique is the famous rice dish called *biriyani*. (See Saffron Chicken Biriyani, page 128, and Fragrant Lamb Biriyani, page 126).

Some Helpful Tools

You do not need special kitchen tools or cookware to cook authentic Indian food at home. All you need is a well-equipped kitchen with sturdy skillets, pots and pans with lids, tongs, good knives, graters, mixing bowls, a rolling pin, a perforated spoon, a sieve, a strainer and a citrus squeezer. I like to use an Indian spice box to hold my most frequently used spices and spice blends. It sits on my kitchen counter where I can quickly grab a pinch of spice when needed. I generally use nonstick pots, saucepans and skillets when cooking Indian food at home because of the relatively long cooking time. Some ingredients, like spices, onions, ginger, garlic and tomatoes, which are typically cooked in small quantities of liquid or fat, tend to stick to conventional pans. If you have regular pots and pans, to prevent sticking, make sure they are heavy bottomed and sturdy. Stir the food frequently. Add more cooking oil as needed. The following tools are not crucial but they will make cooking Indian food a lot simpler and quicker.

Cast-iron skillets and griddles Small cast-iron skillets are ideal for dry roasting spices because they evenly brown them without needing to add any oil or liquid. Always preheat your cast-iron pan before using. A large cast-iron skillet or griddle is excellent for making Indian flatbreads such as Whole-Wheat Griddle Breads (*Chapati*) (page 136) and Flaky Paratha Breads Stuffed with Potatoes (*Aloo Paratha*) (page 139). Traditionally, these breads are cooked in a *tava*, a round concave, cast-iron griddle that is available in South Asian grocery stores. New cast-iron pans should be seasoned before use. To season, rub a relatively thin coat of neutral oil all around the inside of the pan. Place the pan upside-down in a cold oven with a sheet of aluminum foil on the bottom to catch any drips. Set the oven to between 300° to 400°F (150° to 200°C) and let the pan heat for 30 to 60 minutes. Once done, let the pan cool to room temperature. Repeating this process several times is recommended. Never put cold liquid into a very hot cast-iron pan; doing so might crack and damage the pan.

Electric blender When it comes to combining liquids with fresh herbs or spices for sauces, pastes or purées there is nothing more effective than a blender. Blenders with a narrow, tapered base (or basically straight sides) work very effectively to purée thick sauces and pastes, unlike the blender jars with a broader base, which are ideal for blended drinks. Ginger-garlic paste can be made very fast and effectively in a blender. I also use it to grind large amount of whole spices. This works surprisingly well, which I discovered when I started making large quantities of my Home-Style Garam Masala (page 35) and Dhaba Spice (page 34) as take-away gifts for family and friends. I prefer a glass blender jars in my kitchen as plastic absorbs aromas from the spices and herbs. I also have a hand-held blender, also called an "immersion" blender or "smart stick," which I often use to purée vegetables, lentils or beans. This tool is ideal when preparing puréed soups or dals, such as Spinach Soup (page 67) or Broccoli Soup with Walnuts (page 66), as you can purée the food directly in the pan. You need not wait for the liquid to cool, which is advisable when transferring hot liquids to a blender, and it saves you the task of cleaning up a messy blender.

Electric food processor The traditional grinding stone of Indian kitchens, which is heavy and is moved manually, is now replaced with the modern food processor—a time-saving tool par excellence for busy cooks. Essential ingredients like onion, chili peppers, garlic and ginger can be made into pastes very quickly in these electrically powered machines. The food processor can be used to chop or mince vegetables and fresh herbs, and cut down considerably on prep time. I recommend a food processor that has a capacity of between 7 and 10 cups. To pulverize small quantities of ingredients, make sure the blades sit close to the bottom. However, when chopping very small amounts of fresh garlic, onions, chili peppers or ginger, it's more practical to use a Chef's knife.

Electric spice grinder or coffee grinder I highly recommend investing in a spice

grinder or a coffee grinder. It is one of the most important tools that you will use in Indian cooking. I use it to coarsely or finely grind dry whole spices. It grinds spices in seconds and clean up is very simple, and it is not always necessary to clean up after each spice. I personally use the Cuisine Art nut and spice grinder, which is available for under $50. The ability of electric coffee grinders to grind coffee beans also makes them ideally suited for grinding a wide range of spices, such as cumin seeds, cinnamon sticks (broken up), cardamom and bay leaves. They can grind as little as a teaspoon to as much as half a cup. For larger volumes of whole spices a blender works surprisingly well. I strongly recommend that you invest in a spice grinder or coffee grinder as it will make your cooking process very simple and the results very flavorful. If do you use a coffee grinder to grind spices, reserve it for that use only; otherwise, you will end up with cumin-flavored coffee.

Kadhai, kadai, kadahi, karhai or karahi This is a deep pan similar in shape to the Chinese wok. A *kadhai* is traditionally made out of cast iron, although other materials like stainless steel and copper are sometimes used, and nonstick versions also exist. It is ideal for deep-frying Indian style (*talna*) as the rounded bottom allows you to use a relatively small quantity of oil while giving you enough depth in the center to submerge foods. The kadhai is also used for stir-frying vegetables. There are

decorative ones which are best used for serving, not cooking. A small wok about 12 inches (30 cm) in diameter is a close substitute for a kadhai.

Mortar and pestle is a very common tool that is used to crush and grind. The pestle is a heavy bat-shaped object, the end of which is used for crushing and grinding. The mortar is a bowl, typically made of hard wood, ceramic or stone. The ingredients is placed in the mortar and ground, crushed or mixed with the pestle. In Indian kitchens mortars are also used in cooking to prepare ingredients such as ginger and garlic pastes, as well as grinding spices into powder. With the advent of motorized grinders, use of the mortar and pestle has decreased. I still recommend investing in a good stone mortar and pestle as it will come in handy to grind or crush small quantities of ingredients that are needed to flavor the Indian dishes.

A Brief Introduction to Indian Ingredients

This chapter gives a description of some of the most popular and commonly used Indian ingredients. Many of the ingredients and spices used in *My Indian Kitchen* are found in well-stocked supermarkets. These include cumin, coriander, turmeric, mace, black pepper, ginger, paprika, cayenne pepper, cloves, cinnamon and cardamom. Some others are carried in South Asian or Indian food markets. It is also possible to order spices by mail and on the internet (see Shopping Guide, page 155).

Indian cuisine has always been very receptive to spices and ingredients from other cuisines and cultures. For example, in India, and in Indian homes around the world, it is very common to use soy sauce to jazz up Indian stir-fry dishes that are inspired by oriental cuisines. (See Indian Fried Rice, page 130, and Chili Shrimp with Curry Leaves and Coconut, page 103.)

In *My Indian Kitchen* I use some ingredients that are not used in a traditional Indian kitchen. Olive oil is one of them. Even though in most cases Indian recipes call for any neutral-flavored vegetable oil (for example, canola, safflower or corn oil), olive oil is a healthier alternative. I use it to often to drizzle over salads (Pomegranate and Mint Potato Salad, page 56) and sometimes for lighter cooking, such as seafood dishes (Fish Tikka, page 94) and vegetable dishes.

Pita pockets are another great nontraditional food to incorporate into Indian meals. I sometimes use them instead of a naan or *paratha* to make sandwiches (see Spicy Lamb Burgers, page 117) just because they are readily available in supermarkets.

Traditionally whole milk yogurt is hung in a muslin cloth to drain all the whey out to create a creamy thick yogurt, known as "hung curd," that is ideal for many authentic Indian recipes—particularly to marinate chicken or meats and make creamy sauces and dips. Rather than take the time to hang plain yogurt at home, I use either sour cream or the increasingly available thick, Greek-style plain yogurt. Both are perfect alternatives for the Indian thick, creamy yogurt.

STORAGE TIPS FOR SPICES AND HERBS Ideally, it is best to buy all dry spices in their whole form. Whole spices will stay fresh generally five to six months longer than pre-ground spices. It's a good habit to smell ground spices before using them; if their smell is very faint, it's time to replace them or grind a fresh batch. Both whole and ground spices should be stored in a cool, dry, dark place in tightly covered jars. Freshly ground spices are not the same as pre-ground store-bought spices, neither in flavor nor volume. Freshly ground spices are far superior in flavor and aroma to pre-ground spices. Another difference is the volume: freshly ground spices have less volume tablespoon to tablespoon, or ounce to ounce, than pre-ground spices, which settle over time. You might think you would need to use more of the freshly ground spice to compensate for the greater volume of the settled, and therefore denser, pre-ground bottled spice. But because pre-ground spices are so much less potent than freshly ground, the difference in volume is not of consequence. If anything, you might need to add more of the pre-ground spice.

To prolong the life span of fresh herbs, like fresh coriander leaves (cilantro) and mint, wash and dry the leaves with paper towels until the leaves are mostly, but not completely, dried. Store refrigerated, wrapped in kitchen or paper towels, in a ziplock bag.

Asafetida The dried gum like resin from a rhizome of a giant fennel-like plant. It is sold in both lump and ground forms and used in very small quantities because of its strong and pungent flavor, which is somewhat like garlic. I use and recommend the ground version because it comes mixed with rice flour and turmeric powder to mellow the flavor.

Asian chili powder or cayenne pepper This is a red powder made from grinding dried red skins of several types of chili peppers. In India, it is simply called "chili powder." You can substitute cayenne pepper, which is commonly available in supermarkets. The Indian chili powder, which is darker in color than cayenne pepper, is available in Indian grocery stores. It adds a spicy flavor to dishes.

Bay leaves These are long, oval, pointed and smooth leaves of a hardy evergreen shrub. The leaves are dark green when fresh and turn olive green when dry. The fresh leaves are very mild and do not develop their full flavor until several weeks after picking and drying. They are often used whole, or sometimes ground in curries and rice dishes. They are an important ingredient in the Indian spice blend *garam masala*. Bay leaves are also a common fixture in the cooking of many European cuisines (particularly those of the Mediterranean), as well as North and South American cuisines. The bay leaf that is commonly available in North America is similar in appearance to the Indian bay leaf, but its flavor and fragrance are milder than the Indian one. If you cannot find Indian bay leaves, which are often found only in Indian grocery stores, you may use regular bay leaves as a substitute. The difference is very subtle and will not make a difference in the final result.

Cardamom The cardamom plant is native to India and Sri Lanka and is also cultivated in Guatemala, Mexico, Indonesia and other areas of southern Asia. The cardamom pods are harvested just before they are ripe and they are allowed to dry in the sun or sometimes in drying machines. There are two distinct types of cardamom pods used in Indian cooking: the small green pod and large black pod. The green pods are the most common and have exceptional flavor. I use the green pods in all the recipes in this book. Black

Cardamom

cardamom pods are used in Indian rice and meat dishes; however, they are not as commonly available. Cardamom pods are used in almost every part of the cuisine, from savory dishes to curries and desserts. When using cardamom for desserts, the seeds are extracted from the pods and ground to a powder. For curries, stews or rice dishes, the whole pod can be added directly to the food. The sharp and bitter taste of cardamom mellows to a warming sweet taste as it cooks. The pre-ground is more readily available than the pods in the West whereas in India, it is more typical to find the whole pod. The quality of pre-ground cardamom is not as good as freshly grinding the seeds at home. Once the pods are opened or the seeds ground, the flavor and aroma of the cardamom are lost very quickly. I especially recommend freshly grinding the seeds for the dessert and beverage recipes, where the spice often plays a key role. For instructions on how to extract the seeds and grind them, see page 145.

Chili peppers There are more than 150 varieties of chili peppers in the world. That's a lot to keep track, but as a general rule the smaller ones are hotter than the larger ones. The two most common chilies used in Indian cooking are the Cayenne and Thai. The cayenne pepper is green when fresh and red when dried. The Thai variety, sometimes known as "bird's-eye," is smaller and hotter. The Serrano chili is more widely available in the U.S. and is a good alternative to the cayenne and Thai, though it is milder. If you cannot find fresh Cayenne, Thai or Serrano chili peppers, simply use what's available. Fresh chilies are one of the most important ingredients for providing pungency in Indian cuisine. In many regions in India **fresh green chili peppers** are served raw with the food. Often I like to remove the inner membrane and seeds and use only the skin to reduce the heat. Chopping a fresh chili releases capsaicin, and the finer you chop it, the hotter the taste. Sometimes I slit the chilies open, but leave the seeds intact, to release a gentler heat. **Dried red chili peppers** are about 1½ to 2 inches (4 to 5 cm) long, and are usually added to hot oil to infuse their strong flavor into the oil. A quick contact with hot oil enhances and intensifies the flavor of the skins. The Indian dried red chilies are similar to most common types such as the cayenne and *chili de arbol*. **Dried red pepper flakes** are made from hot dried red peppers. Red pepper flakes are generally not made of one type of chili, but from various combinations of ancho, bell, cayenne and more. Often there is a high ratio of seeds, which intensifies the heat of the pepper. The flakes are not very commonly used in traditional Indian cooking. I use them often to intensify my sauces and stir-fry dishes.

Fresh Green Chili Peppers

Dried Red Chili Peppers

Dried Red Pepper Flakes

Cinnamon This highly fragrant spice is the dried inner bark of the laurel tree. It is an important ingredient in Indian cooking, imparting a pleasant aroma to foods. It is sold in powder and stick forms. The whole sticks are used to flavor meats, curry dishes and rice dishes as well as teas.

Coconut milk, coconut meat, shredded coconut In my recipes I use coconut milk, coconut meat and shredded coconut. Coconut milk is produced by crushing the thick white coconut meat that is inside the dark brown coconut shell with water. It is then drained and the soaked coconut meat is squeezed to extract the liquid. As the milk sits, the fat rises to the surface. This fat is skimmed off and sold separately as coconut cream. The cream is much richer and thicker than the milk. Coconut milk and coconut cream are both sold in cans. When using coconut milk for savory recipes, make sure it is not sweetened. Sweetened milk or cream is used in making pastries and cocktails. I prefer to used full-fat coconut milk rather than the "lite" version, which is not as flavorful or creamy. Before opening a can of coconut milk make sure to shake it well as the cream will have risen to the top; shaking the can incorporate the cream into the thinner milk-like liquid to create a smooth, even consistency.

Once the can is opened make sure you store it in the refrigerator covered and use it within 2 to 3 days, as it spoils quickly. Packaged shredded coconut (sometimes called "grated") is available frozen, which is the next best option to freshly grated, and dried, or "desiccated." For the recipes in this book, be sure to purchase unsweetened shredded coconut. While dried unsweetened coconut is easy to find in most supermarkets or health food stores, frozen shredded coconut is available only in Southeast Asian or Indian grocery stores. The dried shredded coconut, however, has significantly less flavor than the frozen or fresh forms and does not give the creamy texture that is desired in Indian curries and stews. If you only have access to dried, unsweetened shredded coconut, soak ½ cup (50 g) of the dried coconut in ½ cup (125 ml) of boiling water for about 15 minutes. Drain the excess water before use. Note that ½ cup of dried coconut is comparable to 1 cup of freshly shredded or frozen shredded coconut. Freshly shredded, or grated, coconut will provide the best flavor and texture in Indian dishes. This requires purchasing a coconut and whacking it apart at home. Here is how to grate fresh coconut at home: Start with a clean looking coconut without cracks or any over powering or rancid smell. It should feel heavy and full of water. You can shake the coconut to hear the water swish. Place the coconut on a clean heavy wooden cutting board or a clean concrete block. Holding the coconut in one hand, tap the coconut lightly on all sides with a hammer to dislodge the insides from the hard brown shell. Then carefully but forcefully hit the shell with the hammer to break it open. Now most of the hard shell should separate from the coconut. Carefully pry off the meat from the brown outer shell with the tip of a well rounded blunt knife. Grate the coconut meat using a handheld grater or cut it into thin slices for Kerala Coconut Beef (page 116).

Coriander leaves Also known as "cilantro," the leaves of this plant, an annual in the parsley family, is one of the most commonly used herbs in Indian cuisine. This herb is generally used uncooked for garnishes, marinades and chutneys. Many dishes also incorporate fresh coriander leaves at various stages of cooking, which dissipates the sharp flavor and aroma

of the herb, leaving a mild flavor. Fresh coriander leaves is highly perishable and prone to wilting. See "Storage Tips for Spices and Herbs," page 22.

Coriander seeds Coriander seeds are ribbed peppercorn-sized and -shaped, pale green to light brown–colored seeds of the coriander (cilantro) plant. They are extremely aromatic, with a spicy hint; yet, taste and aroma is nowhere similar to the leaves of the coriander plant. I always keep them in little quantities in airtight containers, as they lose their flavor with exposure and age. Coriander seeds are also available in a preground form.

Cucumbers Cucumbers are widely used in Indian kitchens and can be served with any Indian meal. Cucumbers can always be found in my refrigerator and are a summertime favorite. The cooling, clean flavor matches well with foods like chilies, coriander leaves (cilantro), cream, garlic, lemon, lime, mint, olive oil, onions, sour cream, tomatoes, vinegar and yogurt. I like to cut them into little finger-sized wedges and serve it with a sprinkle of salt, black pepper, Asian chili powder or cayenne pepper and a heavy dose of freshly-squeezed lemon juice. When purchasing cucumbers, look for smooth, brightly-colored skin. Cucumbers keep well in a plastic bag in the refrigerator for up to ten days. I prefer to use the long seedless variety called "English" cucumbers. They are usually sold shrinkwrapped and they aren't actually seedless—the seeds are just very small. These cucumbers can be eaten without peeling and seeding unlike the common garden-variety salad cucumber.

Cumin seeds These seeds are the best-known and most widely used spice in Indian cuisine. They are either fried whole in hot oil or dry roasted and then used whole or finely ground, according to the recipe. Cumin is warm, intense, and has an almost nutty aroma.

Curry leaves, fresh and dried Curry leaves originate from the Kari tree, a subtropical tree native to India. They are used similarly to how bay leaves are used—mainly used as an aromatic and flavoring for most curries and soups. They are widely used in dishes along the southern coastal regions of India. When starting a curry or soup dish, curry leaves are placed in hot oil to fry until crisp, which makes the oil and the leaves intensely flavorful. It is common to use fresh curry leaves in India rather than dried. You can purchase fresh curry leaves in Indian grocery stores. Dried curry leaves can be purchased from specialty gourmet stores or online (see Shopping Guide, page 155). The best way to store fresh curry leaves is to wash and

Split Red Lentils
(Masoor Dal)

Split Pigeon Peas
(Toor Dal)

Mung Beans
(Mung Dal)

Split Yellow Peas
(Chana Dal)

Dried legumes (lentils, dried beans and peas) In India, all types of dried legumes, be they lentils, peas or beans, are known as *dal*. They are an integral part of Indian meals, being economical, highly nutritious, very low in fat and a good source of carbohydrates, proteins, fibers, minerals and vitamins. Dals are a good substitute for meat, which has more fat and cholesterol. Many common varieties of dals, like chickpeas (*kabuli chana*), kidney beans (*rajmah*), whole green lentils (*sabut moong*) and cow peas (black-eyed peas), are available in conventional supermarket. Some not-so-common varieties that are used in Indian cooking include split pigeon peas (*toor dal*), split black gram, aka "black lentils" (*urad dal*), green lentils or mung beans (*moong dal*), split red lentils (*masoor dal*) and split yellow peas (*chana dal*). To procure these, a trip to an Indian grocery store or an online purchase is necessary (see Shopping Guide, page 155).

Dal dishes come in various forms—thin and soupy (Fiery South Indian Tomato Soup, page 67), thick and creamy (Spicy Urad Beans, page 70), hearty and comforting (Red Kidney Bean Curry, page 75)—and may be the basis of a salad (Mung Dal and Cucumber Salad, page 62) or an integral part of a steamed rice dish (Black-Eyed Peas and Rice, page 127).

There is nothing more comforting and soulful than a bowl of dal topped with some steamed rice. I incorporate dals into my everyday meals—both Indian and non-Indian. I cook my dried legumes the old fashioned way in my kitchen using a pressure cooker. Though this technique is not so popular in North America and Europe, I urge you to give pressure cooking a try: it uses less liquid, has faster cooking times and the food retains all the vitamins and minerals. Once you get used to a pressure cooker I can assure you that you will be eating more dals as part of your daily meals, especially the longer-cooking types. In anticipation that not everyone will have a pressure cooker, or be inclined to use one, the recipes in this book call for common kitchenware, such as saucepans or pots. If you want to experiment with a pressure cooker, simply follow the instructions provided with it; you will find that cooking time is reduced by more than 50 percent!

I often stock my pantry with canned legumes, which I find to be an acceptable substitute for dried and very convenient to use when I'm in a rush. In the dal recipes in this book, I include the option of using commonly available canned peas or beans. Make sure to drain and rinse them thoroughly before using them.

pat them *mostly* dry with paper towels. Store refrigerated, wrapped in kitchen or paper towels in ziplock bags. They will stay fresh for up to a month. For extended use, air dry them completely and store in an airtight container.

Fennel seeds These are the oval pale greenish-yellow seeds of the common fennel plant, a member of the parsley family. They are sweetly aromatic and have an aniselike flavor. In Indian cooking, they are used whole and ground in both sweet and savory dishes. Roasted fennel seeds are sometimes sugarcoated and chewed as a digestive and mouth freshener after Indian meals. They are easily available in most grocery stores.

Fenugreek leaves Known as *methi* when fresh and *kasoori methi* when dried, these leaves are extensively used in Indian cuisine. The slightly perfumed and bitter flavor of the leaves goes very well with curries. The leaves are sold fresh when in season or dried in packets year-round in Indian markets. The dried leaves can also be purchased online (see Shopping Guide, page 155). Frozen chopped fenugreek greens are also now available at some Indian grocery stores. I use the dried version—kasoori methi—in the recipes in this book because of its unique flavor and strong taste. In comparison, fresh methi

(young leaves and sprouts of fenugreek) has a very mild flavor. When fresh, the leaves are eaten as greens and are commonly cooked with potatoes, spinach and paneer and eaten with roti or naan. The dried leaves have a bitter taste and strong aroma and are used in small amounts to flavor dishes. There is no real substitute for this ingredient in Indian recipes, and so I have made its use optional throughout the book.

Fenugreek seeds The fenugreek seeds are bitter yellowish-brown tiny seeds that provide the commercial curry powders with their distinctive aroma. They are used in small quantities because of their strong flavor. The seeds are often oil-roasted and then ground to create a bitter balance in curries in the southern part of India; in the eastern part of India the seeds are stir-fried whole. This is available only in Southeast Asian or Indian grocery stores.

Ginger This is a knobby, pale-brown rhizome of a perennial tropical plant. It is available fresh, dried and ground into powder and as a preserved stem. Ground ginger or preserved ginger is almost never used in Indian cooking. Fresh ginger root has no aroma, but once you peel or cut it, it emits a warm, woody aroma with citrus undertones. When used fresh, it has a peppery hot bite to it. Fresh ginger is used throughout India and is a very common ingredient in Indian cooking. It is often ground into a paste, finely chopped, or made into juice. We use chopped ginger to stir-fry vegetables, crushed ginger or ginger paste in meat stews and legumes and thinly sliced slivers of raw ginger are sometimes sprinkled over curries just before serving. While shopping for fresh ginger, look for hard and heavy root that

snaps easily into pieces. Avoid dry, shriveled roots that feel light for their size. Keep fresh ginger in refrigerator crisper in a plastic bag with a paper towel to absorb moisture (to prevent mold, change towel occasionally). It will last for two or three weeks. To extend its life, you can freeze the ginger. You don't even need to defrost it, and ginger is much easier to grate when frozen.

Ghee This is the Indian version of clarified butter—that is, butter which has its milk solids removed. Ghee is one of the primary cooking fats used in India. Unlike regular clarified butter, the process of making ghee involves melting the butter over a low heat, and then simmering it until all the moisture has evaporated and the milk solids have separated from the fat. The milk solids are then removed to leave a pure fat that is excellent for deep-frying because of its high smoke point. I just love the way ghee infuses food with a delicious flavor and aroma. It has a buttery and a nutty flavor. I often add a few drops to hot rice dishes, dals and curries as finishing oil. Ghee has a very long shelf life and at room temperature will keep up to 4 to 6 months. Store it in a clean airtight plastic or glass jar. Ghee is commonly available in Indian grocery stores and it is typically sold in glass or plastic jars as a solid fat like butter. I have used ghee in many recipes in this book, which I feel brings out the best flavor of those dishes. If you do not have ghee, substitute it with a mixture of equal parts of unsalted butter and neutral-flavored oil.**To make ghee at home:** Melt 1 pound (500 g) of unsalted butter in a heavy-bottomed, medium-size saucepan over medium-low heat. Simmer, stirring occasionally, until the milk solids turn a rich golden color and settle to the bottom of the pan, about 15 to 20 minutes. Initially, the butter will foam and, as it simmers, the foam will subside. Pass the mixture through a fine-mesh strainer lined with cheesecloth or muslin into a sterilized jar. This recipe makes about 2 cups (500 ml) of ghee. *Note*: use either one 12-inch- (30-cm)-square piece of fine muslin or four layers of cheesecloth.

Lentils, *see* **dried legumes**

Mace It is the dark, red lacy membrane that covers the outside of the nutmeg shell. This is skillfully removed after the fruit burst opens, then flattened and dried to become mace, as we know the spice. Mace has a rich, warm, citrusy, spicy aroma and bitter taste, very similar to nutmeg, only stronger. It is often used in small quantities for making spice blends and pastes, such as Dhaba Spice (page 34) and Vindaloo Curry Paste (page 34). Whole mace, or "blades," is often toasted and ground and then mixed with yogurt, herbs and other spices to marinate Indian grilled or roasted meats. Whole mace is also an important ingredient in rice dishes made with basmati rice (such as Saffron Chicken Biriyani (page 128), where it imparts a unique flavor to the dish. This aromatic spice is a good match for the wonderful fragrance of basmati rice. Whole mace is available in Indian or Middle Eastern grocery stores or online (see Shopping Guide, page 155).

Mango Mangoes are native to the Indian sub-continent, where they have been grown for more than 4,000 years. Because the mango seed can't be dispersed naturally by wind or water, due to its large size and weight, it is believed that people who moved from one region to another transported the fruit to new areas. Though mango cultivation has now spread to many parts of the tropical and sub-tropical world, like Brazil, Mexico, west Indies and parts of Florida, nearly half of the world's mangoes are cultivated in India alone. Mangoes are widely used in Indian cuisine. The green unripe mangoes are sour in taste and are used to make chutneys (Sweet Mango Chutney, page 41), pickles (Green Mango Pickle, page 47) and sometimes side dishes like mango *pachadi*, which is similar to Carrot Yogurt Slaw (page 46) in this book. (To make mango pachadi, simply replace the carrots with green unripe mangoes.) Green unripe mangoes are also eaten raw with a sprinkle of salt and red chili powder, which is my favorite way to eat them. *Panna*, a very popular and refreshing summer drink, is made with green unripe mangoes blended with water, mint, sugar, salt, cumin and ice. Ripe mangoes are typically eaten fresh. Sweet Mango Yogurt Lassi (page 152), made by adding mango pulp to yogurt, is the most popular drink in India and Indian restaurants worldwide. Ripe mangoes are used to make desserts (Sweet Mangoes in a Creamy Custard, page 143) and are also used to make savory curries. *Aamras*, sweetened, thick ripe mango pulp with flavor of cardamom, is a popular dish in western India that is served along with Fried Puffed Bread (page 138). The Alfonso mango is considered the sweetest and best of all eating mangoes. For some recipes, I use canned Alfonzo mango purée (available in Indian grocery stores) when they are not in season. When shopping for ripe mangoes look for mangoes with unblemished yellow skin with a red tinge or blush. Avoid mangoes with bruises or soft spots. You can buy green mangoes and ripen them at home by placing them in a brown paper bag on your counter for a week. Ripe mangoes will last 2 to 3 days at room temperature or for up to 5 days in a plastic bag in the refrigerator. You can find green mangoes in most Indian, Southeast Asian or South American markets. When shopping for green mangoes, make sure they are firm and their skins are dark green in color and unblemished. Store them at room temperature uncovered. They will last about 2 weeks.

Mint Mint is an aromatic, almost exclusively perennial, rarely annual, herb with a very refreshing taste. Fresh mint is used in Indian marinades, chutneys, drinks and desserts, and in curries and rice dishes. I also use dried mint for making breads in my kitchen. Chopped fresh mint leaves steeped in a cup of hot water with tea and honey is one of my favorite after dinner beverages. The spearmint variety is most commonly used in Indian cooking. When purchasing mint, make sure the leaves are fresh and green in color without and black spots or cracks. See "Storage Tips for Spices and Herbs," page 22.

Mustard seeds These tiny, round, hot and pungent seeds are from an annual plant of the cabbage family. They are available in white, yellow, brown, or black colors. The white seeds, the largest type, are used to make commercial mustards in the United States; and the yellow and brown seeds are used for European mustards and for pickling. In India, the black seeds are used in cooking and are the source of commonly used oil. Black mustard seeds are used whole and in powdered form. The whole seeds are used in vegetable dishes, curries, appetizers, salads, and dried legumes, while the powder is used to flavor steamed fish, pickles, and, again, curries. Mustard seeds are available at Indian grocery stores and online (see Shopping Guide, page 155).

Oils and fats In Indian kitchens, oil is used alone or in combination with ghee (clarified butter) to fry flavorings at the start of cooking or to deep-fry foods. The oil used depends on the culture and region. When I call for oil, you may use any neutral-flavored vegetable oil (for example, canola, safflower or corn oil). In addition to using unflavored oils, Indians use toasted sesame oil, coconut oil, peanut and mustard oil to impart distinct flavors to dishes. I have not used these oils in my recipes as some are hard to find and they give a very distinct flavor to the food, which, though popular in India, can be an acquired taste for non-Indian. When I call for oil for deep-frying, it's important to use an oil that is relatively stable at high temperatures, such as peanut oil or saf-flower oil. Additionally, olive oil, which is a very healthy oil, can also be used to cook Indian food.

Paprika Known as *kashmiri mirch* in India, paprika is a red powder made from the dried, mild, non-pungent chili peppers. It is mainly used for the rich red color it adds to curries. When added to hot oil, it immediately releases a deep red color. Most Indian paprika comes from Kashmir, hence the name. Kashmiri mirch is available at Indian grocery stores or online (see Shopping Guide, page 155). The easily available, mild Hungarian paprika is a good substitute.

Peppercorns These are one of the oldest-known spices and are often referred to as the king of spices. Peppercorns are the berries of the pepper plant, a branching evergreen creeper that grows mainly in the hot and humid monsoons forests of south west India. The plant is indigenous to India and dates back to 4000 B.C. The very tangy, slightly hot berries grow like clusters of grapes on the pepper plant. Peppercorns range in color from white, green to black. White peppercorns are picked ripe, and their outer skin is removed. Green peppercorns are under-ripe berries that are cured in brine. Black peppercorns are picked under ripe and allowed to dry until

dark black. Black peppercorns are most commonly used and impart an incredible flavor to all curries. The world's top quality black pepper is grown in India in the southwest coastal state of Kerala, and is known as Tellicherry pepper. The recipes in this book call for dry and oil-roasted, ground and crushed black peppercorns.

Pulses, *see* **Dried legumes**

Rice Rice is an indispensable part of Indian meals. It is served as a staple alongside curries and dals and is eaten at least twice a day in India. There are many distinctive kinds of rice grown and sold in the Indian subcontinent. For everyday meals, the type of rice used varies from region to region. While the people in southern regions prefer the locally available red rice or long-grain variety, northerners prefer the aromatic Basmati rice, which grows in the foothills of the Himalayas. One of my favorite varieties of rice, which I grew up eating, is a medium-grain par-boiled rice known as "red boiled rice" or "rosematta rice." It is made by parboiling the rice paddy before husking. After parboiling, the grain is separated from the husk, thereby leaving a part of the bran on the grain, which gives the rice its red or reddish brown color. It can be boiled as any other form of rice, though it takes twice as long to cook and often requires more water. I have not used it in this book because it is only available at Indian grocery stores or online. If you do run across it and would like to try it, I recommend serving it with dishes from the Southwest of India, and in particular with Coconut Chicken Curry (page 110) and Mangalore Fish Curry (page 105). Basmati, which means "queen of fragrance" in Hindi, is the most popular and the best-known rice of India, and it is the most expensive. It has a wonderful

fragrance when cooked with whole spices and is a good match for all Indian dishes. Basmati rice is always used for *puloa* and *biriyani*—two types of rice dishes—for it absorbs flavors beautifully and yet keeps its shape during cooking. Basmati rice, though preferred, is not absolutely necessary when making simpler rice preparations, such as Lemon Rice with Peanuts (page 129) or Mint Rice with Potatoes and Toasted Cumin (page 133). Whereas Basmati rice needs to be soaked prior to being rinsed and drained, ordinary long-grain rice only needs to be rinsed and drained.

Rosewater Rosewater or rose syrup is the leftover liquid remaining when rose petals and water are distilled together. It imparts an intoxicating fragrance of roses to rice dishes, desserts and drinks. Considered very auspicious for its aroma, it is also diluted with water and sprinkled at various religious and cultural ceremonies in India. A teaspoonful may be added to desserts (Watermelon Mint Ice, page 142) and drinks like Sweet Mango Yogurt Lassi (page 152) or to rice dishes to create a unique taste and aroma. Rose water is available in Indian or Middle Eastern grocery stores.

Saffron These intense yellow-orange threads are the dried orange-to-deep-red stigmas of a small purple flower of the saffron crocus, a member of the iris family. It is the world's most expensive spice as it takes almost 75,000 handpicked blossoms to make one pound of saffron. Use saffron sparingly as it just takes four to five strands of saffron to flavor a dish that feeds four. It has a distinctly warm, rich, powerful, and intense flavor. It is available in strands or ground. I recommend the strands for the sake of more assured quality. Gently heat saffron on a dry skillet before using as heat brings out its aroma. There is no acceptable substitute for saffron. Saffron is available in Indian or Middle Eastern grocery stores, gourmet stores and online (see Shopping Guide, page 155).

Salt The most common salt that is used in North America is table salt. It is very fine in texture and is often supplemented with iodine. Table salt, when compared to kosher or sea salt, is much saltier. Sea salt is the most popular salt used in Indian cooking. Measurements used in the recipes in this book are for common table salt. If you prefer to use kosher salt or sea salt, you will most likely need to increase the amount of salt by 10 to 15 percent. However, it is always a good idea to taste and check for seasoning before adding more. **Black salt** (*kala namak*)—Contrary to its name, powdered black salt is purplish pink in color. It is an unrefined sea salt with a very strong and sulfurous taste. It is available in rock or powder form, and is very traditional to India. Its distinctive earthy flavor and aroma helps to bring out the flavor in relishes, salads, raitas and snacks. It is an essential ingredient in making Chaat Masala (page 35). Black salt is a better choice for those on a low-sodium diet because it has a low-sodium content. It is available in Indian grocery stores. Feel adventurous? Try sprinkling ¼ teaspoon of black salt, a pinch of black pepper and squeeze of fresh lime over a chilled glass of Pepsi or Coke to enjoy a *masala cola*, an popular Indian street-style summer beverage.

Star anise This dried, star-shaped, dark-brown pod contains licorice-flavored seeds. The pods grow on an evergreen tree that is a member of the magnolia family. Star anise is used to flavor and add an enticing aroma to both sweet and savory dishes. It is often used on its own or ground with different spices to make blends. This spice is available at Indian and Asian grocery stores, online (see Shopping Guide, page 155) and at many conventional supermarkets.

Sesame seeds These tiny seeds are harvested from a flowering that is widely adapted in tropical regions around the world and is cultivated for its edible seeds. Whole or ground white sesame seeds are used in savory Indian dishes, breads and many sweets. Sometimes the seeds are toasted to heighten their nutty flavor. They come in a host of different colors, depending upon the variety, including white, yellow, black and red. In general, the paler varieties of sesame seeds are used in the West and Middle East, while the black varieties are more common in the East. They are available in most grocery stores.

Tamarind This is the curved brown bean pod of the tamarind tree. The pod contains a sticky pulp enclosing one to twelve shiny black seeds. It is the pulp that is used as a flavoring for its sweet-and-sour fruity aroma and taste. It is used in chutneys, preserves and curries. Tamarind is available in South Asian grocery stores, natural foods stores, and some conventional supermarkets in one or more of the following three ways: in pod form, pressed into a fibrous dried slab, or in jars of tamarind "paste" or "concentrate," which has a jamlike consistency. I use the tamarind paste in the recipes in this book simply because it is the most convenient form to use and is fairly easy to find.

Alternatively to create tamarind juice from the dried slab, soak a walnut-size chunk of the dried pulp (this is equivalent to 1 teaspoon tamarind paste) in ½ cup (125 ml) of warm water for 15 minutes. After soaking the pulp in water, break it up with your fingers, and then mash it with a fork until the liquid is muddy brown in appearance. Strain this mixture before use through a fine-mesh strainer. Using the back of spoon, mash and push the pulp through the fine-mesh strainer to extract any remaining juice.

Turmeric It is a rhizome of a tropical plant in the ginger family. The fresh root is boiled, peeled, sun-dried, and ground into a bright yellow-orange powder. Ground turmeric has a warm, peppery aroma—reminiscent of ginger—and a strong, bitter taste, which mellows upon cooking. It is used to color many curries and is sometimes used as a "poor man's substitute" for saffron due to the similar color it imparts; however, the taste is quite different.

Yogurt Thick and creamy yogurt is made every day in homes across the Indian subcontinent and it is an important part of every meal. It is most commonly enjoyed plain as a mild contrast to spicy foods. Raitas—cooling salads made with yogurt and crunchy vegetables—are very popular. Yogurt is often churned into cooling drinks with spices, and is the base for many desserts. In savory coking, its main role is as a souring agent, though it also aids digestion. In India it is customary to end a meal with either plain yogurt mixed with rice or a glass of Indian spiced "buttermilk" (thinned yogurt with salt, green chilies, ginger and salt which is common in southern India). The best yogurt to use for the recipes in this book is a thick plain natural yogurt made from whole milk. Look for organic whole milk yogurt for the best consistency and flavor.

Chapter 1

Indian Spice Mixes

Indian cooking is all about spices and flavor. To the Indian cook, the two are one in the same: spice equals flavor. I learned this from my mother and grandmother, who often spent several of their afternoon hours preparing the spices to be used for our daily meals. And it is from them that I learned the benefit of grinding fresh spices and most importantly how the subtle flavors hidden within the spices are gently released when they are slightly roasted before being ground.

To understand Indian cooking is to understand how to use spices individually and in combination to enhance food. The specific mixture of spices in the food is referred to as a *masala*, which means a blend of spices or herbs. It is this unique combination of spices or herbs that creates the distinctive taste of each dish. This section includes recipes for masalas and other basic flavor components that form the building blocks of Indian cooking.

Masalas can be in the form of a powder or a paste. Different Indian recipes may call for a different blend of masalas in either form. Often a recipe will call for a just a sprinkling of mustard seeds and ground turmeric, whereas some recipes may call for a masala that is a blend of over twenty different spices. Do not be alarmed! I have not included such elaborate spice blends in this book. In fact, even a minimal use of spices will lend a wonderful, aromatic accent to a dish. So do not hesitate to use just a few spices to create your masalas. Sprinkle cumin seeds when you cook potatoes or add a stick of cinnamon while boiling rice. Even a single spice can bring out the flavor of a dish.

The proportion of ingredients in these spice blends, as well as the amount used in a recipe, can be adjusted to suit your taste. I urge you to be adventurous with the spice blends in this book. Begin by trying the different blends in this section. You will soon be able to identify the unique flavor each brings to a dish. Then experiment with tweaking the spice profiles to arrive at your own personal versions. The only guideline I would suggest is to maintain a balance between the hot flavors (like peppercorn and cloves) and the aromatic flavors (like cardamom, cinnamon and mace).

You can also substitute many of these masalas with store-bought, premade spice mixes. However, for the best flavor, I recommend using freshly blended spices. When making masalas at home, you are able to slightly roast the spices before grinding them into a powder or a paste, an extra step that helps to release the flavors and oils of spices into the blend, thus adding more potency (and magic!) to the spice mixture.

Indian Five Spice Mix *Panch Phoran*

This is the Indian equivalent of Chinese five spice powder. It is a popular blend used in Bengali cuisine. Panch phoron is a colorful blend of equal quantities of cumin seeds, mustard seeds, fenugreek seeds, fennel seeds and nigella seeds. There are two traditional versions of this spice mix: one whole and one ground. When used whole, the spices are added to hot oil before adding the vegetables, lentils or legumes. This method, known as tempering, is a very common technique in Indian cooking. When used in its ground form, this spice blend is added at the very end of the cooking process to flavor dishes. My favorite technique is to coarsely grind the blend and use it to crust fish fillets and chicken breasts. In the recipes in this book I call for using it in its ground form only. But I encourage you to try using the whole seeds. Nigella seeds can be found in Middle Eastern or Indian food stores as well as specialty food markets. They are also known as black onion seeds. If you don't have nigella seeds, substitute celery seeds.

Makes about 1 cup (125 g)
Prep time: 5 minutes
Cook time: 5 minutes

1 tablespoon cumin seeds
1 tablespoon black mustard seeds
1 tablespoon fenugreek seeds (methi seeds)
1 tablespoon fennel seeds
1 tablespoon nigella seeds or celery seeds

1 If you plan to use this spice mixture in its ground form, dry roast the whole spices over medium heat in a small, nonstick skillet, stirring often, until fragrant, 1 to 1½ minutes.

2 Remove the spices from the skillet and set aside to cool completely.

3 Finely or coarsely grind the whole spices in an electric coffee grinder and store in an airtight jar. *Note*: Some recipes call for a coarsely ground blend. Remember to check the recipe you're planning to make to see if this is the case before grinding the spices.

TIPS FOR USING WHOLE PANCH PHORAN If you plan to use the spices whole, simply mix all of the spice together and store in an airtight jar. To use this spice mix in its whole-seed form, you might sauté some of the whole spice mixture in ghee until fragrant and drizzle the mixture on food as a garnish to liven flavor. Alternatively, to make a simple Bengali vegetable dish, add 2 tablespoons of whole Panch Phoran to a tablespoon of hot oil and, when fragrant (about 25 to 30 seconds), add a teaspoon of minced fresh ginger, a pinch of ground turmeric and salt to taste along with a mix of diced, fresh seasonal vegetables (1 pound/ 500 g total). Sauté the vegetables until tender and serve hot as a side dish.

Red Masala Paste

Lal Mirch Masala

The flavor of this paste is something I grew up, and it's one of my favorite flavors. This *masala* paste is frequently used to marinate fish and is used when preparing bone-in coconut chicken curry with fresh curry leaves or a south Indian lamb stew. To make this masala, the spices and dried red chilies are tempered in oil first and then ground to a paste. Traditionally the masala ingredients are ground in a stone grinder, but for convenience I use a food processor or blender. I make this masala paste in large batches. And for a good reason! If you have some on hand, you can whip up a quick flavor-packed meal in minutes. I love to smear this on fish fillets like tilapia, sea bass or halibut and pan-fry them. Sometimes I make a quick curry by boiling meat or vegetables with coconut milk, Red Masala Paste and fresh coriander leaves (cilantro).

Makes about 1¹/₂ cups (600 g)
Prep time: 15 minutes
Cook time: 7 minutes

1 tablespoon oil
15 dried red chili peppers, broken into small pieces
3 tablespoons coriander seeds
1 tablespoon cumin seeds
1 teaspoon black peppercorns
Two ¹/₂-in (1.25-cm) cinnamon sticks
¹/₂ teaspoon fenugreek seeds (optional)
15 cloves garlic
One ¹/₂-in (1.25-cm) piece fresh ginger, peeled
1 tablespoon shredded, unsweetened coconut (frozen, reconstituted dried, or freshly grated) (page 24)
1 teaspoon tamarind paste
¹/₂ teaspoon ground turmeric
About ¹/₂ cup (125 ml) water

1 Heat the oil in a large non-stick skillet over medium heat. Add the chili peppers, coriander, cumin, peppercorns, cinnamon, fenugreek, if using, garlic and ginger. Cook, stirring until aromatic, about 5 to 7 minutes. Remove the spices from the skillet and let cool slightly.
2 Place the spice mixture in a food processor or blender. Add the coconut, tamarind and turmeric. Process the mixture to make a smooth paste adding water a little at a time. Stop occasionally and scrape down the sides of the processor.
3 Transfer to an airtight container. Store the masala in the refrigerator for up to 3 weeks.

Ginger-Garlic Paste *Pissa Adrak Lahsoon*

A lot of Indian recipes call for this smooth, flavorful paste. Although you can easily find this ginger-garlic paste at Asian markets, it is simple enough to make it at home and it keeps well in the refrigerator. Plus the homemade paste gives the dish a much better flavor than the store-bought one. Basically it is just equal amounts of fresh ginger and garlic pulsed together.

Makes about 1¹/₂ cups (500 g)

¹/₂ lb (250 g) ginger (2 pieces, each about 4 in/10 cm in length), peeled and coarsely chopped
¹/₂ lb (250 g) garlic (about 6 to 7 heads), coarsely chopped
¹/₄ cup (65 ml) water

1 Place the ginger and garlic in a food processor or a blender. Add the water and process to make a fine paste.
2 Store the paste in a clean jar with a tight-fitting lid in the refrigerator up to 3 to 4 weeks.

TIP For a longer shelf life always use a clean spoon each time you dip into your masala jar. It is a common habit for new cooks, especially those in training in busy professional kitchens, to use dirty spoons or double dip spice pastes or masalas, which will cause the blend to go rancid sooner than it would otherwise. It's a shame to waste a large batch of this spice paste simply from a bad habit!

Indian Grilling and Roasting Rub

Making your own fresh spice blends and pastes makes a world of difference in your cooking. This is an aromatic blend that I created inspired by aromatic Indian spices and the western grilling rubs. This blend is ideal for marinating steak, fish or chicken. This can be used as a dry rub or can be mixed in oil to create a flavorful marinade. I like to blend this mixture into a coarse mix, where I can feel the crunch of the spices with the food.

Makes about 1 cup (125 g)
Prep time: 5 minutes
Cook time: 5 minutes

2 tablespoons coriander seeds
1 tablespoon fennel seeds
2 teaspoons cumin seeds
1 teaspoon whole cloves
$1/2$ tablespoon black peppercorns
1 tablespoon light brown sugar
1 teaspoon ginger powder
1 teaspoon garlic powder
2 teaspoons dried mint leaves
1 teaspoon salt

1 Dry roast the whole spices in a small nonstick skillet over medium heat, stirring until fragrant, 1 to 2 minutes. Remove the spices from the skillet and set aside to let cool completely.
2 Coarsely grind all the whole spices in an electric coffee grinder with the powdered spices, dried mint leaves and salt. Store in an airtight jar.

Aromatic Spice Mix *Bhuna Masala*

This spice mix is ideal for mildly spiced dishes. I like to use it for a quick meal of grilled fish fillets or chicken breasts. I also use it for finishing sauces and stews.

Makes about $2/3$ cup (75 g)
Prep time: 5 minutes
Cook time: 5 minutes

20 green cardamom pods
1 tablespoon cumin seeds
1 tablespoon coriander seeds
$1/2$ tablespoon black peppercorns
Three 1-in (2.5-cm) cinnamon sticks
6 whole star anise

1 Dry roast the whole spices in a small skillet over medium heat, stirring until fragrant, 1 to 2 minutes. Remove the spices from the skillet and set aside to let cool completely.
2 Grind the whole spices in an electric coffee grinder to a fine powder. Store in an airtight jar up to 4 to 6 weeks.

Vindaloo Curry Paste

Vindaloo Masala

This spicy curry paste reflects the Portuguese influence in the western Indian state of Goa. Its primary flavors come from vinegar and dried red chilies. The term *vindaloo* derives from the Portuguese dish "Carne de Vinha d' Alhos," a dish of meat, usually pork, with vinegar and garlic. Vindaloo is a very popular restaurant curry among westerners who love hot and spicy Indian dishes. This paste is very versatile—use this with broth or water to flavor meat and vegetable curries.

Makes about 1 cup (200 g)
Prep time: 5 minutes plus 1 hour for
   soaking
Cook time: 15 minutes

8 dried red chili peppers
1 cup (250 ml) red wine vinegar
$\frac{1}{2}$ cup (125 ml) water
1 tablespoon sugar
One 1-in (2.5-cm) piece fresh ginger, peeled
2 tablespoons chopped garlic
20 to 25 fresh curry leaves
$\frac{1}{2}$ cup (25 g) cumin seeds
$\frac{1}{2}$ cup (25 g) coriander seeds
2 teaspoons mustard seeds
10 green cardamom pods
Two $\frac{1}{2}$-in (1.25-cm) cinnamon sticks
1 teaspoon ground mace
2 tablespoons black peppercorns
1 teaspoon whole cloves
2 teaspoons salt
4 tablespoons oil

1 Combine the dried red chili peppers, vinegar and water in a small bowl and let soak for about 2 hours.

2 Process the chili peppers and their soaking liquid, the sugar, ginger, garlic, curry leaves, spices and salt in a heavy duty food processor to make a smooth paste. Add more water if necessary.

3 Heat the oil in a large non-stick pan over medium-high heat. Lower the heat to medium and fry the paste for 10 to 12 minutes over medium heat until rich brownish red color. Let it cool, then store in an airtight container for about 2 months in the refrigerator or in ziplock bags for 6 months in the freezer.

Dhaba Spice

Dhaba Masala

Dhabas are small local restaurants or truck stops which are located along the highways of northern India. Dhabas generally serve delicious, heavily spiced dishes preferred by many travelers. Marinated meat, chicken, fish or cheese is given a distinct flavor with this versatile mixture of spices made famous by the dhabas.

Makes about $\frac{2}{3}$ cup (75 g)
Prep time: 5 minutes
Cook time: 5 minutes

2 tablespoons cumin seeds
2 tablespoons coriander seeds
One $\frac{1}{2}$-in (1.25-cm) stick cinnamon
1 teaspoon whole cloves
1 teaspoon fennel seeds
1 teaspoon Asian chili powder or cayenne pepper
1 teaspoon ground turmeric
1 teaspoon garlic powder
1 teaspoon ground mace
1 teaspoon salt

1 Dry roast the whole spices in a small skillet over medium heat, stirring until fragrant, 1 to 2 minutes. Remove the spices from the skillet and set aside to let cool completely.

2 Grind the whole spices in an electric coffee grinder with the ground spices and salt to a fine powder. Store in an airtight jar.

Green Chili Masala

Hara Mirch Masala

Hara means green and usually made with fresh herbs like coriander leaves (cilantro) and/or mint leaves and green chili peppers. This can be used as a marinade or as dipping chutney.

Makes about 1 cup (300 g)
Prep time: 10 minutes

1/2 lb (250 g) fresh coriander leaves (cilantro), washed and drained
6 fresh green chili peppers, coarsely chopped
1 tablespoon coarsely chopped garlic
2 teaspoons peeled and coarsely chopped fresh ginger
1 teaspoon cumin seeds
1/2 cup (50 g) shredded, unsweetened coconut (frozen, reconstituted dried, or freshly grated) (page 24)
2 tablespoons water
1 teaspoon sugar
3 tablespoons freshly-squeezed lime juice
Salt, to taste

1 Remove and discard the coriander stems. Coarsely chop the leaves.
2 Place the coriander leaves, chili peppers, garlic, ginger, cumin, coconut and water in a food processor and process to a paste.
3 Transfer to a bowl. Stir in the sugar, lime juice and salt. Use immediately or refrigerate, covered, until ready to be used. This *masala* will keep for about 4 days in a well-sealed container in the refrigerator.

Home-Style Garam Masala

Garam Masala

Garam masala, literally "hot spice," is the most popular spice blend used in Indian cooking. It is the basic essence of Indian cooking. There are as many versions of garam masala as there are chefs. This recipe is what I use very often in my kitchen. It is important that the spices are blended fresh as needed. Many store-bought blends aren't roasted and tend to be very poor in flavor. Try this recipe and you will never buy a ready-made version.

Makes about 2/3 cup (75 g)
Prep time: 5 minutes
Cook time: 5 minutes

2 tablespoons cumin seeds
1 tablespoon coriander seeds
1 tablespoon black peppercorns
One 1/2-in (1.25-cm) stick cinnamon
10 green cardamom pods
1 teaspoon whole cloves
1 teaspoon fennel seeds
5 bay leaves

1 Dry roast the whole spices in a small skillet, over medium heat, stirring until fragrant, 1 to 2 minutes. Remove the spices from the skillet and set aside to let cool completely.
2 Grind the spices, with the bay leaves, in an electric spice grinder to a fine powder and store in an airtight jar for up to 4 to 6 weeks.

Chaat Masala

Chaat is a commonly used term to describe street snacks of India. These small dishes are infused with a complex blend of sweet, tangy and spicy flavors. This is always seasoned with a spice mix called *chaat masala*. Like any other Indian spice blends each one has their own regional variation throughout India. This spice blend is great in more than just snacks. You can use it to jazz up your salads, dressings, fresh fruit, fruit juices and grilled meats. This spice blend is easily available pre-mixed at Indian grocery stores.

Makes about 1 1/2 cups (200 g)
Prep time: 5 minutes
Cook time: 5 minutes

1 tablespoon cumin seeds, roasted and ground
4 tablespoons dried green mango powder (amchoor)
2 tablespoons ginger powder
2 tablespoons ajwain seeds, ground (optional)
1 tablespoon finely ground sea salt, preferably black salt (kala namak), or 2 teaspoons common table salt
2 teaspoons Asian chili powder or cayenne pepper
1 teaspoon ground asafetida (optional)

Mix all the spices together and store in an airtight container. The shelf life is about 1 month at room temperature or about 6 months if stored in the refrigerator.

A NOTE ABOUT THE INGREDIENTS *Amchoor* is a green mango powder. Unripe, sour green mangoes are sliced and dried in the sun and then ground. Amchoor, a key ingredient in chaat masala, is one of the many souring agents used in Indian cooking. *Ajwain* (also known as *ajowan caraway*, carom seeds or mistakenly as bishop's weed), is an uncommon spice except in certain areas of Asia. This small, grayish egg-shaped spice is commonly used in Indian cuisine. Raw ajwain smells almost exactly like thyme, however, it is more aromatic and less subtle in taste, as well as slightly bitter and pungent. It tastes like thyme or caraway, only stronger. It is only available in stores as a whole seed. Amchoor and ajwain are available at Indian grocery stores, specialty stores or online (see Shopping Guide, page 155).

Chapter 2

Chutneys and Accompaniments

A typical Indian meal is not complete if without chutneys and other accompaniments. Chutneys add that little bit of "something extra" to every bite of a meal. They are usually made with fruits or vegetables, and are often flavored with sugar, vinegar, or yogurt or a blend of different spices. Chutneys can be sweet, sour, spicy or tangy in taste, and they can also be dry or wet.

Indian chutneys are usually freshly made each day. They generally use ingredients that are seasonal and regional. Hence, chutneys do not usually contain preservatives and are supposed to be eaten within a few days.

The word chutney means "something which is crushed," and chutneys were traditionally made using a mortar and a pestle. However, the advent of modern cooking gadget means that we can use a food processer or a blender to easily create these wonderful accompaniments and add that "something extra" without a lot of effort.

In this chapter I have included a variety of my favorite chutneys, raitas, and other accompaniments spanning the entire range of tastes and textures. These accompaniments provide a contrasting flavor and texture that perfectly complements the meal. For example, raitas—the most common and popular Indian accompaniment—act as a coolant for curries and other fiery hot Indian dishes. No Indian meal is complete without at least one accompaniment, and fancy meals may have as many as five or more accompaniments. I've made suggestions throughout for pairing main dishes with accompaniments; but, I hope you have fun trying your own combinations to see what you like best.

Plum Tomato Chutney with Mustard Seeds *Tamatar Sarso ki Chutney*

This creation is inspired by the south Indian flavors of curry leaves and mustard seeds. I often serve this as a dip with flatbreads (pages 134–139), chips or crisped *pappadum* (page 55). It also goes well with Masala Lamb Chops (page 121) or Crunchy Potato and Corn Croquettes (page 52). It can be made in advance and served warm or at room temperature. I like to use red wine vinegar in this recipe, but you can use any vinegar or lemon juice as a substitute. This chutney keeps for up to one week in the refrigerator.

Makes about 1 cup (400 g)
Prep time: 15 minutes
Cook time: 15 minutes

1 tablespoon coriander seeds
1 teaspoon cumin seeds
$^1/_2$ teaspoon black peppercorns
$^1/_4$ cup (65 ml) oil
2 teaspoons black mustard seeds
5 to 6 fresh or dried curry leaves, torn
2 dried red chili peppers, broken in half
1 tablespoon minced garlic
1 small red onion, minced (about
   $^1/_4$ cup/50 g)
$^1/_2$ teaspoon paprika
Salt, to taste
2 plum tomatoes, chopped (about
   1$^1/_2$ cups/225 g)
2 tablespoons tomato paste
2 tablespoons white vinegar
$^1/_2$ cup (125 ml) water

1 Grind the coriander, cumin and peppercorns to a fine powder in a spice or a coffee grinder.
2 Heat the oil in a small saucepan over medium heat and add the mustard seeds, curry leaves and dried red chili peppers. Reduce the heat to the lowest setting and cover the pan. When the spluttering subsides add the garlic and onion. Stir a few seconds and then add the finely ground spices, paprika and salt. Continue to cook, while stirring, another 2 minutes.
3 Add the chopped tomato, tomato paste, vinegar and water. Reduce the heat to low, and cook, stirring occasionally, about 10 to 15 minutes. The chutney is ready when it becomes thick and fragrant and is reduced to about 1 cup (400 g). Serve hot or cold. Store in an airtight container in the refrigerator.

Garlic and Peanut Chutney

Moong-Phalli aur Lahssun ki Chutney

There is nothing like freshly made, tangy, spiced chutney to accompany crispy snacks, breads, curries and rice dishes. Made with peanuts, garlic and tamarind, this chutney has a good sharp clean flavor. Serve this as a spread with Spicy Lamb Burgers (page 117) or alongside warm Basmati Rice with Whole Spices (page 132).

Makes 1 cup (250 g)
Prep time: 15 minutes
Cook time: 5 minutes

$^1/_2$ cup (75 g) roasted, unsalted peanuts
10 large cloves garlic, peeled
2 fresh green chili peppers
4 tablespoons chopped fresh mint leaves
3 tablespoons tamarind paste
$^1/_4$ **cup (65 ml) water**
1 teaspoon sugar
Salt, to taste
1 tablespoon oil
1 teaspoon black mustard seeds
5 fresh or dried curry leaves
1 teaspoon sesame seeds

1 Process the peanuts, garlic, green chili peppers, and mint leaves in a food processor or a blender until minced. Add the tamarind paste, water, sugar and salt, and mix again to make a smooth purée. Add more water if needed for blending. Taste and adjust the seasonings by adding more salt, if needed, or more fresh green chili peppers, if you want it spicier.
2 Heat the oil in a large saucepan over medium-high heat. Add the mustard seeds, reduce the heat to low and cover the pan. When the sputtering subsides, add the curry leaves and sesame seeds and cook for 30 seconds, stirring constantly. This technique is called tempering or *tarhka*.
3 Add the tamarind mixture to the pan and simmer over low heat for 2 minutes. Cool and serve immediately or refrigerate up to 2 weeks.

Mint Chutney

Pudine ki Chutney

This green chutney is the most popular chutney throughout India. Every household adds its own special touch and ingredients and there are hundreds of variations on this chutney. Mint chutney can be served with any Indian snacks, breads or grilled meats and poultry. This chutney can be refrigerated for up to a week or frozen up to two to three months.

Makes 1 cup (250 g)
Prep time: 10 minutes

2 to 4 medium fresh green chili peppers
2 cups (60 g) packed fresh mint leaves
4 tablespoons fresh lime juice
$^1/_4$ **cup (65 ml) water**
1 teaspoon sugar
Salt, to taste

1 Process the chili peppers and mint leaves in a food processor or a blender until minced. Scrape the sides with a spatula. As you process, drizzle in the fresh lime juice and water and process until the chutney is smooth.
2 Add the sugar and salt. Taste and adjust the seasonings if needed. Transfer to a bowl and serve immediately or refrigerate for future use.

South Indian Coconut Chutney

Nariyal ki Chutney

This condiment complements crispy Indian snacks, breads, pancakes, grilled fish or chicken dishes perfectly. If you cannot find fresh coconut, use either unsweetened desiccated or shredded dried coconut that has been soaked in warm water to soften. I love to eat this with Split Pea Fritters (page 60) but it goes well with anything fried.

Makes 2 cups (600 g)
Prep time: 10 minutes
Cook time: 5 minutes

1 lb (500 g) shredded, unsweetened coconut (frozen, reconstituted dried, or freshly grated) (about 3 cups) (page 24)
2 fresh green chili peppers
One 1/2-in (1.25-cm) piece fresh ginger, peeled and coarsely chopped
1/2 tablespoon tamarind paste
1 bunch fresh coriander leaves (cilantro) (about 1/4 lb/125 g), stemmed
Salt, to taste
1 tablespoon oil
1 teaspoon black mustard seeds
1 dried red chili pepper, broken in half
5 fresh or dried curry leaves, torn

1 Blend together the coconut, green chili peppers and ginger in a food processor or a blender until smooth. Add the tamarind paste and fresh coriander leaves and process, scraping the sides of the bowl or jar a few times with a spatula until as smooth as possible. Add the salt and transfer to a serving bowl.

2 Heat the oil in a small, nonstick saucepan over medium-high heat and add the mustard seeds, dried red chili pepper and curry leaves. Reduce the heat to low and cover the pan until the spluttering subsides. This cooking technique is called tempering or *tarhka*.

3 Quickly add to the chutney and stir lightly as a garnish. Serve immediately or refrigerate for up to 1 week.

Sweet Mango Chutney

Mitha Aam Chutney

Unripe green mangoes are used in this sweet and slightly sour mango chutney. This condiment is especially good when paired with fish, bread and vegetable dishes. The possibilities are endless. Try it with Fried Puffed Bread (page 138), called *poori*, Tandoori Chicken (page 112) or store-bought plain *pappadum*. You might even try smearing it on bread instead of peanut butter like I do. Store the cooled chutney in a clean, airtight container at room temperature, and to increase the shelf life of this chutney for up to two to three months, store it out of direct light or preferably in a cool place. Eat responsibly because this chutney can be addictive.

Makes about 4 cups (700 g)
Prep time: 20 minutes
Cook time: 30 minutes

3 tablespoons butter
One 1-in (2.5-cm) cinnamon stick
4 green cardamom pods
1 tablespoon fennel seeds
4$^1/_2$ lbs (2 kg) green (unripe) mangoes
 (about 4 to 5 large mangoes), peeled
 and sliced
1 lb (500 g) granulated sugar (2$^1/_4$ cups)
1 lb (500 g) light brown sugar (2 cups,
 packed)
1 teaspoon Asian chili powder or
 cayenne pepper
1 tablespoon salt
1 cup (250 ml) malt vinegar

1 Melt the butter in a large saucepan over medium heat. Add the cinnamon stick, cardamom pods and fennel seeds, and sauté for 30 seconds. Add the mangoes, sugars, Asian chili powder or cayenne pepper, salt and vinegar. Mix thoroughly.

2 Reduce the heat to low and cook, stirring occasionally, until the sugar dissolves and the mangoes are softened, about 20 to 30 minutes. Be careful not to overcook as the consistency will become thick as the mixture cools. The consistency should be like a preserve or a jelly. Store in an airtight container at room temperature.

Spicy Apricot Chutney

Khubani Chutney

Sweet and spicy, this chutney goes well with grilled chicken or fish. I particularly enjoy it with Five Spice Blackened Salmon (page 104) and Salmon Kebabs (page 95). And it tastes equally good on plain toasted bread. It is very simple to make and will keep in the refrigerator, stored in an airtight container, for six to eight weeks, ready for use whenever you wish. This chutney makes a great takeaway gift for your guests.

Makes about 4 cups (1 kg)
Prep time: 10 minutes
Cook time: 30 minutes

$^1/_2$ lb (250 g) dried apricots (about 1$^1/_2$ cups), soaked overnight in 2 cups (500 ml) of water
One $^1/_2$-in (1.25-cm) piece fresh ginger, peeled
4 tablespoons chopped fresh mint leaves
2 cups (400 g) sugar
$^1/_4$ cup (65 ml) freshly-squeezed lemon juice
1 teaspoon salt
$^1/_2$ teaspoon ground green cardamom
2 teaspoons black pepper
1 teaspoon Asian chili powder or cayenne pepper
1 cup (100 g) golden raisins
$^3/_4$ cup (100 g) almonds, chopped

1 Drain the soaked apricots and squeeze out the excess moisture.
2 Grind the ginger and mint into a smooth paste using a spice grinder or mortar and pestle.
3 Cook the apricot, ginger and mint paste, sugar and lemon juice in a small saucepan over medium heat for 5 minutes. Add the rest of the ingredients and cook on low heat until it thickens, stirring occasionally, for about 20 to 30 minutes.
4 Remove from the heat and let cool. Place the chutney in a sterilized jar. Seal the jar with a tight-fitting lid and store in the refrigerator.

Cucumber and Onion Chaat

Kheera Pyaz ka Chaat

This refreshing and deliciously crunchy relish can be served with any Indian meal. It is yummy on a hot summer's day! And there are endless variations—try adding diced radish, carrots or apples to give this a twist when entertaining. This relish is a very common fixture of Indian meals, adding a flavorful bit of raw crunch with cooked foods, just as *raita* does. Serving combinations are limitless but my favorites are with Tandoori Chicken (page 112), Pepper Chicken (page 108), Five Spice Blackened Salmon (page 104) and Spicy Lamb Burgers (page 117).

Serves 4
Prep time: 15 minutes

2 medium seedless cucumbers (about 1$^1/_2$ lbs/750 g total), peeled and cut into $^1/_4$-in (6-mm) dice
1 large onion (about $^1/_2$ lb/250 g), cut into $^1/_4$-in (6-mm) dice
1 tomato (about $^1/_3$ lb/150 g), cut into $^1/_4$-in (6-mm) dice
4 tablespoons chopped fresh coriander leaves (cilantro)
Salt, to taste
2 teaspoons Chaat Masala (page 35)
2 tablespoons freshly-squeezed lemon juice
$^1/_4$ teaspoon Asian chili powder or cayenne pepper
1 teaspoon cumin seeds, roasted and coarsely ground

Mix together all of the ingredients in a medium mixing bowl. Serve immediately.

Spiced Garlic

Poondu Kolumbu

This traditional south Indian side dish is known as Poondu Kolumbu in the south or Lahsooni Kari in the north, which simply means "garlic curry." The pungent flavor of garlic is well complemented by the spices and tangy tamarind and tomatoes. Do not be put off by the quantity of garlic, although you might not want to prepare garlic curry if you are likely to be in close proximity to anyone for the following two days. Due to its potent flavor, it is best served as part of a larger meal, as one might serve a condiment. Serve this with Flaky Paratha Breads Stuffed with Potatoes (page 139) or any flatbread of your choice, or, for one of my favorite combinations, with Spicy Mixed Beans and Lentils (page 73) and Basmati Rice with Whole Spices (page 132). I also like to use this as a spread on toasted baguette.

Serves 4
Prep time: 15 minutes
Cook time: 30 minutes

3 tablespoons oil
1^1/$_4$ cups (150 g) garlic cloves, peeled
1 teaspoon fenugreek seeds
^{1}/$_2$ teaspoon cumin seeds
2 dried red chili peppers
1 tablespoon plus ^{1}/$_2$ cup (125 ml) water
^{1}/$_2$ teaspoon black mustard seeds
^{1}/$_2$ teaspoon fennel seeds
10 fresh or dried curry leaves
2 onions (about ^{3}/$_4$ lb/350 g total), minced
2 fresh green chili peppers, chopped
^{1}/$_2$ teaspoon ground turmeric
^{1}/$_2$ teaspoon Asian chili powder or cayenne pepper
Salt, to taste
2 tomatoes (about ^{3}/$_4$ lb/350 g total), diced
2 teaspoons tamarind paste

1 Heat 1 tablespoon of the oil in a skillet over low heat. Add ^{1}/4 cup (25 g) of the garlic cloves, the fenugreek, cumin and dried red chili peppers and fry for about 1 minute, until the garlic is golden brown. Remove with a slotted spoon and drain on paper towels. Transfer the cooked garlic and spices to a blender along with the 1 tablespoon of water and process to a fine paste. Set aside.

2 Heat the remaining 2 tablespoons of oil in a large saucepan over medium heat. Add the mustard seeds, let them splutter, and then add the fennel seeds, curry leaves, onions and green chili peppers. Cook for about 5 minutes, until the onions are soft. Add the turmeric, Asian chili powder or cayenne pepper and salt, followed by the diced tomatoes. Stir well and cook for an additional 4 to 5 minutes with the remaining ^{1}/2 cup (125 ml) of water.

3 Stir in the remaining cup of garlic cloves, the cooked garlic paste and the tamarind paste. Lower the heat and cook gently, stirring frequently, for 15 to 20 minutes until the sauce is thick and the garlic is soft. The mixture will get thicker as it cools down.

Avocado and Roasted Cumin Raita

Makhanphal aur Bhuna Jeera Raita

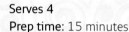

I cannot get enough of this creamy *raita* with Lemon and Saffron Chicken Kebabs (page 108)—and hot Whole-Wheat Griddle Breads (page 136)—my idea of the perfect lunch. Avocados often tend to be hard and not always ripe when you buy them in the supermarket. You may have to buy them a few days before you need them to ensure that they are soft to the touch and fully ripe when you're ready to make this raita.

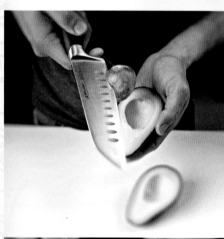

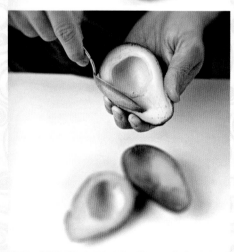

Serves 4
Prep time: 15 minutes

2 large ripe avocados (about 1 lb/500 g total)
2¹/₂ cups (610 g) plain yogurt, whisked until smooth
1 tablespoon freshly-squeezed lime juice
2 teaspoons cumin seeds, toasted and ground
1 teaspoon black peppercorns, toasted and ground
Salt, to taste
4 tablespoons minced fresh coriander leaves (cilantro)

1 Hold one of the avocadoes gently with one hand and with a large, sharp knife in the other hand, cut the avocado lengthwise around the pit. Open the two halves to expose the pit. Scoop out the pit with a spoon. Then scoop out the avocado flesh from the skin and chop it into 1-inch (2.5-cm) dice. Repeat with the other avocado.
2 Place the yogurt in a medium mixing bowl. Mix in the avocado, lime juice, half the ground cumin and black pepper and salt. Add the fresh coriander leaves and mix well.
3 Serve cold sprinkled with the remaining ground spices and salt.

Avocado and Roasted Cumin Raita

Cucumber and Yogurt Raita

Kheera Raita

Raita, a traditional yogurt-based condiment, is served with every Indian meal. All raitas are refreshing, and this version, with its cooling combination of cucumber and mint, is one of the most popular. Serve this raita as a dip with any appetizer or with spiced rice dishes like Fragrant Lamb Biriyani (page 126), Saffron Chicken Biriyani (page 128) and Black-Eyed Peas and Rice (page 127). Proportions of a raita do not have to be precise—you may customize it by adding more or less chili pepper or herbs, depending on your taste. You will find millions of uses for this simple dip, including making it thinner (with a little milk) and using it as a salad dressing.

Serves 4
Prep time: 15 minutes

2 cups (500 g), plain yogurt, whisked until smooth
2 small seedless cucumbers, grated (with or
   without the skin)
1 tomato, chopped (1 cup/150 g)
1 fresh green chili pepper, minced (with seeds)
1 tablespoon minced fresh mint leaves
1 tablespoon minced fresh coriander leaves
   (cilantro)
1 teaspoon Chaat Masala (page 35)
Salt, to taste

1 Place the yogurt in a serving dish and stir in the cucumbers, tomatoes, green chili pepper, mint and fresh coriander leaves.
2 Sprinkle the Chaat Masala on top and swirl lightly to mix. Add the salt to taste, keeping in mind that Chaat Masala has salt in it. Serve cold.

Pineapple and Beet Raita

Chukandar aur Annanas Raita

This seasoned creamy yogurt dip is a simple but delicious way to serve beets. It can be served with Indian bread and rice dishes. I like to serve this raita with Baked Garlic Naan (page 134) or Flaky Paratha Breads Stuffed with Potatoes (page 139). Sour cream is added to this dish to make it extra creamy and delicious, but it is not an essential ingredient. It will taste equally good with just plain yogurt.

Serves 4
Prep time: 15 minutes
Cook time: 15 minutes

2 medium beets (about $^3/_4$ lb/ 350g total)
2 cups (500 g) plain yogurt, whisked until smooth
1 cup (230 g) thick, Greek-style plain yogurt or sour cream, whisked
$^1/_2$ pineapple (about $^1/_2$ lb/250 g) peeled, eyes removed, cored and diced
3 tablespoons minced green onion (scallion)
1 teaspoon garlic powder
1 fresh green chili pepper, minced
Salt, to taste
$^1/_2$ teaspoon black pepper
2 tablespoons chopped fresh coriander leaves (cilantro), for garnish

1 Place the beets in a small pan with water to cover by approximately 2 inches (5 cm) and bring to a boil over high heat. Reduce the heat to medium-low, cover the pan, and simmer until tender, about 15 minutes. Remove the beets from the pan and let them cool until they are easy to handle. Peel and dice the beets. Set aside until completely cooled. Refrigerate if needed.
2 Mix together the 2 cups (500 g) of yogurt and the 1 cup (230 g) thick, Greek-style plain yogurt or sour cream in a bowl. Add the cooked beets, pineapple, green onion, garlic, minced green chili pepper, salt and black pepper; mix well. Garnish with the fresh coriander leaves and serve.

Carrot Yogurt Slaw   Gaajar Pachadi

Pachadi, a type of slaw, is a common staple in South Indian homes. Pachadis are typically flavored with mustard seeds and curry leaves. Here I have included other ingredients to add my personal touch. This side dish works well as a part of a large meal or can be served with traditional flatbreads like Whole-Wheat Griddle Breads (page 136) or Baked Garlic Naan (page 134) for a healthy snack or light meal. I like to top this slaw with seafood dishes like Masala-Crusted Tilapia (page 97) or Masala-Baked Red Snapper (page 96). This slaw keeps for up to two to three days in the refrigerator.

Serves 4
Prep time: 20 minutes

$^1/_4$ cup (60 g) plain yogurt
2 tablespoons sesame seeds, toasted and ground
2 teaspoons cumin seeds, toasted and ground
1 lb (500 g) carrots (about 5 to 6), peeled and grated
Salt, to taste
2 teaspoons oil
$^1/_2$ teaspoon black mustard seeds
5 fresh or dried curry leaves
1 fresh green chili pepper, slit and deseeded
$^1/_4$ teaspoon Asian chili powder or cayenne pepper
$^1/_4$ teaspoon ground turmeric
1 tablespoon freshly-squeezed lemon juice
2 tablespoons minced fresh mint leaves, for garnish

1 Mix together the yogurt, sesame seeds and cumin in a small bowl until well blended. Add the grated carrot and salt. Set aside.
2 Heat the oil in a small skillet over medium heat. Add the mustard seeds, let them splutter, and then add the curry leaves and green chili pepper. Cook for about 30 seconds, stirring, until the spices are aromatic. This cooking technique is called tempering, or *tarhka*. Stir in the Asian chili powder or cayenne pepper and turmeric.
3 Pour the flavored oil over the carrot mixture. Add the lemon juice and toss gently. Serve cold topped with the mint leaves.

Green Mango Pickle *Harae Aam ki Chutni*

My friend's son, all of nine years, goes rock climbing on weekends. Call me old fashioned . . . but does that even come close to the thrill of climbing guava and mango trees, and taking challenges from friends as to who can reach the highest branch with the plumpest, juiciest fruit? Like probably every child growing up in India, I have fond memories of climbing mango trees or aiming a slingshot at a neighbor's mango tree—I have even been chased by an irate *mali* (gardener) and sometimes the owner of the property. As a kid, I used to snack on diced raw green mangoes simply dipped in chili powder and salt. Later I learned how to make this into a pickle in my home kitchen in India and it remains one of my favorite condiments. There are thousands of different variations of mango pickle recipes, and you will find a version of it in every home, no matter where you are in India. This recipe is one of my favorites. Don't be alarmed by the amount of chili powder used in this recipe. Indian pickles are indeed very potent and are flavored with a lot of salt, chili peppers and oil, which helps to preserve them. Serve Green Mango Pickle with any rice dish. I love to eat this pickle with Lemon Rice with Peanuts (page 129) or Tamarind Rice (page 131) and wash it all down with a glass of Salted Lassi (page 152). This pickle will keep nicely in the refrigerator for a couple of months.

Makes about 3 cups (500 g)
Prep time: 15 minutes plus 8 hours for resting the mangoes in salt
Cook time: 10 minutes

3 green mangoes (1¼ lbs/600g total), peeled and cut into small dice (about ¼-in/6-mm)
¾ cup (75 g) salt
1½ cups (375 ml) oil
1 tablespoon black mustard seeds
1 teaspoon fennel seeds
1 teaspoon fenugreek seeds
2 dried red chili peppers, broken into small pieces
10 fresh or dried curry leaves
2 tablespoons ground turmeric
½ cup (50 g) Asian chili powder or cayenne pepper

1 Place the diced mangoes in a medium bowl. Sprinkle the salt over the top, toss and set aside for 6 to 8 hours. Drain the liquid from the mango and set aside.
2 Heat the oil in a skillet over medium heat; add the mustard seeds, fennel seeds, fenugreek seeds, dry red chili peppers and curry leaves. When the seeds splutter, turn the heat off and add the mangoes, turmeric and Asian chili powder or cayenne pepper. Mix well and cool completely. Store the pickle in a clean sterilized jar. This pickle tastes better as it ages. Refrigerate after opening.

Chapter 3

Appetizers

In this chapter, you will learn how to make some of my favorite appetizers, ranging from fritters, crispy fish fingers, Indian-spiced meatballs, and kebabs, to the famous *samosa*, or stuffed and fried turnovers. Many are served with chutneys and all go great with drinks. To balance out the meal—these tasty appetizers are not exactly fat-free—I included some healthy and flavorful salads, which will no doubt be appreciated by all your guests!

Appetizers and salads are a very important part of an Indian meal. Typically, salads are served with the meal rather than as a first course, whereas appetizers may be served either some time before the meal or at "tea time" with a cup of steaming hot *masala* (spiced) tea. In most Indian families, tea time is in the early evening or late afternoon, with dinner following a few hours later. Appetizers are usually spicy in taste, can also be eaten as a light snack served at tea time or before a meal.

Most Indian meals usually contain a salad and/or chutney. In comparison with the more heavily spiced chutneys, Indian salads are very lightly spiced and are usually made with either fresh fruits or vegetables. It is not very common to eat a salad made with poultry or seafood in India. Shrimp and Apple Salad (page 57) is not a traditional dish; it is my take on a seafood salad with Indian flavors which I enjoy eating as a light lunch.

Shrimp Bruschetta

These simple but innovative bruschetta with an Indian twist are delicious served as finger food at cocktail parties or as a starter. Best of all, these bruschetta can be whipped up at a moment's notice, allowing you to feed unexpected guests and look like a gourmet cook. Try not to eat them all yourself while you make them.

Serves 4
Prep time: 15 minutes
Cook time: 10 minutes

4 large cloves garlic
2 tablespoons oil
$^1/_2$ teaspoon black mustard seeds
5 fresh or dried curry leaves
1 cup (250 g) shallots, sliced
$^1/_2$ lb (250 g) fresh, medium-size shrimp (about 15 to 18), peeled, deveined and cut in half lengthwise
$^1/_4$ teaspoon crushed red pepper
$^1/_4$ teaspoon ground turmeric
1 small fresh green chili pepper, minced
1 tablespoon lemon juice
$^1/_2$ teaspoon salt
1 baguette, cut into $^1/_2$-in (1.25-cm) slices on the bias
Extra-virgin olive oil, for drizzling over toasts
2 tablespoons chopped fresh coriander leaves (cilantro) (optional)

1 Smash 3 of the garlic cloves with the side of a large knife. Leave the remaining clove whole.

2 Heat the oil in a large skillet or wok over high heat. Add the mustard seeds and, when they start to pop, add the 3 smashed garlic cloves, curry leaves and sliced shallots. Cook, stirring, 3 to 4 minutes or until the shallots are soft.

3 Stir in the shrimp, crushed red pepper, turmeric, green chili pepper, lemon juice and salt. Cook for 2 to 3 minutes or until the shrimp are cooked. Taste for seasoning and add more salt if needed. Set aside.

4 Toast or grill each piece of bread and rub with the whole garlic clove. Drizzle each toast generously with extra-virgin olive oil and top with the shrimp mixture. Garnish with the fresh coriander leaves. Serve warm or at room temperature.

Serves 4
Prep time: 20 minutes
Cook time: 15 minutes

4 skinless, white fish fillets (about 1¹⁄₂
    lbs/750 g), such as tilapia or halibut,
    cut into thin strips, about ¹⁄₂-in
    (1.25-cm) thick
Juice of 2 lemons
Salt
¹⁄₂ tablespoon ground coriander
1 cup (120 g) all-purpose flour
1¹⁄₄ cups (300 ml) water
One 2-in (5-cm) piece fresh ginger,
    peeled and minced
1 tablespoon minced garlic
1 teaspoon cumin seeds
1 teaspoon Asian chili powder or
    cayenne pepper
2 tablespoons minced fresh mint leaves
Oil, for deep-frying
Lemon wedges, for serving

1 Wash and clean the fish strips and pat dry on paper towels. Combine the lemon juice, ¹⁄₂ teaspoon of salt and coriander in a bowl. Add the fish strips and let marinate for 1 hour in the refrigerator. Remove the fish from the marinade and place on paper towels to remove any excess liquid.
2 Stir the flour and water together in a medium bowl until completely smooth. Add the ginger, garlic, cumin seeds, Asian chili powder or cayenne pepper and mint leaves.
3 Heat 2 inches of oil in a *kadhai*, small wok or large saucepan over medium heat to 325°F (160°C) on a deep-fry or candy thermometer. To gauge the temperature of the oil without a thermometer, drop a piece of bread about 1-inch (2.5-cm) square into the oil, turning the piece of bread often as the oil heats up. When the oil reaches 325°F (160°C), the bread will begin to brown quickly and turn golden brown all over—like a crouton—in about 40 seconds. Dip the fish fingers into the flour mixture to evenly coat, and deep-fry until golden brown and crisp, about 6 minutes. Remove with a slotted spoon and drain on paper towels. Transfer to a serving dish and serve hot with lemon wedges.

Crispy Masala Fish Fingers
Macchi Kae Pakorae

Here is an Indian version of pub-style fried fish. Buy the freshest fish available and be sure to use clean oil for deep-frying. I like to use cod for this recipe. Other suitable fish for this recipe are tilapia, snapper, halibut, sea bass, whiting and sea bream. Serve with Plum Tomato Chutney with Mustard Seeds (page 38) and a glass of chilled ale for a delicious cocktail snack.

Spicy Paneer Cheese Kebabs

Panner Kae Kebab

This is a variation on the classic tandoori appetizer known as *paneer tikka*. In this version, paneer cheese is marinated with spiced sour cream and cooked under a broiler. These kebabs can be served as a part of an elaborate Indian meal or as an appetizer. Because they're equally delicious at room temperature, they make a great picnic food as well.

Serves 6
Prep time: 15 minutes
Cook time: 15 minutes

1 cup (230 g) thick, Greek-style plain yogurt or sour cream
1 tablespoon minced garlic
2 tablespoons peeled and minced fresh ginger
1 teaspoon Chaat Masala (page 35)
1$^1/_2$ teaspoons Home-Style Garam Masala (page 35)
3 teaspoons Asian chili powder or cayenne pepper
1 fresh green chili pepper, minced
$^1/_2$ teaspoon cumin seeds, toasted and ground
$^1/_2$ teaspoon coriander seeds, toasted and ground
1 teaspoon salt
$^1/_2$ lb (250 g) paneer cheese cut into 3-in (7.5-cm) pieces about $^1/_2$-in (1.25-cm) thick
Lemon wedges, for garnish

1 Mix together the Greek-style plain yogurt or sour cream, garlic, ginger, Chaat Masala, Home-Style Garam Masala, Asian chili powder or cayenne pepper, green chili pepper, cumin, coriander and salt in a medium bowl.
2 Place the paneer cheese in a mixing bowl. Pour the yogurt mixture over the paneer and gently mix together, making sure that all the paneer pieces are well coated. Cover and marinate in the refrigerator for 3 to 4 hours.
3 Preheat the broiler to high, making sure the rack is close to the heat source to ensure a golden brown color. Grease a sheet pan.
4 Drain the marinade and transfer the paneer cheese piece by piece to the sheet pan.
5 Broil on the top rack until golden brown, about 5 minutes on each side. Do not overcook as paneer will toughen. Serve hot with lemon wedges.

Crunchy Potato and Corn Croquettes

Aloo aur Makki ki Tikki

These potato cakes are packed with crunchy corn, very simple to prepare and is one of India's popular comforting street food. These are traditionally served topped with Northern Chickpea Curry (page 69) and Mint Chutney (page 39) as a perfect teatime snack. If you don't have time to prepare homemade chutney, try serving it with store-bought Asian chili sauce—one of my favorite and delicious time-saving shortcuts.

Makes 12 to 14 croquettes
Prep time: 30 minutes plus 1 hour to chill the patties
Cook time: 10 minutes

1 lb (500 g) potatoes, boiled and mashed
$^1/_2$ cup (100 g) corn kernels, fresh or frozen
4 fresh green chili peppers, minced
4 tablespoons chopped fresh coriander leaves (cilantro)
3 teaspoons Chaat Masala (page 35)
1 teaspoon salt
1 cup (90 g) dried bread crumbs
2 tablespoons oil

1 Mix together the mashed potatoes, corn, green chili peppers, chopped fresh coriander leaves, Chaat Masala and salt in a large bowl until well blended.
2 Spread the bread crumbs on a plate or in a shallow bowl. Using your hands moistened with water, roll a small ball, about the size of a golf ball, of the potato mixture and dump it into the plate or bowl with the bread crumbs. Roll the ball around in the bread crumbs until coated. Then press down on the ball to form a flattened 2 to 3-inch (5 to 7.5-cm) round cake. Press the cake on the bread crumbs to evenly coat and put it on a plate. Continue to shape the rest of the mixture into cakes. Chill at least for 1 hour.
3 Heat 1 tablespoon of the oil in a large, nonstick skillet over medium heat and fry the first batch of cakes—6 to 7 at a time—until golden brown, about 3 to 4 minutes on each side. Heat the remaining 1 tablespoon of oil in the skillet and fry the remaining cakes. Drain on paper towels. Serve hot.

Spiced Meatballs

Sukka Kofta

Petite and light, these meatballs are the perfect finger food—enough to whet your guests' appetites, but not enough to fill them. For a unique and flavorful twist, sometimes I like to make them with Dhaba Spice (page 34). Simply replace the coriander, cumin, Asian chili powder, and Home-Style Garam Masala with Dhaba Spice. Though lamb is the traditional choice, ground beef can be used instead of lamb—it works really well in this recipe.

Makes 30 meatballs
Prep time: 30 minutes
Cook time: 15 minutes

1 lb (500 g) ground lamb or beef
4 tablespoons chopped fresh coriander
  leaves (cilantro)
1 fresh green chili pepper, minced
¼ teaspoon coriander seeds, crushed
¼ teaspoon cumin seeds, crushed
¼ teaspoon Asian chili powder or
  cayenne pepper
½ teaspoon Home-Style Garam
  Masala (page 35)
½ teaspoon salt
1 egg, lightly beaten
½ cup (45 g) dried bread crumbs
½ cup (60 g) all-purpose flour
4 tablespoons oil
Two 1-in (2.5-cm) cinnamon sticks
5 green cardamom pods
2 bay leaves
1 teaspoon fennel seeds
2 tablespoons thick, Greek-style plain
  yogurt or sour cream
2 tablespoons tomato purée
1 cup (250 ml) warm water

1 Line a sheet pan with plastic wrap.
2 Combine the ground lamb or beef, fresh coriander leaves, green chili pepper, coriander, cumin, Asian chili powder or cayenne pepper, Home-Style Garam Masala, salt, egg and bread crumbs in a large mixing bowl. Mix well using your hands.
3 Dip your hands in water and form about 30 meat balls, each about the size of a golf ball. Place on the prepared tray. Cover with plastic wrap and place in the refrigerator for 15 minutes to chill.
4 Spread the flour on a plate. Roll the meatballs in the flour and shake off any excess.

5 Heat the oil in a large nonstick skillet over medium heat. Add the cinnamon sticks, cardamom pods, bay leaves and fennel, and quickly stir. Immediately place the meatballs in the skillet in a single layer and fry them until they are browned on all sides, about 10 minutes.
6 Beat together the Greek-style plain yogurt or sour cream, tomato purée and warm water in a small bowl. Pour this mixture all over the meatballs. Cover, reduce the heat to low and simmer for 20 to 30 minutes, making sure the meatballs are not sticking to the bottom of the skillet.
7 Take the meatballs out of the sauce and transfer them to a serving platter without the whole spices. To serve, spoon a little sauce over the top and stick a toothpick into each meatball.

Smoky Eggplant Dip

Baingan ki Chutney

This is my twist on the famous Indian dish known as *Baingan Bharta* (page 84). It shares similarities to the more widely known Middle Eastern baba ghanoush, where the eggplants are grilled whole over a flame and then mashed to a pureé. The great thing about this recipe is that the eggplants can be roasted ahead. If you happen to have your grill fired up, and have eggplants on hand, throw them on the hot grill. Half your work will be done! When roasted ahead, the whole eggplants should be stored in ziplock bags in the refrigerator for up to three to four days. I like to add sour cream to this dip to give it an ultra creamy texture and flavor. One of my favorite ways to serve this dip is spread on wedges of toasted naan breads—as a sort of Indian bruschetta.

Serves 6
Prep time: 15 minutes
Cook time: 20 minutes

2 medium eggplants, about 1 lb (500 g) total
3 tablespoons oil
2 tablespoons minced fresh green chili pepper
1 large onion, minced (1 cup/200 g)
2 medium tomatoes, minced (1³/₄ cups/350 g)
4 tablespoons minced fresh coriander leaves (cilantro)
1 tablespoon Dhaba Spice (page 34) (substitute store-bought or Home-Style Garam Masala, page 35)
Salt, to taste
¹/₂ cup (115 g) thick, Greek-style plain yogurt or sour cream
2 sprigs fresh coriander leaves (cilantro), for garnish

1 Flame-char the whole eggplants on a gas grill or over the open flame of a gas burner, turning constantly until blackened and soft. Alternately, roast the eggplants in a preheated 375°F (190°C) oven on a sheet pan for about 15 to 20 minutes until completely soft and lightly burnt. Let cool until easy to handle, and then peel and mash the eggplant flesh.
2 Heat the oil in a large wok or saucepan over medium-high heat; add the minced green chili pepper and onion, and cook, stirring constantly, until golden, about 7 minutes. Add the tomatoes, minced fresh coriander leaves and cook, stirring occasionally, until the tomato juices evaporate, about 5 minutes.
3 Mix in the mashed eggplant, Dhaba Spice and salt. Reduce the heat to medium-low and cook, stirring and mashing with the back of a wooden spoon occasionally, about 10 to 15 minutes. Take it off the flame and cool completely. Mix in the Greek-style plain yogurt or sour cream until completely incorporated. Transfer to a serving dish, and serve cold garnished with the fresh coriander sprigs.

NOTE Dhaba Spice can be replaced with *garam masala,* which can be more readily found premixed in stores.

Masala Pappadums

Serves 4
Prep time: 10 minutes
Cook time: 4 minutes if using grill or gas flame, 30 seconds if deep-frying

4 store-bought pappadums, flavor of your choice
1 large red onion (about ¹/₂ lb/250 g), finely chopped
1 large tomato (about ¹/₂ lb/250 g), deseeded and finely chopped
4 tablespoons fresh coriander leaves (cilantro), chopped
2 fresh green chili peppers, deseeded and finely chopped
2 tablespoons chopped roasted peanuts
Juice of 2 limes
¹/₄ teaspoon salt
1 teaspoon Chaat Masala (page 35)

Pappadum, sometimes called *papad*, are dried disks of dough made from legume flours. They are often flavored with chili pepper, black pepper, garlic and cumin seeds. Some will be brittle and so thin that they're almost translucent, while others will be relatively thick and made perhaps from a different kind of legume. Pappadums are a great way to bring additional flavor and texture to an Indian meal. Sometimes they are just the added touch that completes a meal. Cooked pappadums can be served as is or stuffed or topped with toasted coconut, chopped herbs, spice mixtures, ground meats and nuts. Here is a quick recipe for Masala Pappadums. I prefer and recommend the lijjat brand, just because they are known for their famous pappadums in India, and they are easily available around the world in Indian grocery stores.

1 Roast the pappadums over the open flame of a gas burner or over a BBQ grill (approximately 1 minute per disc, turning frequently to expose both sides evenly to the heat. They will crinkle up into beautiful shapes almost at once. Alternately, slide them one at a time into a large skillet filled with hot oil (325°F/160°C)—they will instantly start to expand and change color. With a pair of tongs, try to hold each one under the surface of the oil until the whole disk has cooked, 5 to 7 seconds per pappadum. Remove from the fryer, drain excess oil, and stack them to cool and become crisp. (*Note*: while the pappadum is still hot and soft, you may shape it up into a cone or a pocket for a stylish presentation.)

2 Toss the onion, tomato, fresh coriander leaves, green chili peppers, peanuts, lime juice and salt in a medium mixing bowl. Spread the mixture evenly on the pappadums. Right before serving sprinkle on the Chaat Masala.

HOW TO MAKE CRISPED PAPPADUMS There are several different ways to cook the pappadums, all of which should result in nicely crisped pappadums. The most common methods to crisp pappadums are to deep-fry them in oil or roast them over a gas burner or a grill. While still hot, they can be shaped into pockets, rolls or any desired shapes before they cool and become crisp. To make crisped pappadums, follow Step 1 for Masala Pappadums.

Pomegranate and Mint Potato Salad

Aloo aur Anardana ki Chaat

This yummy salad, garnished with fresh pomegranate seeds and mint, is ideal for a lazy Sunday brunch. The combination of extra-virgin olive oil, red pepper flakes, mint and pomegranate seeds is heavenly! Its sweet and tart, slightly spicy flavors go very well with Indian flatbreads and lentil dishes.

Serves 4
Prep time: 20 minutes
Cook time: 15 minutes

$1\frac{1}{2}$ lbs (750 g) potatoes, peeled, boiled and diced
$\frac{3}{4}$ cup (125 g) split yellow peas (chana dal), soaked overnight and boiled until tender
$\frac{1}{2}$ cup (100 g) fresh pomegranate seeds (from 2 pomegranates)
4 tablespoons chopped fresh mint leaves
1 red onion (about $\frac{1}{3}$ lb/150 g), diced
1 cup (150 g) red cherry tomatoes, halved

Lemon-Honey Dressing
3 tablespoons freshly-squeezed lemon juice
2 teaspoons honey
3 tablespoons extra-virgin olive oil
Salt, to taste
$\frac{1}{2}$ teaspoon dried red pepper flakes
2 teaspoons cumin seeds, toasted and coarsely ground

1 Whisk together all the ingredients for the Lemon-Honey Dressing in a small bowl until well blended. Set aside.
2 Mix together the potatoes, yellow split peas, $\frac{1}{4}$ cup (50 g) of the pomegranate seeds, mint, onion and tomatoes in a large mixing bowl. Pour on the Lemon-Honey Dressing and toss gently.
3 Transfer to a glass serving bowl and sprinkle on the remaining $\frac{1}{4}$ cup (50 g) of pomegranate seeds. Serve chilled.

TIPS FOR REMOVING POMEGRANATE SEEDS Cut off the crown end of the pomegranate and discard. Score the rind of the pomegranate lengthwise into about 4 to 6 segments, but be sure not to cut all the way through. Soak the pomegranate upside down in a bowl of cold water for 5 to 10 minutes. Working over the bowl of water, break apart the rind of the pomegranate and remove the seeds from the membrane with your fingers. The seeds will sink to the bottom of the bowl. With a slotted spoon, remove the rind and membrane from the bowl. Drain the seeds in a sieve. Pat the seeds dry with a paper towels. Use immediately or store in an airtight container in the refrigerator for up to 2 days.

Pomegranate and Mint Potato Salad

Shrimp and Apple Salad *Jhinga ka salaad*

This flavorful salad is my idea of the perfect light lunch. To make a simple variation of this salad, add thinly sliced garden vegetables, such as carrots and radish, and fresh mint for a light summer meal. Serve with Avocado and Roasted Cumin Raita (page 44) on the side.

Serves 4
Prep time: 15 minutes
Cook time: 5 minutes

1 lb (500 g) fresh, medium-size shrimp (about 30 to 35), peeled, deveined and cut in half lengthwise
2 tablespoons oil
2 tablespoons freshly-squeezed lemon juice
2 teaspoons minced garlic
$^1/_2$ tablespoon Home-Style Garam Masala (page 35)
1 teaspoon salt
1 tablespoon tomato purée or tomato ketchup
1 small red bell pepper (about $^1/_4$ lb/125 g), cut into $^1/_2$-in (1.25-cm) dice
1 small red onion (about $^1/_4$ lb/125 g), cut into $^1/_2$-in (1.25-cm) dice
2 tomatoes (about $^3/_4$ lb/350 g), quartered
2 fresh green chili peppers, slit open lengthwise and deseeded
2 tablespoons chopped fresh coriander leaves (cilantro)
$^1/_4$ cup (25 g) sliced almonds, toasted
1 apple, peeled cored and cut into thin wedges
4 cups (250 g) mixed salad greens
4 lemon wedges, for garnish

1 Combine the shrimp, 1 tablespoon of the oil, 1 tablespoon of the lemon juice, garlic, Home-Style Garam Masala and salt in a bowl. Toss to evenly coat the shrimp. Cover and place in the refrigerator to marinate for at least 1 and up to 2 hours.
2 Heat the remaining 1 tablespoon of oil in a medium saucepan over medium heat. Add the shrimp and sauté until slightly brown, about 3 to 4 minutes. Add the tomato purée and cook, while stirring, for 1 minute. Transfer to a mixing bowl and let cool. Add the diced bell pepper and onion and toss to combine. Refrigerate until chilled.
3 When ready to serve, add the tomatoes, green chili peppers, fresh coriander leaves, almonds and apple wedges. Toss and serve over mixed greens garnished with the lemon wedges.

NOTE If you don't have a can of tomato purée already open, or have plans for making a tomato sauce in the near future, you can use an equal amount of tomato ketchup instead of the tomato purée, which gives the salad an underlying touch of sweet-tart flavor.

Samosas Three Ways

Samosas, a type of stuffed and fried pastry, are one of the most popular snack foods in India, and one of the most popular Indian foods worldwide. (They are often one of the first Indian foods to be sold in supermarkets outside India). They make excellent appetizers. Making them at home is simple, though making the *samosa* pastry dough does take some patience. You can use store-bought phyllo dough or puff pastry instead. Each of the filling variations is enough to fill four samosas, or one recipe of samosa pastry.

Serves 4
Prep time: 30 minutes
Cook time: 15 minutes

Samosa Pastry

2 cups (240 g) all-purpose flour
$1/2$ teaspoon salt
4 tablespoons plus 1 teaspoon oil
4 tablespoons water, plus more if needed

Potato and Peas Filling

4 tablespoons oil
1 teaspoon mustard seeds
1 onion (about $1/3$ lb/150 g), diced
1 teaspoon ground coriander
1 teaspoon Asian chili powder or cayenne pepper
1 teaspoon salt
$1/2$ teaspoon ground turmeric
2 potatoes (about $11/4$ lbs/600 g), peeled and diced
1 cup (130 g) green peas, fresh or frozen (shelled from 1 lb/500 g fresh pea pods or about half of one 10-oz/300-g package frozen peas)

Kheema Filling

4 tablespoons oil
1 large onion (about $3/4$ lb/350 g), chopped
1 tablespoon tomato paste
2 fresh green chili peppers, minced
1 tablespoon chopped garlic
1 teaspoon Asian chili powder or cayenne pepper
1 teaspoon salt
1 teaspoon Home-Style Garam Masala (page 35)
1 cup (250 ml) water
$1/2$ lb (250 g) ground lamb
4 tablespoons chopped fresh coriander leaves (cilantro)

Paneer and Spinach Filling

1 potato (about $1/2$ lb/250 g)
3 tablespoons oil
1 teaspoon cumin seeds
2 small green chili peppers, minced
1 onion (about $1/3$ lb/150 g), chopped
1 cup (100 g) grated Paneer Cheese (page 83)
2 cups (100 g) packed spinach leaves, washed
$1/2$ teaspoon ground turmeric
$1/2$ teaspoon salt
$1/2$ teaspoon Home-Style Garam Masala (page 35)
4 tablespoons chopped fresh coriander leaves (cilantro)

1 To make the Samosa Pastry: Sift the flour and salt into a bowl. Add the 4 tablespoons of oil and rub it in with your fingers until the mixture resembles coarse breadcrumbs. Slowly add about 4 tablespoons water and form the dough into a stiff ball, adding more water if needed.

2 Knead the dough for about 5 to 7 minutes on a floured surface until smooth. Make a ball. Rub the remaining 1 teaspoon of oil on the surface and set aside for at least 30 minutes, making sure it is tightly wrapped with plastic wrap. While the Samosa Pastry is resting, make the samosa filling of your choice and proceed to Step 6.

3 To make the Kheema Filling: Heat the oil in a skillet over medium heat and fry the onion until soft and golden, about 3 to 4 minutes. Add the tomato paste, minced green chili peppers, chopped garlic, Asian chili powder or cayenne pepper, salt, Home-Style Garam Masala and water, and bring to a boil. Stir in the ground lamb, reduce the heat to low and simmer, covered, until the lamb is cooked and the mixture is thickened, about 15 to 20 minutes. Stir in the fresh coriander leaves and set aside to cool.

4 To make the Potato and Peas Filling: Heat the oil in a skillet over medium heat. Add the mustard seeds and when they start to pop, add the onion and fry until soft.

Add the ground coriander, Asian chili powder or cayenne pepper, salt and ground turmeric, and cook, stirring constantly, for about 30 seconds. Add the potatoes and green peas. Cover and cook for 15 minutes, stirring frequently, until the potatoes are cooked. Remove from the heat and set aside.

5 To make the Paneer and Spinach Filling: Boil the potato in salted water until cooked, about 10 minutes. Drain and let cool slightly. Peel and mash in a small bowl. Set aside. Heat the oil in a skillet over medium heat. Add the cumin seeds, chili peppers and onion and fry for 3 to 5 minutes. Stir in the grated paneer, mashed boiled potato, spinach, ground turmeric, salt and Home-Style Garam Masala and cook until soft, about 4 minutes. Mix in the fresh coriander leaves and let cool.

6 When you are ready to fill the samosas, divide the Samosa Pastry into 8 balls. It is important to work with one ball of dough at time and to keep the other dough balls covered while working to prevent drying. Take a ball and roll it out into a 7-inch (18-cm) round. Cut it in half with a sharp knife. Working with one of the half-circles, with the straight edge positioned at the top, fold one of the sides inward to the center. With your finger, rub a little water on top of the folded edge. Now take the

other side and fold it inward, overlapping the moistened dough edge to form a cone. Press the two edges together. Fill the cone with about 2 tablespoons of the filling of your choice. Do not over fill the samosa. It is very important to make sure there is at least a ¼-inch (6-mm) wide border of dough along the top to make sure the filling does not come out while frying. With your finger, rub a little water along the inside edge of the dough at the top of the cone. Close the top of the cone by firmly pressing the open edges together. Press the top seam down with back side of the fork or flute it with your fingers. Fill the rest of the samosas.

7 Heat 2 inches of oil in a *kadhai*, small wok or large saucepan over medium heat to 325°F (160°C) on a deep-fry or candy thermometer. To gauge the temperature of the oil without a thermometer, drop a piece of bread about 1-inch (2.5-cm) square into the oil, turning the piece of bread often as the oil heats up. When the oil reaches 325°F (160°C), the bread will begin to brown quickly and turn golden brown all over—like a crouton—in about 40 seconds. Deep-fry the samosa in batches, turning frequently until golden brown and crisp. Remove with a slotted spoon and drain on paper towels. Serve hot or at room temperature.

Wrapping the Samosas

Split Pea Fritters

Dal kae Pakorae

During the monsoon season in India, people crave hot, fried snacks and tea. There can be nothing more consuming than seeing rain soaked mountains in front of you, freshly washed asphalt roads, couples sharing umbrellas, and raincoat-clad children returning from school splashing water onto each other from puddles—all while sitting on a bench on the roadside curb and sipping hot chai and nibbling snacks like these fritters! The restaurants and tea shops of Udipi, a city and region in coastal southwestern Indian state of Karnataka (and my home town), are famous for their snacks and variety of vadas (lentil- and rice-based fritters). The cuisine from this region of India, and especially its vegetarian delicacies, are popular all over India. The region is so famous for its food that restaurants serving its cuisine are known as "udupi" restaurants. These split pea fritters, known as *chaatambade* or *dal vada*, are just one of the many famous vadas from Udupi. This crunchy and incredibly tasty snack is traditionally made with split yellow peas (*chana dal*) and subtly flavored with green chili peppers, ginger and fresh coriander leaves (cilantro). I have added spinach for an added twist. If you do not care for spinach, use one-half pound (250 g) fresh dill instead—the result is equally delicious. Serve with South Indian Coconut Chutney (page 40) or Garlic and Peanut Chutney (page 39).

Serves 4
Prep time: 30 minutes plus 1 hour to soak lentils
Cook time: 15 minutes

2¹⁄₂ cups (425 g) split yellow peas (chana dal)
¹⁄₂ lb (250 g) fresh spinach, washed, stemmed and finely chopped

1 red onion (about ¹⁄₃ lb/150 g), minced
2 fresh green chili peppers, minced
One 1-in (2.5-cm) piece fresh ginger, peeled and minced
10 fresh or dried curry leaves, minced
4 tablespoons chopped fresh coriander leaves (cilantro)
1¹⁄₂ teaspoons salt
Oil, for deep-frying

1 Place the *chana dal* in a large bowl, cover with water, and set aside to soak for at least an hour. Put the soaked *dal* into a strainer and drain thoroughly. Transfer the dal to a blender and process for 2 to 3 minutes to a coarse paste without adding any water. It is important that some of the dal remains whole to give the fritters a crispy texture.

2 Transfer the coarse dal paste to a mixing bowl and add the chopped spinach, red onion, green chili peppers, ginger, curry leaves, fresh coriander leaves and salt. Mix thoroughly to make a thick paste.

3 Divide the mixture into golf ball–size portions and gently roll and press each between your palms to form small, round patties. The mixture should yield about 20 patties.

4 Heat 2 inches of oil in a *kadhai*, small wok or large saucepan over medium heat to 325°F (160°C) on a deep-fry or candy thermometer. To gauge the temperature of the oil without a thermometer, drop a piece of bread about 1-inch (2.5-cm) square into the oil, turning the piece of bread often as the oil heats up. When the oil reaches 325°F (160°C), the bread will begin to brown quickly and turn golden brown all over—like a crouton— in about 40 seconds. Deep-fry the patties in batches for 5 minutes, or until deep golden. Remove with a slotted spoon and drain on paper towels. Serve hot.

Potato and Onion Fritters

Aloo aur Pyaz kae Pakora

Traditionally known as *pakora, bhajis* or *bhajiyas*, these fried morsels are a very popular street food of India and are a common item on every Indian restaurant menu. They are served with chutney or even tomato ketchup and are ideally eaten hot and crisp right out of the pan because they get soggy as they cool. I like to use the double-fry method, which entails lightly frying the pakoras in advance, allowing them to cool and then either refrigerating them in an airtight container or ziplock bags for up to a week or freezing them up to a month. To reheat, I bring them to room temperature before refrying them in hot oil. Serve pakoras with one or more chutneys of your choice or tomato ketchup.

Serves 6
Prep time: 30 minutes
Cook time: 15 minutes

- 1 large onion (about ¹/₂ lb/250 g), thinly sliced
- 1 large potato (about ²/₃ lb/300 g), peeled and finely shredded
- 5 cups (250 g) packed spinach leaves, washed and chopped
- 2 cups (220 g) chickpea flour (besan), sifted
- 4 tablespoons chopped fresh coriander leaves (cilantro)
- One ¹/₂-in (1.25-cm) piece fresh ginger, peeled and minced
- 1 fresh green chili pepper, minced
- ¹/₄ teaspoon coriander seeds, crushed
- ¹/₂ teaspoon ground Asian chili powder or cayenne pepper
- ¹/₄ teaspoon cumin seeds, crushed
- 1 teaspoon salt
- ¹/₄ teaspoon baking powder
- 1³/₄ cups (425 ml) water
- Oil, for deep-frying
- 1 or more chutneys of your choice or tomato ketchup, for serving

NOTE Chickpea flour, also known as *besan*, is a finely ground flour made from chickpeas (*chana dal*). It is widely used all over India to make breads and batters for coating deep-fried vegetables and also to thicken sauces. When using chickpea flour it is crucial to sift it. Sifting gets rid of any lumps and incorporates air into the flour for a smooth texture. Chickpea flour is available in any South Asian grocery store or online (see Shopping Guide, page 155).

1 Mix together the onion, potatoes, spinach, chickpea flour, fresh coriander leaves, ginger, green chili pepper, coriander seeds, Asian chili powder or cayenne pepper, cumin, salt and baking powder in a large bowl. Gradually mix in the water to make a thick batter. (Onions will expel water, so adjust the quantity of water based on the consistency.)

2 Heat 2 inches of oil in a *kadhai*, small wok or large saucepan over medium heat to 325°F (160°C) on a deep-fry or candy thermometer. To gauge the temperature of the oil without a thermometer, drop a piece of bread about 1-inch (2.5-cm) square into the oil, turning the piece of bread often as the oil heats up. When the oil reaches 325°F (160°C), the bread will begin to brown quickly and turn golden brown all over—like a crouton—in about 40 seconds.

3 Using a metal spoon, take a small portion of batter and shape roughly into a ball. Carefully drop it into the hot oil, and continue with the rest of the batter, frying them in batches to as not to overcrowd. Deep-fry for 3 to 4 minutes or until the pakoras are cooked and have a crunchy, evenly browned exterior. Remove with a slotted spoon and drain on paper towels. Serve immediately while still hot.

Mung Dal and Cucumber Salad

Kheera aur Mung Dal ka Salaad

With its crisp texture and superb combination of flavors, this salad works well with almost any Indian meal. And if you make sure all the ingredients are fresh, and then you can't really go wrong. In Southern India, where I grew up, it is very traditional to serve this salad during festivals and ceremonies. I recall eating this salad alongside other staples like rice, *rasam* and *pappadum* on a banana leaf as part of a festival meal. Today, I particularly enjoy it with Masala-Crusted Tilapia (page 97) or Masala Lamb Chops (page 121). You can use store bought sprouted beans for a quicker version, just add double the quantity of dried beans to sprouted beans for this recipe.

Serves 4
Prep time: 15 minutes
Cook time: 2 minutes

3 tablespoons mung beans (moong dal)
4 cucumbers (about 1 lb/500 g), peeled, cut in half lengthwise and thinly sliced
1/4 cup (10 g) fresh coriander leaves (cilantro), chopped
1 tablespoon shredded, unsweetened coconut (frozen, reconstituted dried, or freshly grated) (page 24)
1 fresh green chili pepper, deseeded and finely chopped
Juice of 1 lemon
1/2 teaspoon salt
1 teaspoon oil
1/4 teaspoon black mustard seeds
1 tablespoon plain yogurt

1 Boil the mung beans in water until they split, about 20 to 30 minutes. Drain the excess water and let the mung beans cool.
2 Mix together the cucumber, boiled mung beans, fresh coriander leaves, coconut, green chili pepper, lemon juice and salt in a large mixing bowl. Set aside.
3 Heat the oil in a small skillet over medium heat and add the mustard seeds. When they sputter, take the pan off the heat and stir in the yogurt. Add this mixture to the salad and toss well. Serve immediately.

Fruit Chaat

Phal ki Chaat

This cool, juicy fruit salad is all about simplicity and freshness! It's particularly refreshing on a hot day in summer. The fruit combination listed below is one of my favorites, but you may use any tropical fruits that are available in season. Garnish with fresh pomegranate seeds if in season for a burst of color and crunchy texture.

Serves 6
Prep time: 15 minutes

**1 small pineapple (about 1 lb/500 g),
   peeled, cored and diced**
**1 cup (150 g) seedless red grapes,
   halved**
**1 cup (150 g) seedless green grapes,
   halved**
1 orange, peeled and cut into segments
**1 ripe mango (about 1 lb/500 g), peeled
   and diced**
**3 tablespoons freshly-squeezed lime
   juice**
1/4 cup (65 ml) mango juice
2 teaspoons Chaat Masala (page 35)
**4 tablespoons chopped fresh mint
   leaves**
**1/4 cup (50 g) pomegranate seeds, for
   garnish (optional) (see page 56 for
   tips on extracting seeds)**

1 Place all the prepared fruits, lime juice, mango juice and Chaat Masala in a large bowl.
2 Toss well to mix, then sprinkle with the fresh mint leaves and pomegranate seeds, if using.

Chapter 4

Soups and Dals

Typically, Indian meals are served family style—all dishes, including soups, are served together at the same time rather than as separate courses. However, even though soup is served with other dishes, it is supposed to be consumed first, before one proceeds with the rest of the meal. Indian soups can range from mild to heavily spiced and are eaten all year round.

In general, Indian soups tend to be thin. Whether they are lentil-, vegetable- or meat-based, they are almost never thickened with starch, unlike Western soups. The recipes for soups in this chapter are vegetarian, as is representative of Indian cuisine. Meat broths are not common in India.

Dals, on the other hand, though souplike in consistency, are much thicker than a typical western soup. They are made with dried legumes, especially lentils, and add much needed protein to a meal. Dals are eaten along with the meal, and often treated like an additional vegetable. They are also mixed with white rice to add flavor to the rice.

Dals are probably the most common and significant dishes in India—no Indian meal is complete without them. They are eaten in all parts of India in various forms ranging from spicy to mild and from vegetarian to some with meats incorporated into it to make it a complete meal.

Broccoli Soup with Walnuts

Akhroth aur Hara Phool Gobi ka Soop

Even though broccoli isn't eaten in India, I've come to love its flavor. Though this easy-to-prepare recipe is basically a cream of broccoli soup, there is nothing basic about it. The exotic flavors of Indian spices give it a distinctive taste and the walnuts provide a nice crunchy contrast to the smooth texture of the soup. It can be made with light cream or, for a healthier alternative, whole or even skim milk. I like to serve this soup with Flaky Paratha Breads Stuffed with Potatoes (page 139) or Plain Naan (page 134).

Serves 4
Prep time: 15 minutes
Cook time: 30 minutes

1 teaspoon black peppercorns
4 whole cloves
5 green cardamom pods, crushed
One ¹/₂-in (1.25-cm) stick cinnamon
1 bay leaf
2 tablespoons butter
1 small onion (about ¹/₄ lb/125 g), chopped
4 large cloves garlic, minced
One 1-in (2.5-cm) piece fresh ginger, peeled and chopped
6 cups (500 g) broccoli florets (from 2 lbs/1 kg broccoli)
1 teaspoon Home-Style Garam Masala (page 35)
Salt, to taste
7 cups (1.75 liters) vegetable stock or water
1 cup (250 ml) heavy cream
2 tablespoons chopped walnuts, for garnish

1 Make a spice pouch by placing the peppercorns, cloves, cardamom, cinnamon and bay leaf in a small piece of cheese cloth and tie the cloth closed with a knot.

2 Melt the butter in a medium saucepan over medium heat. Add the onion, garlic, ginger, broccoli, Home-Style Garam Masala and salt. Cook, stirring constantly, for 1 minute. Add the vegetable stock or water and the spice pouch. Simmer for 20 to 25 minutes, or until the broccoli is tender. Remove from the heat and discard the spice pouch. Let the soup cool slightly.

3 Purée the cooled soup in a food processor or blender until smooth. Force the soup through a strainer into a clean saucepan. Add the heavy cream and bring the soup to a simmer. Ladle into soup bowls and serve hot garnished with the walnuts.

TIP Don't discard the broccoli stalks—you can turn the leftover stalks into salads. Peel the stalks, cut lengthwise into matchsticks and cook with the florets or eat raw mixed in with other salad vegetables.

Spinach Soup

Palak ka Soop

Whereas traditional Indian cooks do not use flour as a thickening agent, an Anglo-Indian neighbor of mine in India used to make delicious soups using roux cooked with ghee instead of butter. After some experimentation in my own kitchen, I realized that ghee makes an excellent roux. This recipe is the re-creation of my memory of the wonderful roux-thickened soup that I had once in my neighbor's home. You can use butter as an option instead of ghee. Serve with Baked Garlic Naan (page 134).

Serves 5
Prep time: 15 minutes
Cook time: 30 minutes

2 tablespoons ghee (clarified butter) or butter
2 tablespoons all-purpose flour
1 teaspoon Home-Style Garam Masala (page 35)
One 1-in (2.5-cm) piece ginger, peeled and chopped
2 teaspoons minced garlic
1 lb (500 g) fresh spinach, washed and tough stems removed
5 to 6 black peppercorns
4 bay leaves
Salt, to taste
White pepper, to taste
6 cups (1.5 liters) water or vegetable stock

1 Melt the ghee or butter in a medium saucepan over medium heat. Add the flour and cook, stirring constantly, until a sandy texture is created, about 1 minute. Add the Home-Style Garam Masala, ginger, garlic and spinach, and sauté for 1 or 2 minutes. Add the black peppercorns, bay leaves, salt, white pepper and water or vegetable stock, and simmer for 15 to 20 minutes. Let cool slightly.

2 Remove the bay leaves. Purée the soup in a blender or food processor, or with a hand-held mixer. Return the soup to the pan and simmer for another 5 minutes until slightly thickened. Ladle into soup bowls and serve hot.

Fiery South Indian Tomato Soup *Rasam*

Rasams are thin south Indian soups made with *dal*, or lentils. Every household in the south Indian home has its own variation of this popular tangy and spicy soup, which is often served as a digestive drink before a meal and also as an accompaniment with rice. This recipe is the traditional way to make *rasam*—there is an alternate short-cut method using store-bought rasam powder, which is readily available in ethnic stores (my favorite brand is MTR). If you are using store-bought rasam powder, add it along with the lentils and water and bring it to a boil. Just be sure to read the instructions on the packet for the ratio of powder to the broth as each brand has slightly different ingredients in it. I like to use a pinch of *asafetida* in my rasam as this is how my mother made it at home, and it is a common ingredient in south Indian cooking. Asafetida's mild garlicky flavor adds a nice dimension to the soup, plus it is said to have beneficial digestive properties. Rasam soup is traditionally served with Plain Basmatic Rice (page 124) as part of the main meal rather than as a first course.

Serves 4
Prep time: 15 minutes
Cook time: 30 minutes

2 tomatoes (about $^3/_4$ lb/350 g), coarsely chopped
$^1/_2$ cup (100 g) split pigeon peas (toor dal), washed
$^1/_4$ teaspoon ground turmeric
2 teaspoons salt
2 fresh green chili peppers, slit open lengthwise
7 cups (1.75 liters) water
1 tablespoon oil
2 teaspoons black mustard seeds
2 teaspoons cumin seeds, crushed
3 dried red chili peppers, broken in half
10 fresh or dried curry leaves
3 cloves garlic, smashed
Pinch of asafetida (optional)
2 teaspoons black pepper
1 tablespoon tamarind paste
4 tablespoons chopped fresh coriander leaves (cilantro)

1 Purée the coarsely chopped tomatoes in a blender. Set aside.
2 Place the lentils, turmeric, salt, green chili peppers and 4 cups (1 liter) of the water in a medium saucepan. Bring the mixture to a boil over high heat. Once boiling, reduce the heat to low and simmer, covered, until the lentils have become soft and mushy.
3 Heat the oil in a large saucepan over medium heat and add the mustard seeds. When they crackle and pop, add the cumin seeds, red chili peppers, curry leaves, garlic and asafetida, if using. Cook, while stirring, about 30 more seconds. This cooking technique is called tempering or *tarhka*. Add the tomato purée, black pepper and remaining 3 cups (750 ml) of water and bring to a boil.
4 Add the cooked lentils and tamarind paste and bring to a boil once more. Stir in the fresh coriander leaves and serve hot.

Indian-Style Lentil Soup

Dal Shorba

For this hearty lentil soup, you can use any lentils you like. Other lentils I like to use for this recipe are the French green lentils or the Indian red lentils (*sabut masoor dal*). Serve this with a piece of Indian flatbread, either Baked Garlic Naan (page 134) or Whole-Wheat Griddle Breads (page 136) with a crisped *pappadum* (page 55) for a perfect winter lunch.

Serves 4
Prep time: 15 minutes
Cook time: 45 minutes

1 tablespoon oil
1 onion (about 1/3 lb/150 g), thinly sliced
2 tablespoons minced garlic
2 fresh green chili peppers, chopped
One 1-in (2.5-cm) piece fresh ginger, peeled and
   minced
1 tomato (about 1/3 lb/150 g), diced
2/3 cup (120 g) split red lentils (masoor dal)
1/3 cup (50 g) split yellow peas (chana dal)
1/3 cup (50 g) mung beans (moong dal)
1 cup (50 g) packed spinach, washed and tough
   stems removed
1 teaspoon Asian chili powder or cayenne pepper
1 teaspoon Home-Style Garam Masala (page 35)
1 teaspoon salt
5 cups (1.25 liters) water
4 tablespoons chopped fresh coriander leaves
   (cilantro)

1 Heat the oil in a large saucepan over medium heat. Add the onion, garlic, green chili peppers, ginger and tomato. Cook, stirring frequently, until the onions become translucent, about 1 minute.
2 Add the rest of the ingredients, except the coriander leaves, and bring to a boil. Reduce the heat to low and simmer, stirring frequently, for 30 to 40 minutes, or until the beans are completely cooked, adding more water if necessary.
3 Ladle the soup into serving bowls and garnish with the chopped coriander leaves.

Northern Chickpea Curry

Northern Chickpea Curry

Chana Masala

This chickpea dish is unquestionably one of the most popular vegetable curry dishes in northern India, and the most versatile. It is served as a one-dish meal at any time—for breakfast, lunch or dinner—or as a snack. Try serving this with Fried Puffed Bread (page 138), Crunchy Potato and Corn Croquettes (page 52) or Samosas (page 58). I've used ghee in the recipe, though it can be easily substituted with canola or vegetable oil.

Serves 4

Prep time: 15 minutes plus 8 hours soaking time if using dried chickpeas

Cook time: 30 minutes (1 hour, 15 minutes if using dried chickpeas)

2 cups (350 g), dried chickpeas (kabuli chana), soaked overnight and drained, or three 15^1/$_2$-oz (439-g) cans chickpeas, drained and rinsed well

4 cups (1 liter) water plus ^{1}/$_2$ teaspoon salt for cooking dried peas

^{1}/$_2$ cup (125 ml) oil

1 tablespoon plus 1 teaspoon Ginger-Garlic Paste (page 32)

8 dried red chili peppers, broken in half

1 tablespoon plus 1 teaspoon coriander seeds, crushed

1 tablespoon plus 1 teaspoon cumin seeds, crushed

2 onions (about ^{3}/$_4$ lb/350 g), minced

4 fresh green chili peppers, slit open lengthwise

One 1-in (2.5-cm) piece fresh ginger, peeled and chopped

2 tomatoes (about ^{3}/$_4$ lb/350 g), chopped

2 teaspoons salt

2 teaspoons Home-Style Garam Masala (page 35)

1 teaspoon Asian chili powder or cayenne pepper

1 cup (250 ml) water

2 tablespoons freshly-squeezed lemon juice

1 teaspoon dried fenugreek leaves (kasoori methi) (optional)

4 tablespoons chopped fresh coriander leaves (cilantro)

1 If using dried chickpeas, bring the soaked and drained peas, water and ^{1}/$_2$ teaspoon of salt to a boil in a large saucepan over high heat. Reduce the heat to low and simmer, covered, until the peas are tender, about 45 minutes. Drain the peas, rinse with cold water, and drain again. Set aside.

2 Heat the oil in a medium saucepan over medium heat. Add the Ginger-Garlic Paste and fry for about 30 seconds, stirring constantly. Add the red chili peppers, crushed coriander and cumin seeds and fry for 15 to 20 seconds, stirring constantly, until fragrant.

3 Add the onions, green chili peppers and ginger, and cook over medium heat, stirring often, until the onions are uniformly dark brown in color, about 10 to 12 minutes. Make sure the onions don't stick to the pan, adding a little water if necessary. Add the tomatoes, salt, Home-Style Garam Masala and Asian chili powder or cayenne pepper and cook, stirring constantly, for about 30 seconds. Add the 1 cup (250 ml) of water and chickpeas and bring to a simmer. Cook gently, partially covered, for 15 minutes, stirring occasionally. Stir in the lemon juice, fenugreek and fresh coriander leaves. Taste for seasoning and add more salt if needed. Serve hot.

Spicy Urad Beans

Dhaba Dal

This *dal* is named after the Indian roadside eatery called *dhaba*. These dhabas satisfy millions of hungry travelers, workers and truck drivers who pass along the rural roads and highways all over India. To cook this dish faster, put all of the ingredients in a pressure cooker. For convenience, you can substitute the homemade Dhaba Spice with store-bought *garam masala* powder. Serve this rich and creamy lentil delicacy with freshly prepared Plain Basmati Rice (page 124) or Whole-Wheat Griddle Breads (page 136) and slices of raw onions and some homemade pickles—Green Mango Pickle (page 47) is a good choice.

Serves 6
Prep time: 15 minutes
Cook time: 55 minutes

5 cups (1.25 liters) water
1 cup (175 g) split black gram
   (urad dal)
1/2 teaspoon ground turmeric
1 teaspoon Asian chili powder
   or cayenne pepper
1/2 teaspoon salt

Tempering Oil
1/2 cup (1 stick/115 g) plus
   1 tablespoon butter
2 teaspoons cumin seeds
1/2 tablespoon minced garlic
1/2 tablespoon peeled and
   minced fresh ginger
1 small onion (about 1/4 lb/
   125 g), minced
1 small tomato (about 3 oz/
   85 g), chopped
1/4 cup (65 ml) tomato purée
4 tablespoons tomato paste
2 fresh green chili peppers, slit
   open lengthwise
2 teaspoons Dhaba Spice
   (page 34)
1 cup (250 ml) water
3 tablespoons freshly-squeezed
   lemon juice

1 Bring the water, the *urad dal*, turmeric, Asian chili powder or cayenne pepper and salt to a boil in a large saucepan over high heat. Reduce the heat to low and simmer until the *dal* is tender, about 30 to 40 minutes.) Check occasionally during cooking and add more water if necessary. (Urad dal tends to absorb water while cooking and become very thick.) When the dal is done, drain any excess water and set aside.

2 To prepare the Tempering Oil: Heat half of the butter in a large saucepan over medium-high heat. Add the cumin, garlic, ginger and onion and cook until browned, about 1 minute.

3 Add the cooked urad dal, chopped tomato, tomato purée, tomato paste, green chili peppers and Dhaba Spice. Mix well, add the water and bring to a boil. Taste for seasoning and add more salt if needed.

4 Melt the remaining butter in a small saucepan. Finish with the lemon juice and stir in the melted butter. Serve hot.

Yellow Mung Beans with Spinach

Yellow Mung Beans with Spinach

Dal Palak

Lentils, or *dal*, are prepared almost daily in many Indian homes. They are rich in nutrients and equally tasty. This particular combination of spinach and lentils is one of my favorite meals. I like to eat Dal Palak with fresh baked bread or over Plain Basmati Rice (page 124) laced with butter. This dish is the perfect complement to fiery hot meat curries.

Serves 4
Prep time: 15 minutes
Cook time: 30 minutes

1 tablespoon oil
1 teaspoon black mustard seeds
1 red onion (about $^1/_3$ lb/150 g), chopped
2 large cloves garlic, crushed
1 teaspoon ginger powder
$^1/_2$ teaspoon Home-Style Garam Masala (page 35)
1 small tomato (about 3 oz/85 g), chopped
1 cup (200 g) split pigeon peas (toor dal), rinsed and drained
2 cups (500 ml) water
3 cups (150 g) packed fresh spinach leaves, washed and chopped, or 1 cup (200 g) frozen chopped spinach, thawed
$^1/_2$ cup (125 ml) coconut milk
Salt, to taste
2 tablespoons chopped fresh coriander leaves (cilantro)
1 teaspoon black sesame seeds, toasted

1 Heat the oil in a large saucepan over medium heat. Add the mustard seeds—they should sizzle upon contact with the hot oil. Add the onion, garlic, ginger powder, Home-Style Garam Masala and cook, stirring constantly, until the spices are fragrant, about 1 minute. Add the tomato and cook for another 30 seconds.
2 Add the lentils and water and bring to a boil over medium-high heat. Reduce the heat to low, cover partially, and simmer until the lentils are tender but still firm, about 15 to 20 minutes. Add more water if you want the dal to be thinner.
3 Stir in the spinach, coconut milk and salt, cover and simmer until the spinach is cooked, about 3 minutes longer. Serve hot, garnished with the fresh coriander leaves and sesame seeds.

Black-Eyed Peas with Mushrooms

Lobhiya Khumb Masala

Lobhiya, known as "black-eyed peas," in the West, are cooked in a variety of ways in India. In this recipe, the addition of cumin, cinnamon and mushrooms makes for a comforting and flavorful dish. Serve with any meat or vegetarian main dish and some warm Whole-Wheat Griddle Breads (page 136) for a wonderfully satisfying evening meal.

Serves 6
Prep time: 15 minutes plus 8 hours soaking time if using dried black-eyed peas
Cook time: 55 minutes (1 hour, 15 minutes if using dried black-eyed peas)

1 cup (175 g) dried black-eyed peas (lobhiya), soaked overnight and drained, or one 15.5-oz (439-g) can black-eyed peas, rinsed and drained
4 cups (1 liter) water plus ¹/₂ teaspoon salt for cooking dried peas
¹/₄ cup (65 ml) oil
2 teaspoons cumin seeds
One 1-in (2.5-cm) cinnamon stick
1 red onion (about ¹/₃ lb/ 150 g), chopped
1 tablespoon minced garlic
¹/₂ lb (250 g) button mushrooms, cleaned and sliced (about ³/₄ cup/250 g)
1 lb (500 g) tomatoes, blanched, peeled and chopped (about 2¹/₂ cups /500 g)
2 teaspoons ground coriander
1 teaspoon ground cumin
¹/₂ teaspoon ground turmeric
¹/₂ teaspoon paprika
Salt, to taste
3 tablespoons chopped fresh coriander leaves (cilantro)

1 If using dried black-eye peas, bring the soaked and drained peas, water and ¹/₂ teaspoon of salt to a boil in a large saucepan over high heat. Cover and simmer over low heat until the peas are tender, about 45 minutes. Drain the peas, rinse with cold water, and drain again. Set aside.

2 Heat the oil in a large heavy-bottomed skillet or saucepan over medium heat. Add the cumin seeds and cinnamon stick and let them sizzle for 10 seconds. Add the onion and garlic and cook, stirring frequently, until soft and starting to brown, about 5 minutes. Add the mushrooms and fry for 1 to 2 minutes. Add the tomatoes, ground coriander, cumin, turmeric, paprika and salt and a little water, if needed. Cover and cook over low heat for 10 minutes, until tender.

3 Add the cooked or canned black-eyed peas to the tomato and mushroom mixture and simmer, uncovered, for 10 minutes. Stir in the fresh coriander leaves. Serve hot.

Black-Eyed Peas with Mushrooms

Spicy Mixed Beans and Lentils *Pancharatni Dal Fry*

Whether eating at home or dining out, no Indian meal is complete without a bowl of *dal*, or lentils. I remember eating this very popular lentil dish at a random north Indian restaurant on a highway that runs from Pune to Mumbai. Containing five different legumes, this "jewel" of a dal is more elaborate than many (*panch* means "five" and *rattan* means "jewels") and is a true delicacy. Adjust the quantity of chili peppers according to your spice level. Serve with Plain Basmati Rice (page 124) or Whole-Wheat Griddle Breads (page 136).

Serves 6
Prep time: 15 minutes
Cook time: 45 minutes

7 cups (1.75 liters) water
1/4 cup (40 g) split green lentils (moong dal)
1/4 cup (40 g) split red lentils (masoor dal)
1/4 cup (40 g) split yellow peas (chana dal)
1/4 cup (50 g) split pigeon peas (toor dal)
1/4 cup (40 g) split black gram (urad dal)
1 teaspoon salt, plus more if needed
1 teaspoon ground turmeric
3/4 cup (160 g) ghee (clarified butter) or oil
1 1/2 teaspoons cumin seeds
1 tablespoon minced garlic
1 1/2 tablespoons peeled and minced fresh ginger
1 large onion (about 1/2 lb/ 250 g), finely chopped
1 large tomato (about 1/2 lb/ 250 g), finely chopped
2 fresh green chili peppers, minced
2 tablespoons ground coriander
1 teaspoon Asian chili powder or cayenne pepper
4 tablespoons chopped fresh coriander leaves (cilantro)
1/4 teaspoon Home-Style Garam Masala (page 35)

1 Bring the water, all five lentils, salt and turmeric to a boil in a large saucepan. Reduce the heat to low and simmer until the beans are tender, about 30 to 40 minutes. Add more water during cooking if necessary.

2 While the lentils are cooking, heat the ghee or oil in another large saucepan over medium-high heat. Add the cumin seeds, garlic, ginger and onion, and cook until golden, about 1 minute. Add the tomato, green chili peppers, ground coriander and Asian chili powder or cayenne pepper. Reduce the heat to medium and cook, stirring constantly, until the tomato is soft. Add the cooked lentils and mix well, adding more water as needed. (Most lentil dishes tend to get very thick as they cook). Taste for seasoning and add more salt if needed.

3 Add the fresh coriander leaves and mix in. Transfer to a serving dish, sprinkle the Home-Style Garam Masala over the top and serve.

Delicious Everyday Dal

Masaladar dal Lahsooni

Thanks to my profession I have been fortunate to have had the opportunity to taste foods from the best restaurants across the globe. But nothing, to this day, comforts me more than the simple luxury of a home cooked meal of rice and *dal*, which is staple for most Indian households. While growing up, this was one of my mom's standard everyday dals. It's very versatile, going well with practically any Indian dish, and is immensely satisfying. When I feel like indulging in one of my all-time favorite comfort foods, I simply ladle this dal over Plain Basmati Rice (page 124) topped with generous dollops of melted ghee.

Recently, on a friend's advice, I added to my plate of dal and rice a simple mixture of boiled and mashed potatoes and eggs, spiked with Indian Five Spice Mix (page 31) and some diced, cooked onions. Borrowing my friend's favorite comfort food recipe and adding it to mine was indeed the highlight of dinner that evening. Do feel free to add mashed and spiced potatoes to this dish as an accompaniment, for that extra level of comfort! Green Mango Pickle (page 47) and crisped *pappadum* (page 55) are also very good served on the side. I like to use split red lentils (masoor dal), which is available in Indian and Middle Eastern grocery stores, but you can make this dal with any split lentil.

Serves 6
Prep time: 15 minutes
Cook time: 45 minutes

2 cups (350 g) dried, split lentils of your choice, washed and drained
7 cups (1.75 liters) water
1 teaspoon ground turmeric
1½ teaspoons salt and more, to taste
3 tablespoons oil
2½ teaspoons cumin seeds
2 dried red chili peppers, broken in half
6 to 8 fresh or dried curry leaves
2 tablespoons chopped garlic
1 tablespoon peeled and minced fresh ginger
2 fresh green chili peppers, minced
1 teaspoon Asian chili powder or cayenne pepper
4 tablespoons minced fresh coriander leaves (cilantro)
Juice of ½ lime

1 Bring the lentils and water to a boil in a heavy pot. Remove any surface scum that collects on top. Add the turmeric and 1½ teaspoons of salt and reduce the heat to low. Cover, leaving the lid slightly ajar, and simmer gently for 20 to 30 minutes, or until the lentils become soft and mushy and have absorbed all the cooking liquid. Stir often to prevent sticking. Set aside

2 Heat the oil in a large saucepan over medium heat. Add the cumin seeds and let them sizzle for 3 to 4 seconds. Add the dried red chili peppers, curry leaves, garlic, ginger, green chili peppers and Asian chili powder or cayenne pepper. Cook, stirring constantly, for 30 seconds. Add the cooked lentils to this mixture. Mix well, adding more water as needed. Taste for seasoning and add salt if needed.

3 Stir in the fresh coriander leaves and lime juice. Transfer to a serving bowl, serve hot.

Red Kidney Bean Curry

Rajmah Masala

Rajmah is one of my favorite comfort foods. I cook it at least once a week at home. This north Indian staple goes well with Plain Basmatic Rice (page 124) and Whole-Wheat Griddle Breads (page 136). Usually the beans are cooked in a pressure cooker in Indian homes, which cuts down the cooking time and also makes the beans very tender. Cooking the beans in a conventional pot works just a well—it will just take longer. For a shortcut, canned beans may also be used.

Serves 4

Prep time: 15 minutes plus 8 hours soaking time if using dried kidney beans

Cook time: 55 minutes (1 hour, 20 minutes if using dried kidney beans)

2 cups (350 g) dried red kidney beans (rajmah), soaked overnight and drained, or two 15.5-oz (439-g) cans kidney beans, rinsed and drained

10 cups (2.5 liters) water plus $^1/_2$ tablespoon salt for cooking dried beans

$^1/_2$ cup (125 ml) oil

1 tablespoon cumin seeds

1 large onion (about $^1/_2$ lb/250 g), minced

4 tablespoons Ginger-Garlic Paste (page 32)

3 fresh green chili peppers, minced

3 large tomatoes (about $1^1/_2$ lbs/ 750 g), minced

3 teaspoons ground coriander

2 teaspoons Asian chili powder or cayenne pepper

Salt, to taste

2 teaspoon Home-Style Garam Masala (page 35)

4 tablespoons chopped fresh coriander leaves (cilantro)

2 tablespoons butter

1 If using dried kidney beans, bring the soaked and drained beans, water and salt to a boil in a large saucepan. Reduce the heat to low, cover, and simmer until the beans are tender, about 45 to 50 minutes. Drain the beans but reserve the cooking liquid. Set aside.

2 Heat the oil in a large heavy-bottomed skillet or saucepan over medium heat. Add the cumin seeds and let them sizzle for 10 seconds. Add the onion and cook, stirring frequently, until soft and starting to brown, about 5 minutes. Add the Ginger-Garlic Paste and fry for 1 to 2 minutes, until soft. Add the green chili peppers, tomatoes, ground coriander, Asian chili powder or cayenne pepper, salt and 1 cup (250 ml) of the reserved bean-soaking liq-uid or water. Cover and cook over low heat until the *masala* is cooked, about 5 minutes.

3 Add the cooked or canned red kidney beans to the tomato gravy and simmer, adding more of the bean-soaking liquid or water as needed, for 5 to 10 minutes. Stir in the Home-Style Garam Masala, fresh coriander leaves and butter. Serve hot.

Chapter 5

Vegetable and Cheese Dishes

In this chapter, you will learn how to make some of the myriad of tasty and tantalizing vegetarian dishes that form such an important part of the Indian diet. Typically, vegetables are either braised or sautéed, combined with garlic and spices, and served with rice or curries. For vegetarians and meat eaters alike, vegetable dishes are a key part of every Indian meal. In fact, vegetables are probably the most important part of any Indian meal—the choice of the accompanying chutneys, salads and dals being determined after the main vegetable dish has been decided. And usually there is also a secondary vegetable dish in the meal menu.

Milk and milk products also play an important role in Indian meals and are considered to be an important source of protein in the Indian diet. Paneer, or "Indian cottage cheese," is one of the most popular milk products, and is the basis of several interesting vegetarian dishes.

Hyderabadi Mixed Vegetables *Hyderabadi hara Subzi*

This dish has the classic flavors from Hyderabad, a city in the south of India known for its rich, complex and highly spiced cuisine. This flavorful combination of seasonal vegetables, fresh green chili peppers, curry leaves, spices and coconut goes especially well with Lemon Rice with Peanuts (page 129) and Pepper Chicken (page 108).

Serves 4
Prep time: 20 minutes
Cook time: 20 minutes

1 red onion (about $^1/_3$ lb/150 g), coarsely chopped
$^1/_4$ cup (25 g) shredded, unsweetened coconut (frozen, reconstituted dried, or freshly grated) (page 24)
3 tablespoons plus 2 cups (500 ml) water
1 handful fresh coriander leaves and stems (cilantro) (about 4 oz/ 125 g) plus 4 tablespoons minced fresh coriander leaves (cilantro)
2 fresh green chili peppers
$^1/_4$ cup (65 ml) oil
12 shallots (about $^1/_4$ lb/125 g total), peeled and cut into wedges
10 fresh or dried curry leaves
2 or 3 cloves garlic, crushed
One $^1/_2$-in (1.25-cm) piece fresh ginger, peeled and chopped
1 teaspoon salt, plus more if needed
$^1/_2$ teaspoon ground turmeric
1 teaspoon ground coriander
1 teaspoon ground cumin
1 cup (130 g) green peas, fresh or frozen (shelled from 1 lb/500 g fresh pea pods or about half of one 10-oz/300-g package frozen peas)
$^1/_4$ lb (125 g) fresh green beans, trimmed and cut into 1-in (2.5-cm) lengths
1 carrot, peeled and diced (about $^3/_4$ cup/112 g)
1 small potato, peeled and diced (about $^3/_4$ cup/130 g)
2 cups (500 ml) coconut milk

1 Place the red onion, coconut, 3 tablespoons of the water, handful of fresh coriander with stems and green chili peppers in a blender or food processor and process to a smooth paste. Set aside.
2 Heat the oil in a large saucepan over medium heat. Add the shallots, curry leaves, garlic, ginger and fry for 2 to 3 minutes, stirring constantly, until soft. Add the coconut paste and the salt and cook, uncovered, stirring frequently, for about 5 minutes. This technique is called *bhunao*.
3 Add the turmeric, coriander, cumin and all the vegetables, and fry for another minute. Add the remaining 2 cups (500 ml) of water and cover. Cook, stirring occasionally, for 15 to 20 minutes or until the vegetables are tender.
4 Add the coconut milk and minced fresh coriander leaves. Mix well and taste for seasoning, and add more salt if needed. Serve hot.

Street-Style Grilled Corn on the Cob

Street-Style Grilled Corn on the Cob

Bhutta

This style of corn on the cob, flavored with lemon and spices and cooked over hot charcoals, is sold by street vendors all over India. Sometimes the corn is coated with a sprinkling of different spice blends, depending on the region or the vendor's personal taste. For an extra special Indian flavor, try to use black salt (*kala namak*); otherwise, another sea salt or kosher salt will do.

Serves 4
Prep time: 5 minutes
Cook time: 15 minutes

4 ears fresh corn, shucked (save 4 large leaves)
1 lemon, cut in half
1 tablespoon Chaat Masala (page 35)
1 teaspoon Asian chili powder or cayenne pepper
$1/4$ teaspoon salt (sea salt, kosher salt or, preferably, Indian black salt)
Onion and Cucumber Chaat (page 42), for serving
Plum Tomato Chutney with Mustard Seeds (page 38), for serving

1 Preheat a grill, preferably charcoal for the best flavor, to high heat.
2 Grill the corn directly over the heat for about 5 minutes, turning constantly, until slightly golden brown and lightly burnt.
3 Squeeze the lemon juice all over the corn. Sprinkle with the Chaat Masala, Asian chili powder or cayenne pepper and salt. Serve each ear on top of a fresh corn leaf with a side of Onion and Cucumber Chaat and Plum Tomato Chutney with Mustard Seeds.

Stir-Fried Vegetables with Yogurt

Subz Jhalfrazie

Subz Jhalfrazie is an elegant and colorful mixed vegetable dish that will make any meal look and taste special. It is a spicy dish with the unique flavor of dried fenugreek leaves (*kasoori methi*) and yogurt. If you cannot find kasoori methi, this dish is still worth making and quite delicious. And, if you do not have green onions, you can substitute regular white onions or shallots. Serve with main dishes like Malabar Crab Curry (page 98), Spicy and Fragrant Lamb Curry (page 119) or Chicken Curry in a Hurry (page 109).

Serves 6
Prep time: 15 minutes
Cook time: 20 minutes

1/2 cup (125 ml) oil
One 1-in (2.5-cm) piece fresh ginger, peeled and chopped
2 tablespoons chopped garlic
1 bunch green onions (scallions) (about 1/4 lb/125 g), white part only, chopped
1/4 lb (100 g) fresh green beans, trimmed and cut into 1-in (2.5-cm) lengths
1 small zucchini (about 1/4 lb/125 g), diced
1 carrot, peeled and diced (about 3/4 cup/112 g)
1 small potato, peeled and diced (about 3/4 cup/130 g)
1 cup (100 g) broccoli florets or 1 cup (200 g) cauliflower florets
1/2 teaspoon ground turmeric
1 teaspoon Asian chili powder or cayenne pepper
1 tomato (about 1/3 lb/150 g), chopped
2 fresh green chili peppers, chopped
4 dried red chili peppers, broken in half
4 tablespoons chopped fresh coriander leaves (cilantro)
1 cup (245 g) plain yogurt, whisked
4 tablespoons dried fenugreek leaves (kasoori methi) (optional)
1 1/2 cups (375 ml) water
3 teaspoons salt, plus more if needed

1 Heat the oil in a *kadhai*, wok or large sauté pan over medium heat. Add the ginger and garlic, and sauté over medium heat for 30 seconds. Add the green onions and sauté for 30 seconds. Add the green beans, zucchini, carrot, potato, broccoli or cauliflower florets, and sauté 1 minute, stirring constantly. Stir in the turmeric and Asian chili powder or cayenne pepper. Add the tomato, green chili peppers, red chili peppers and fresh coriander leaves and sauté for another minute.

2 Stir in the yogurt and fenugreek leaves, if using. Add the water and salt and bring to a boil. Lower the heat and simmer until the vegetables are cooked and the liquid has evaporated, about 5 minutes. Taste for seasoning and add more salt if needed.

Bengali Potatoes with Spices

Bengali Potatoes with Spices

Bengali Aloo

The potato is called the "king of vegetables" in India and in my kitchen it rules. Potato dishes are loved by everyone, and they go with everything. If you love potatoes every which way, you will love this exotically spiced but simple dish. For this recipe, I like to use a coarse grind of the Indian Five Spice Mix (page 31), which gives a crunchy texture to the dish. If you do not have the time to make this spice blend simply use an equal amount of store-bought *garam masala*. Day-old boiled potatoes work very well for this dish. Serve this as side dish with Masala Lamb Chops (page 121), Marinated Roast Leg of Lamb (page 118) or Pork Tenderloin with Mango Salad (page 119).

Serves 6
Prep time: 15 minutes
Cook time: 30 minutes

3 large potatoes (about 2 lbs/1 kg)
4 tablespoons oil
1 onion (about 1/3 lb/150 g), cut into 3/4-inch (2-cm) dice
1 green bell pepper, cut into 3/4-inch (2-cm) dice (about 1 cup/175 g)
1 tomato (about 1/3 lb/150 g), diced
1 teaspoon salt
2 tablespoons coarsely ground Indian Five Spice Mix (page 31)
4 tablespoons minced fresh coriander leaves (cilantro)

1 Combine the potatoes with enough cold water to cover, in a large saucepan. Bring to a boil over high heat and cook, uncovered, until tender, about 15 to 20 minutes. Drain well and set aside to cool. Peel the potatoes and cut into 3/4-inch (2-cm) dice. Set aside.
2 Heat the oil in a nonstick skillet over medium heat. When hot, add the onion and bell pepper and cook, stirring frequently, until they are slightly cooked, 2 to 3 minutes. Add the tomato, salt and the Indian Five Spice Mix and cook for another minute. Add the diced potatoes and stir them around for about 1 minute to allow the flavors to mix. Taste for seasoning and sprinkle on more salt if needed. Cook for another 3 minutes or so to let the potatoes heat through. Sprinkle on the coriander leaves, mix in, and serve.

Spicy Coconut Green Beans *Beans Poriyal*

I love the combination of mustard seeds, shredded coconut and vegetables in this dish. Poriyals are a type of lightly seasoned sautéed, or "dry," vegetable dishes from southern India. They emphasize the flavor of fresh vegetables cooked in their own juices and moisture. Serve this dish alongside Masala-Baked Red Snapper (page 96) or Coconut Chicken Curry (page 110).

Serves 6
Prep time: 10 minutes
Cook time: 15 minutes

4 tablespoons oil
3 teaspoons black mustard seeds
One 1-in (2.5-cm) piece fresh ginger, peeled and chopped
1 tablespoon minced garlic
2 teaspoons cumin seeds
4 dried red chili peppers
10 fresh or dried curry leaves
1¹/₂ lbs (750 g) green beans, preferably thin French beans, trimmed and cut on the diagonal into 1-in (2.5-cm) lengths
1 teaspoon ground coriander
¹/₄ teaspoon ground turmeric
1¹/₄ teaspoons salt
1 cup (100 g) shredded, unsweetened coconut (frozen, reconstituted dried, or freshly grated) (see page 24)
1¹/₂ cups (375 ml) water
Juice of ¹/₂ lemon

1 Heat the oil in a wide, heavy pot over medium heat. When hot, add the mustard seeds and cook, stirring constantly, until they sputter and pop, about 30 seconds. Immediately add the ginger, garlic, cumin seeds, red chili peppers and curry leaves and cook, stirring constantly, for about 1 minute. Add the beans, coriander, turmeric, salt and coconut and cook, stirring frequently, for 3 to 4 minutes, until fragrant.

2 Add the water and bring to a simmer. Cover and cook until the beans are tender, about 7 to 10 minutes. Remove the cover, add the lemon juice and cook, stirring often, until all of the water is evaporated. Taste for seasoning and add more salt if necessary. Serve hot.

Spicy Coconut Green Beans

Paneer Cheese

Paneer, which is also known as "Indian cottage cheese," is made by curdling milk with something acid, lemon juice or vinegar, and then separating the curds from the whey. This soft, spongy cheese with its sweet, milky aroma is preservative-free, has no artificial additives, and can be made with low-fat or whole milk. Paneer does not need to be used only in Indian dishes. I sometimes serve it as part of an antipasto platter, giving it an Italian twist with salt, pepper, chopped fresh basil and balsamic vinegar, or as a Caprese Salad, layered with slices of fresh plum tomato and basil.

Makes 1 lb (500 g)
Prep time: 10 minutes
Cook time: 30 minutes

1 gallon (3.75 liters) low-fat or whole milk
1 cup (250 ml) freshly-squeezed lemon juice (4 to 6 lemons) or white vinegar
One 3-feet (1-meter)-square piece of fine muslin or 4 layers of cheesecloth

1 Place the milk in a heavy-bottomed pot and bring to a boil, stirring constantly, over medium-high heat. As soon as the milk comes to a boil, add the lemon juice and lower the heat to medium. Continue to stir until the milk curdles and separates into curds, which resemble cottage cheese, and whey 1 to 2 minutes. Remove from the heat. Let it sit for 5 minutes.

2 Drape the muslin or cheesecloth over a large pan and pour the curdled milk over it. As you do this, the whey drains through the cloth into the pan, and curdled paneer cheese remains in the cloth. Tie the ends of the cloth together and hang over a sink to drain. Allow to drain 3 to 5 minutes.

3 Twist the cloth around the cheese, and then place the cheese between two plates. Place a large pan of water or a heavy saucepan on the top plate and let the cheese drain further, 10 to 20 minutes.

4 Remove the weight off the cheese (which, by now, should have compressed into a chunk), cut into desired shapes and sizes, and use as needed. Store in an airtight container in the refrigerator 4 to 5 days or freeze up to 4 months.

Variation:

Flavored Paneer Cheese

Paneer cheese can also be made with about 1 cup (200 g) chopped fresh herbs like basil, tarragon or mint. Or, you may add about 2 tablespoons of toasted cumin seeds or toasted fennel seeds to the above recipe to give it a different texture and flavor. Store in an airtight container in the refrigerator 4 to 5 days or freeze up to 4 months.

Smoky Fire-Roasted Eggplant *Baingan Bharta*

I love the smoky aroma and taste of this eggplant delicacy, which is cooked with onions, tomatoes and spices and served over Whole-Wheat Griddle Breads (page 136). Though the eggplant is traditionally charcoal-smoked, the smoking can also be done over a gas burner on a stove top or under the broiler. This dish also goes nicely alongside Masala-Crusted Tilapia (page 97) or even Tandoori Chicken (page 112).

Serves 6
Prep time: 10 minutes
Cook time: 30 minutes

4 "baby" eggplants (Asian or Italian) or 2 large eggplants (globe variety), about 2¹/₂ lbs (1.25 kg) total
³/₄ cup (185 ml) ghee (clarified butter) or oil
1 teaspoon cumin seeds
1 red onion (about ¹/₃ lb/ 150 g), finely chopped
One 1-in (2.5-cm) piece fresh ginger, peeled and chopped
1 teaspoon paprika
Salt, to taste
2 tomatoes (about ³/₄ lb/ 350 g), chopped
3 fresh green chili peppers, minced
4 tablespoons chopped fresh coriander leaves (cilantro)

TIP When selecting eggplants, choose ones that are shiny and seem light for their size. They will have fewer seeds.

1 Preheat a grill to medium heat or a broiler to 325°F (160°C) and set the oven rack 5-inches (12.5 cm) below the heat source.
2 Flame-char the whole eggplants on the gas grill, turning constantly, until blackened and soft, about 15 minutes. Alternatively, you may roast the eggplants under the preheated broiler on a sheet pan until completely soft and lightly burnt and the skin starts peeling off, about 15 to 20 minutes.
3 Immerse the grilled or roasted eggplants in cold water to cool. Remove the skin and stem and coarsely chop the flesh. (You should have nearly 2 cups/500 g chopped eggplant.) Set aside.
4 Heat the ghee or oil in a saucepan over medium heat. Add the cumin and sauté until it begins to crackle, about 30 seconds. Add the onion and cook until transparent, about 2 minutes. Add the ginger and cook, stirring constantly, for 30 seconds.
5 Reduce the heat to medium-low. Add the paprika, salt and tomatoes and cook until the fat starts to leave the sides, about 2 minutes. Add the chopped eggplant and green chili peppers and cook, stirring constantly, until soft and mushy, about 4 to 5 minutes. Stir in the chopped coriander leaves and serve hot.

Pumpkin with Coconut *Kaddu Narialwalla*

Pumpkin is available all year-round in India and is widely used in savory as well as sweet dishes. If pumpkin is not available, try to use a close cousin, such as butternut squash. The skin of winter squashes is thick and hard, and difficult to peel, so it is best to cut the pumpkin into manageable-size pieces first. Serve this dish with Whole-Wheat Griddle Breads (page 136) and Traditional Lamb Curry (page 115).

Serves 4
Prep time: 15minutes
Cook time: 30 minutes

1 lb (500 g) pumpkin
2 tablespoons oil
¹/₂ teaspoon cumin seeds
2 dried red chili peppers, broken in half
One 1-in (2.5-cm) cinnamon stick
6 fresh or dried curry leaves
1 onion (about ¹/₃ lb/150 g), chopped
1 teaspoon ground coriander
1 teaspoon light brown sugar
Salt, to taste
1 cup (100 g) shredded, unsweetened coconut (frozen, reconstituted dried, or freshly grated) (page 24)
¹/₄ cup (65 ml) water
4 tablespoons minced fresh coriander leaves (cilantro), for garnish

1 Using a large sharp knife, carefully cut the pumpkin in half. Lay the flat side down on a cutting board and then cut the halves into wedges. Remove the skin and seeds. Cut the pumpkin flesh into 1-inch (2.5-cm) dice.
2 Heat the oil in a large heavy skillet over medium-high heat. Add the cumin, red chili peppers, cinnamon stick, and curry leaves and fry briefly, until fragrant. Add the onion and cook, stirring frequently, until golden brown, about 5 minutes.
3 Add the pumpkin; lower the heat to medium, and cook, stirring constantly to prevent sticking, for 5 minutes. Add the ground coriander, brown sugar and salt. Cook until the pumpkin is softened, about 15 minutes.
4 Add the coconut and stir to break up lumps and blend it into the pumpkin mixture. Add the water and cook an additional 2 to 3 minutes, stirring to prevent sticking. Taste for seasoning and add more salt if necessary. Garnish with chopped fresh coriander leaves.

Mushrooms and Corn in a Spicy Curry *Makki Khumb Masala*

India is home to some vibrant vegetarian dishes made according to ancient recipes. Though corn is not a part of India's ancient vegetarian cuisine, it has been incorporated into a myriad of dishes using cooking techniques that have been developed over many centuries. This recipe—a colorful maize and mushroom combination cooked with fresh herbs—is always a crowd-pleaser at my parties. If you cannot find fresh corn you can substitute frozen corn kernels. This dish goes very well with Madras Chicken (page 114), Masala Lamb Chops (page 121) or Lemon and Saffron Chicken Kebabs (page 108) and a helping of Plain Basmati Rice (page 124).

Serves 4
Prep time: 15 minutes
Cook time: 20 minutes

1 lb (500 g) fresh mushrooms
³⁄₄ cup (185 ml) oil
1 large onion (about ¹⁄₂ lb/250 g), minced
4 fresh green chili peppers, minced
2 tablespoons Ginger-Garlic Paste (page 32)
2 teaspoons Asian chili powder or cayenne pepper
¹⁄₄ cup (65 ml) water
2 tomatoes (about ³⁄₄ lb/350 g), chopped
1¹⁄₂ cups (280 g) fresh or frozen corn kernels (from 3 ears fresh corn or one 10-oz/300-g package)
2 teaspoons salt
1 small green bell pepper, cut into 1-in (2.5-cm) dice (³⁄₄ cup/130 g)
2 teaspoons Home-Style Garam Masala (page 35)

1 Wipe the mushrooms with a damp cloth to remove all dirt, cut off the stems, and cut them into bite-size pieces. Depending on the size, you may need to cut them in half or quarters or, if they are very small, leave them whole.
2 Heat the oil in a large, heavy skillet over medium-high heat. Add the onion and sauté until golden brown, about 2 to 3 minutes. Add the green chili peppers, Ginger-Garlic Paste, Asian chili powder or cayenne pepper and water and fry for 1 minute, stirring constantly. Add the chopped tomatoes and cook, stirring frequently, until the fat separates from the *masala*. This technique is called *bhunao*.
3 Add the corn, mushrooms and salt and bring to a boil. Reduce the heat to medium-low and simmer until the liquid has evaporated. Taste for seasoning and add more salt if needed.
4 Stir in the diced green bell pepper and Home-Style Garam Masala and bring to a boil. Serve hot.

Cauliflower with Ginger and Cumin

Adraki Gobhi

This dish pairs well with any *dal* and flatbread. With its delightfully soft texture, it is the perfect side dish to serve with some of the heavier meat curries. For a quick snack or a meal on the run, I love to create a tasty roll-up with this dish and a freshly made Whole-Wheat Griddle Breads (page 136).

Serves 4 to 6
Prep time: 15 minutes
Cook time: 15 minutes

5 tablespoons oil
3 teaspoons cumin seeds
2 teaspoon fennel seeds
1 large onion (about $^1/_2$ lb/250 g), minced
2 tablespoons Ginger-Garlic Paste (page 32)
1 teaspoon ground turmeric
2 teaspoons Asian chili powder or cayenne pepper
2 teaspoons ground coriander
1 cup (250 ml) water
1 small tomato (about 3 oz/85 g), chopped
1 teaspoon salt
1 large head cauliflower (about 2 lbs/ 1 kg), cut into florets (stem discarded or reserved for other use)
2 teaspoons Home-Style Garam Masala (page 35)
One 2-in (5-cm) piece fresh ginger, peeled and cut into thin strips
4 tablespoons minced fresh coriander leaves (cilantro)

1 Heat the oil in a large skillet over medium heat. When hot, add the cumin and fennel. Cook, stirring until the seeds begins to brown, about 30 seconds. Add the onion; cook stirring for about 1 minute until slightly brown. Add the Ginger-Garlic Paste, turmeric, Asian chili powder or cayenne pepper, coriander, $^1/_2$ cup (125 ml) of the water, the tomato and salt. Sauté for another minute until the fat leaves the *masala*. This technique is called *bhunao*.

2 Add the cauliflower and cook, stirring, until it begins to brown, about 1 minute. Add the remaining $^1/_2$ cup (125 ml) of water. Cover and cook until the cauliflower is tender, about 10 minutes. Add the Home-Style Garam Masala, ginger and coriander leaves and cook until the masala is dry, about 1 minute. Serve hot.

Stir-Fried Okra

Bhindi Subzi

Bhindi Subzi is simply divine with any Indian meal. If you have previously cooked okra and ended up with slimy results, you may be turned off to making it at home. But don't be! You need only follow my aunt's three cardinal rules: always wipe okra dry before cutting it, always cook it without a lid, and do not stir it too much while cooking. Following her tips will ensure that the okra does not have a slimy texture. If you prefer okra crispy, deep-frying is a good option. Always pick out the smallest okra as they will be the most tender. Frozen cut okra may be used in place of fresh if it is out of season. Serve this as a side dish with a saucy curry or a *dal* and some Plain Naan (page 134) or rice of your choice.

Serves 4
Prep time: 15minutes
Cook time: 15 minutes

1 lb (500 g) fresh tender okra, rinsed
  and patted dry or 1 lb (500 g) cut
  frozen okra
$^1/_2$ cup (125 ml) oil
2 teaspoons cumin seeds
1 large onion (about $^1/_2$ lb/250 g),
  sliced
$^1/_2$ teaspoon ground coriander
$^1/_2$ teaspoon ground cumin
$^1/_2$ teaspoon Asian chili powder or
  cayenne pepper
$^1/_4$ teaspoon ground turmeric
$^1/_2$ teaspoon salt
Juice of $^1/_2$ lemon

1 Trim the ends off each okra pod and cut into small segments about approximately $^1/_2$-inch (1.25-cm) in length.
2 Heat the oil in a nonstick skillet over medium-high heat. Add the cumin seeds—they should sizzle upon contact with the hot oil. Quickly add the onion and cook, stirring frequently, until golden, about 3 to 4 minutes. Add the okra and fry, stirring every now and then, for 10 minutes. The onion will be dark brown by this time. Add the ground spices and salt and sauté for another 5 minutes. Add the lemon juice and cook, stirring gently, for another minute. Serve hot.

Puréed Spinach with Cheese Balls

Palak Paneer Kofta

I like to cook this rich dish for festive occasions and formal dinners. Cheese balls, or *kofta*, are coated in a creamy spinach sauce. The best result comes from using fresh spinach, but you can use frozen spinach as an alternative. The cheese koftas can be made ahead of time and refrigerated. You can also omit the sauce and serve just the koftas as an appetizer with any of the chutneys or dips or serve them rolled up in flatbreads to make delicious wraps.

Serves 4
Prep time: 40 minutes
Cook time: 40 minutes

Oil, for deep-frying

Cheese Balls
1 lb (500 g) Paneer Cheese (page 83), grated and mashed
1 potato (about 1/2 lb/250 g) potato, boiled, peeled and mashed
1 tablespoon plus 1 teaspoon cornstarch
2 teaspoons salt
1/2 teaspoon white pepper

Spinach Sauce
2 lbs (1 kg) spinach, washed and tough stems removed
3 1/2 tablespoons oil
1 teaspoon minced garlic
1/2 cup (125 ml) tomato purée
1/2 teaspoon Asian chili powder or cayenne pepper
1/4 teaspoon ground turmeric
1/2 teaspoon ground coriander
1 teaspoon salt, or to taste
1 cup (250 ml) water
1 cup (250 ml) cream
1/2 teaspoon Home-Style Garam Masala (page 35)
2 teaspoons dried fenugreek leaves (kasoori methi), crushed (optional)

1 To make the Cheese Balls: Blend together all the ingredients in a large mixing bowl. Mix well and divide this mixture into 16 equal-sized balls. Refrigerate for at least an hour.

2 Heat 2 inches of the deep-frying oil in a *kadhai*, small wok or large saucepan over medium heat to 325°F (160°C) on a deep-fry or candy thermometer. To gauge the temperature of the oil without a thermometer, drop a piece of bread about 1-inch (2.5-cm) square into the oil, turning the piece of bread often as the oil heats up. When the oil reaches 325°F(160°C), the bread will begin to brown quickly and turn golden brown all over—like a crouton—in about 40 seconds. Deep-fry the Cheese Balls in batches until golden brown. Remove with a slotted spoon and drain on paper towels. Set aside.

3 To make the Spinach Sauce: Bring a large saucepan of water to a boil. Place the spinach in the boiling water and cook until it's just done, about 3 minutes. Drain in a colander and rinse under cold water. Purée the spinach in a blender or a food processor until smooth, adding a little water if necessary. Set aside.

4 Heat the 3 1/2 tablespoons of oil in a skillet over medium heat. Add the garlic and sauté for 30 seconds, until slightly brown. Add the spinach purée and cook, while stirring, for about 2 minutes. Add the tomato purée, Asian chili powder or cayenne pepper, turmeric, coriander, salt and water. Cook for about 5 minutes. Stir in the cream, Home-Style Garam Masala and dried fenugreek leaves, if using. And the fried Cheese Balls and let simmer for about 3 to 5 minutes, gently stirring from time to time. Remove from the heat.

5 Using a spoon, carefully transfer the Cheese Balls to a serving plate (they break apart easily, so be careful). Pour the Spinach Sauce on top and serve hot.

Zucchini with Lentils and Roasted Garlic

Masala Zucchini aur Dal ki Subzi

Serves 6
Prep time: 15 minutes
Cook time: 40 minutes

1 cup (200 g) split pigeon peas (toor dal), rinsed and drained
$1/2$ teaspoon ground turmeric
2 teaspoon salt
4 cups (1 liter) water
2 tablespoons oil
6 large garlic cloves, crushed
1 teaspoon cumin seeds
1 small onion (about $1/4$ lb/125 g), thinly sliced
4 small zucchini (about 1 lb/500 g), cut into $1/4$-in (6-mm)-thick half moons
1 tablespoon ground coriander
1 tablespoon ground cumin
$1/2$ teaspoon paprika
2 tablespoons chopped fresh coriander leaves (cilantro)
1 teaspoon Home-Style Garam Masala (page 35)

The combination of lentils, vegetables, garlic and cumin gives this satisfying side dish a unique flavor that goes perfectly with Kerala Coconut Beef (page 116) or Stir-Fried Shrimp (page 103) and Plain Basmati Rice (page 124) or Whole-Wheat Griddle Breads (page 136). If zucchini is not available, use other common squashes such as summer squash (*ghia*) or calabash, aka bottle gourd (*doodhi*). The addition of lentils in this side dish makes it a nutritious main dish for vegetarians with rice or bread and a *raita* or plain yogurt.

1 Place the lentils, turmeric, salt and water in a large saucepan. Bring to a boil, skimming off any surface scum that collects on the top. Reduce the heat and simmer, covered, until the lentils are cooked, about 15 to 20 minutes. Transfer to a serving bowl. Cover the bowl and keep warm.

2 Heat the oil in a medium saucepan over medium heat. Add the garlic and sauté until golden brown. Add the cumin seeds—they should sizzle upon contact with the hot oil. Quickly add the onion and zucchini and cook for 10 to 15 minutes.

3 Add the ground coriander and cumin and continue to cook until the zucchini is cooked, about 10 minutes.

4 Remove the pan from the heat, add the paprika, and immediately pour over the hot lentils. Swirl lightly to mix and sprinkle on the fresh coriander leaves and Home-Style Garam Masala. Serve with your choice of Indian breads or rice.

Stir-Fried Paneer Cheese with Bell Peppers

Kadhai Paneer

A *kadhai* is an Indian version of a Chinese wok, which Indian cooks use to make a variety of dishes. However, for a dish to be considered a "kadhai dish" it must have the flavor combination of onions, peppers, ginger, garlic, dried red chili peppers and a blend of select Indian spices. This recipe is a classic way of making a kadhai dish, which I learned while I was working at a restaurant in New Delhi. The paneer can be substituted with mixed vegetables, seafood or chicken. (See Stir-Fried Shrimp, page 103). My favorite version is Kadhai Anda, which includes hard-boiled eggs. I always make some extra Kadhai Spice Blend for making kadhai dishes and store it in an airtight container for later use. If you find that you enjoy this Indian-style stir-fry, as I do, you will reach for this spice blend often. This dish goes best with flatbreads like Baked Garlic Naan (page 134) or Whole-Wheat Griddle Breads (page 136).

Serves 4
Prep time: 20 minutes
Cook time: 15 minutes

3 tablespoons oil
1 tablespoon minced garlic
2 fresh green chili peppers, slit open
   lengthwise
1 tablespoon plus 1 teaspoon peeled
   and minced fresh ginger
3/4 cup (185 ml) tomato purée
1/2 cup (125 ml) water
1 green bell pepper, diced (1 cup/175 g)
1 red bell pepper, diced (1 cup/175 g)
1 lb (500 g) Paneer Cheese (page 83),
   diced
2 teaspoons crushed, dried fenugreek
   leaves (kasoori methi) (optional)
1 1/2 teaspoons Home-Style Garam
   Masala (page 35)
2 teaspoons salt
4 tablespoons minced fresh coriander
   leaves (cilantro)

Kadhai Spice Blend
6 dried red chili peppers
1 tablespoon plus 1 teaspoon coriander
   seeds
1 tablespoon plus 1 teaspoon cumin
   seeds

1 To make the Kadhai Spice Blend: Grind the red chili peppers, coriander and cumin seeds in a spice grinder to make a coarse powder. Set aside.

2 Heat the oil in a wok or a saucepan over medium heat. Add the minced garlic and fry until light brown, about 1 minute. Add the green chili peppers, ginger and tomato purée and sauté for 30 seconds. Then add the Kadhai Spice Blend and cook for 30 seconds, stirring constantly. Add the water and cook until the fat leaves the *masala*, about 2 minutes. This technique is called *bhunao*.

3 Add the green and red bell peppers and cook over medium heat for 30 seconds. Add the diced paneer and simmer stirring gently for 2 to 3 minutes. Sprinkle on the fenugreek leaves, if using, Home-Style Garam Masala, salt and fresh coriander leaves. Stir and serve hot.

Variation:

Kadhai Anda

Eggs, or *anda* in Hindi, are a commonly used ingredient in Indian cooking. To make this kadhai dish simply replace the paneer cheese in the above recipe with 4 hard-boiled eggs, cut in half. This is a delicious variation which goes well with Whole-Wheat Griddle Breads (page 136).

Stir-Fried Paneer Cheese with Bell Peppers

Mangalore Spiced Potatoes *Mangalore Aloo Masala*

This spicy, yellow-tinged potato dish gets its signature flavor from curry leaves, mustard seeds, turmeric and *asafetida*—a favorite spice combination from Mangalore, a coastal region in the southwestern part of India. This sautéed dish is very versatile. When mashed, it is used as a filling for breads, such Flaky Paratha Breads Stuffed with Potatoes (page 139), and it makes a tasty accompaniment to a larger meal. I like to serve it with Masala Lamb Chops (page 121) or Pork Vindaloo (page 120) and some Plain Basmati Rice (page 124). I sometimes replace the green peas with fresh spinach or mustard greens. Day-old boiled potatoes work very well for this dish, just make sure the potatoes are slightly over cooked so that they get mashed up when you sauté them.

Serves 4
Prep time: 20 minutes
Cook time: 10 minutes

1¹/₂ lbs (750 g) potatoes (about 2 large potatoes)
1 cup (130 g) green peas, fresh or frozen (shelled from 1 lb/500 g fresh pea pods or about half of one 10-oz/300-g package frozen peas), optional
3 tablespoons oil
2 teaspoons black mustard seeds
2 fresh green chili peppers split open lengthwise
10 fresh or dried curry leaves
Dash of asafetida (optional)
¹/₂ teaspoon ground turmeric
1 teaspoon salt, plus more if needed
4 tablespoons chopped fresh coriander leaves (cilantro)

1 Combine the potatoes with plenty of cold water to cover, in a large saucepan. Bring to a boil over high heat and cook, uncovered, until very tender, about 15 to 20 minutes. (In the meantime, if using frozen peas, remove them from the freezer to allow them to defrost.) Drain the potatoes well and set aside to cool. Peel the potatoes and coarsely chop.
2 Heat the oil in a nonstick skillet over medium heat. When hot, add the mustard seeds. When the mustard seeds pop and splatter, add the green chili peppers, curry leaves and asafetida, if using. Fry for about 30 seconds, stirring constantly. Add the green peas, cooked potatoes, turmeric, salt and fresh coriander leaves and cook, stirring frequently, until the potatoes are heated through and the peas are cooked, about 3 to 5 minutes. Check the seasoning and sprinkle on more salt if needed.

Chapter 6

Fish and Seafood

For Indians living in coastal areas or inland near fresh water lakes, ponds and streams, fish and seafood are an important part of the daily diet—only those following a strict vegetarian diet are likely to abstain from this excellent source of protein. And, since geographically one-half of India is a peninsula, surrounded by the Indian Ocean, Bay of Bengal and Arabian Sea, and most of the country is well traversed by rivers and streams and dotted with small lakes, this is a significant part of the population. In these areas, an ample supply of fresh fish or seafood is available year-round and meals and accompanying dishes are planned around the fish or seafood dish. I grew up in Udupi, a small town on the western coast of India. We were never far from local fish markets or fresh seafood. I walked to the market often, looking at baskets of fresh seafood, as well as dried and salted fish. (The dried and salted fish are delicacies in these regions and is used in making fish chutneys and pickles.) My family's favorite fish dish, which was a staple at our home, was Mangalore Fish Curry (page 105).

The most common method of cooking and serving fish and seafood in Indian homes is as a curry and so it is usually accompanied by rice. Other popular techniques are pan-frying and deep-frying. When fish or seafood is pan-fried, it is coated with spices, when deep-fried, it is coated with a batter or a crust. Baking and grilling is not done very often in homes in India. In restaurants, in addition to the traditional home-style cooking methods, fish may be baked in a *tandoor* oven to create tandoori-style fish dishes or grilled. In this chapter, you can learn how to make several traditional fish and seafood dishes like Mangalore Fish Curry (page 105), Stir-Fried Shrimp (page 103) and Malabar Crab Curry (page 98) along with some nontraditional Indian-inspired dishes like Spicy Scallops with Grilled Pineapple Chutney (page 101) and Masala-Crusted Tilapia (page 97).

The most popular fish and seafood in India are Indian mackerel, pomfret (*pompano*), *hilsa* (similar to shad fish), *rohu* (most popular fish in northeastern India), black sea bream, sardines, shrimps, mussels and squid. Although these varieties are different from what is available in waters in other parts of the world, most fish in American and European fish markets are comparable to Indian varieties, and most take well to Indian flavors. Most Indian recipes can be made with varieties that are easy to find in the West, such as sea bass, halibut, salmon, snapper, haddock, cod or even swordfish.

Fish Tikka *Macchli ke Tikke*

The sweet and tart cucumber-onion relish perfectly complements the delicate flavors of this *tikka*, which basically means "chunk" and is applied to many Indian dishes featuring bite-size pieces of food. I love to use swordfish for tikka—being thick and firm, it's a good option for skewering and takes well to Indian spices and seasonings. To keep things simple I use a readymade tandoori seasoning. Alternatively, Dhaba Spice (page 34) or Home-Style Garam Masala (page 35) may be used to flavor the fish. Serve this over salad greens for a flavorful light meal.

Serves 4
Prep time: 15 minutes
Cook time: 15 minutes

1 red onion (about $1/3$ lb/150 g), thinly sliced
2 teaspoons salt
3 lemons
1 teaspoon sugar
1 tablespoon minced fresh coriander leaves (cilantro)
4 swordfish or mahi mahi steaks (about $1^1/_2$ lbs/750 g total), cut into chunks
Four 12-inch (30-cm) bamboo skewers, soaked in water for 30 minutes
1 tablespoon store-bought tandoori seasoning, Dhaba Spice (page 34) or Home-Style Garam Masala (page 35)
3 small cucumbers (about $1^1/_2$ lbs/750 g total), thinly sliced on the diagonal
1 to 2 tablespoons oil

1 Put the sliced onion in a mixing bowl and sprinkle with 1 teaspoon of the salt. Leave for 20 minutes. Rinse the onion slices under cold water. Squeeze dry and return to the bowl with the juice of 1 of the lemons, the sugar and fresh coriander leaves. Toss to combine. Set aside.
2 Slice the remaining 2 lemons into thick slices. Thread the swordfish chunks and lemon slices onto the skewers. Season with the remaining 1 teaspoon of salt, tandoori seasoning, Dhaba Spice or Home-Style Garam Masala and set aside.
3 Add the cucumber to the bowl with the pickled onion and toss until well mixed.
4 Heat a large nonstick skillet over medium-high heat. Drizzle the oil to evenly coat the pan. Place the skewers in the hot oil and cook for 2 minutes on each side. Serve with the onion-cucumber relish.

Salmon Kebabs

Serves 4
Prep time: 20 minutes
Cook time: 15 minutes

1¼ lbs (600 g) salmon fillets, skinned
3 tablespoons finely chopped fresh
   coriander leaves (cilantro)
2 tablespoons Indian Grilling and
   Roasting Rub (page 33)
1 to 2 tablespoons dried bread crumbs
8 bamboo skewers, soaked in water for
   30 minutes
2 tablespoons oil
Chutney of your choice, for serving

1 Chop the salmon meat by using a knife or a food processor, being careful not to pulverize the meat. Mix together the salmon meat, fresh coriander leaves, and Indian Grilling and Roasting Rub and 1 tablespoon of the bread crumbs in a bowl. Take about ¼ cup (75 g) of the mixture and, with moistened hands, form a little patty directly onto a skewer, leaving about 1 inch (2.5 cm) open on either end. Firmly press the salmon mixture onto a skewer. This is your test skewer. If the test patty adhered to the skewer, follow Step 2, but divide the dough into 7 equal portions instead of 8. If the patty does not adhere to the skewer, remove the patty from the skewer and return it to the bowl with the rest of salmon mixture. Sprinkle on additional tablespoon of bread crumbs and thoroughly mix in.

2 Divide the mixture into 8 equal portions (or 7 portions, if the test patty worked). Using your hands, with your palms slightly wet, form a little patty directly onto a skewer. (Make sure the patties are firmly attached to the skewers before putting them onto the preheated and oiled pan.)

3 Preheat a large, shallow skillet over medium heat. Add the oil. When hot, place the skewers in the skillet.

4 Cook the skewers until the salmon is just cooked through, about 2 to 3 minutes per side. Remove the skewers from the pan and serve immediately with the chutney of your choice.

Skewered minced fish on a stick is not very common in Indian cooking. This is my twist on minced meat kebabs that are popular in India. This dish makes a very elegant presentation and is a good choice for a cocktail party. Fresh coriander leaves (cilantro) adds a delicate citrusy fragrance to this delicious salmon dish. I love to serve this with Spicy Apricot Chutney (page 42) or Cucumber and Yogurt Raita (page 45).

Masala-Baked Red Snapper
Masaladar Oven ki Macchi

This recipe is inspired by a memorable trip I took to Cochin, a port city in Kerala, a state in southern India. Cochin's unique "You buy, I cook" beach-side food stalls offer good, fresh seafood and beautiful views of the ocean. First you choose your own "catch of the day" from one of the fishmongers opposite the fishing nets and then one of the nearby "fast food" shacks will cook it for you. On one occasion, I picked out a whole red snapper, which was grilled wrapped in banana leaves with some local ingredients and spices. It is a great way of cooking a whole fish—keeping the head on the fish makes for a great presentation. I like to serve this fish dish with Lemon Rice with Peanuts (page 129) or Tamarind Rice (page 131) and Spicy Coconut Green Beans (page 82). The pink color of the snapper contrasts nicely with the green beans. If you cannot find fresh snapper you can substitute another whole firm-fleshed fresh fish, such as trout or pickerel. This recipe will feed four when served with rice and one or more vegetable dishes.

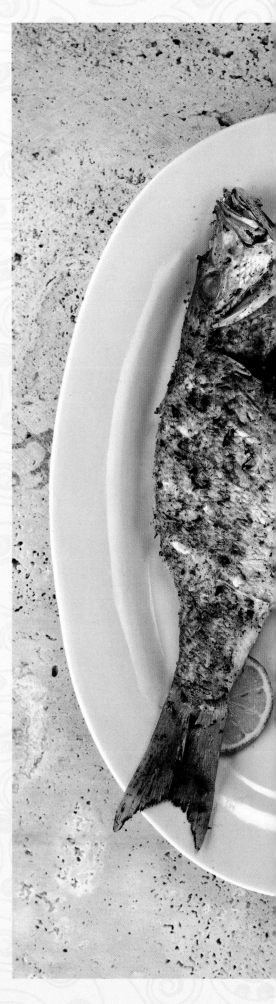

Serves 2 to 4
Prep time: 15 minutes
Cook time: 45 minutes

1 whole red snapper (about 2 lbs/1 kg), cleaned and scaled
$^1/_2$ cup (125 ml) freshly-squeezed lime juice
$^1/_2$ teaspoon grated lime zest
2 tablespoons oil, plus extra to coat the baking dish
2 teaspoons salt
1 cup (300 g) Green Chili Masala (page 35)
Aluminum foil

1 Preheat the oven to 400°F (200°C).

2 Score the skin of the fish in a diamond pattern. Combine the lime juice, lime zest, 1 tablespoon of the oil and the salt in a shallow pan. Rub the fish all over with the lime juice mixture.

3 Rub the Green Chili Masala mixture into the slits in the fish skin and into the fish's cavity. Lay the fish on a large sheet of foil. Pour on the remaining 1 tablespoon of oil and spread it over the top of the fish.

4 Lightly coat a shallow baking dish with oil to prevent the foil from sticking. Wrap the aluminum foil fairly tightly around the fish, making sure that the package is well sealed. Place it in the prepared baking dish.

5 Bake for about 30 minutes, but start checking after 20 minutes. The exact time will depend on the size and thickness of the fish. To test, peel back a little of the foil and press on the flesh at the thickest part of the fish. It should yield a little and feel soft. The other test is to unwrap more of the fish and test the texture of the flesh: if it flakes with a fork, it is cooked.

6 To serve, lift sections of the top fillet off the bone and place on a platter. Pour the excess pan juices on top of the fish. When the first side is finished, flip the fish over to serve the second fillet.

Masala-Baked Red Snapper

Masala-Crusted Tilapia

Bhuni Masala Macchli

Tilapia, an otherwise dull fish, is easily perked up with a rub of Indian spices. Though not traditionally used in Indian cooking, here I have used garlic powder to create a blackened crust on the fish. Fresh garlic will not give the desired texture. Serve this fish with any of the rice dishes or, my favorite way, with a simple salad like Mung Dal and Cucumber Salad (page 62) or just mixed greens.

Serves 4
Prep time: 15 minutes
Cook time: 30 minutes

4 tilapia, or other firm white fish, fillets (about 1¹/₄ to 1¹/₂ lbs/600 to 750 g total)
2 tablespoons oil
Juice of 2 limes

Indian Blackened Seasoning
1 tablespoon Asian chili powder or cayenne pepper
1 teaspoon garlic powder
2 teaspoons cumin seeds, toasted and coarsely ground
2 teaspoons fennel seeds, toasted and coarsely ground
2 teaspoons Home-Style Garam Masala (page 35)
1 teaspoon salt

1 Combine the ingredients for the Indian Blackened Seasoning on a plate. Dredge the fillets in the spice mixture to coat.
2 Heat the oil in a large nonstick skillet over medium-high heat. Fry the fish until just opaque in the center, 2 to 3 minutes per side, gently turning it when half-done. Squeeze the lime juice on the fish and serve immediately.

NOTE: While cooking this fish or any other pan-fried fish dishes, lift the pieces carefully with a spatula and do not turn them more than twice.

Malabar Crab Curry

Malabari Kekda Kari

My grandmother (*ajji*) used to make this flavorful spicy curry from the west coast of India on special occasions. We used to dunk hot *dosa* into this steaming hot curry, but today, to simplify my time in the kitchen, I serve this curry with Plain Basmati Rice (page 124). In this recipe, the tomatoes are a welcome addition to this rich coconut-based curry. This curry is made with whole crabs, cut up. If using fresh crabs, be on the look-out for live crabs and have your fish monger clean them before you bring them home. Frozen crabs make a decent substitute, but the flavor of the curry is nowhere near to when using fresh crabs.

Malabar Crab Curry

Serves 4
Prep time: 15 minutes
Cook time: 20 to 25 minutes

8 live medium-size crabs, such as blue or snow or 2 lbs (1kg) frozen whole crab, crab claws or king crab legs (not previously cooked)

1 cup (100 g) shredded, unsweetened coconut (fresh, frozen or recon-stituted dried, page 24)

2 fresh green chili peppers

$^1/_3$ cup (80 ml) plus 2 cups (500 ml) water

$^3/_4$ cup (185 ml) oil

1½ teaspoons black mustard seeds

2 dried red chili peppers

10 fresh or dried curry leaves

1 onion (about $^1/_3$ lb/150 g), chopped

4 tablespoons Ginger-Garlic Paste (page 32)

$^1/_2$ teaspoon Asian chili powder or cayenne pepper

$^1/_2$ teaspoon ground turmeric

2 teaspoons salt, plus more if needed

1 large tomato (about $^1/_2$ lb/250 g), chopped

4 tablespoons chopped fresh coriander leaves (cilantro), for garnish

1 To clean a whole crab, hold the crab in one hand and lift up the shell where it forms a point to remove the top shell. Clean the crab making sure the spongy, inedible gills from either side of the body are removed. Cut off the "face" of the crab where it joins the lower shell and remove the internal organs by scraping them out with a knife. Clean and wash the crabs thoroughly.

2 To cut a whole crab, using a strong knife, remove the legs from the body of the crab and set aside. Cut the body into 2 to 3-inch (5 to 7.5-cm) pieces. Or, you can leave the body whole if you prefer.

3 Place the coconut, green chili peppers and $^1/_3$ cup (80 ml) of the water in a food processor or blender and process to make a very smooth paste.

4 Heat the oil in a large skillet or wok over medium heat. Add the mustard seeds and sauté until they begin to pop. Add the dried red chili peppers and curry leaves and stir for 5 seconds. Quickly add the onion and sauté until a light golden color. Add the Ginger-Garlic Paste and cook, stirring constantly, until the liquid has evaporated, about 2 to 3 minutes. Add the Asian chili powder or cayenne pepper, turmeric and salt and cook for 30 seconds to allow the flavors to intensify.

5 Add the chopped tomato and crab and cook until the oil leaves the *masala*. Add the coconut paste and the remaining 2 cups (500 ml) of water; bring to a boil stirring occasionally. Cover, reduce the heat to low, and simmer for 15 to 20 minutes. Check for seasoning and add more salt if needed. Garnish with the fresh coriander leaves and serve hot.

Tandoori Skewered Shrimp

Jhinga Kebab

This is a perfect summer meal for a grill, but can be cooked on a grill pan on the stovetop too for an equally delicious result. This dish can be served as a salad or appetizer, but I like it best as a light meal served with Avocado and Roasted Cumin Raita (page 44). To make things simple, this recipe calls for store-bought tandoori seasoning. If you cannot get your hands on a tandoori seasoning spice, replace it with store-bought or Home-Style Garam Masala (page 35). When my mother prepared this dish—which was one of my father's favorites—she would serve it without the salad greens and fruits. I like the mix of flavor the greens and fruit provide, and the greens make me feel light and healthy—which is something you want on a hot summer evening!

Serves 2 to 4
Prep time: 10 minutes
Cook time: 10 minutes

16 fresh jumbo shrimp, peeled but with tail on
4 wooden skewers, soaked in water for 30 minutes
1 tablespoon store-bought tandoori seasoning
Salt, to taste
Oil, for oiling grill racks or broiler pan
2 cups (50 g) loosely packed red or green leaf lettuce
1 cup (150 g) seedless, diced watermelon
2 oranges, peeled and cut into segments
4 tablespoons chopped fresh coriander leaves (cilantro)
Juice of 2 limes

1 Preheat the grill to high heat. If broiling the shrimp, preheat the broiler to high heat and set the oven rack 4 inches (10 cm) below the heat source.

2 Thread 4 shrimp onto each skewer. Sprinkle with the tandoori seasoning and salt.

3 To grill the shrimp: Oil the hot grill grate and place the shrimp skewers over high heat for about 2 minutes on each side.

4 To broil the shrimp: Place the shrimp on an oiled broiler pan and broil for about 2 minutes on each side.

5 Arrange the lettuce on a serving platter. Top with the orange slices and watermelon cubes and tandoori shrimp skewers. Sprinkle evenly with the fresh coriander leaves and lime juice and serve.

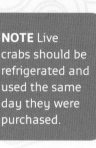

NOTE Live crabs should be refrigerated and used the same day they were purchased.

Stir-Fried Telicherry Mussels

Kallumakai Varuthathu

If being a chef is my passion, then traveling is my soul! India has a variety of geographic as well as culinary contours. Every region, even small towns, has flavors and recipes specific to its culture and local ingredients. During a recent trip to Telicherry, a south Indian town in the state of Kerala, I tasted this delicate stir-fry on the go, and this is my earnest attempt to recreate its flavors. Telicherry, apart from its artistic and talented circus artists, is also famous for its peppercorns—this dish uses a generous amount. *Kallumakai*, or *kadukka*, means "mussels" and *varuthathu* means "fried" in Malayalam, a language spoken in this region, which is a good description of this simple but delicious recipe. Traditionally this dish is flavored with the juice of *kokum*, a prunelike black fruit indigenous to India, which imparts a sour flavor. I have used lime juice and tomatoes to recreate the sourness in this dish. This recipe serves four as an appetizer and two as a main dish when served with Plain Basmati Rice (page 124). Use Telicherry peppercorns if you can for an extra-authentic flavor.

Serves 2 to 4
Prep time: 20 minutes
Cook time: 15 minutes

2 lbs (1 kg) fresh mussels
1 teaspoon ground turmeric
Salt, to taste
4 tablespoons oil
2 teaspoons cumin seeds
3 tablespoons chopped garlic
1 large red onion (about 1/2 lb/250 g),
   chopped
2 tomatoes (about 3/4 lb/350 g), chopped
Juice of 1 lime
5 tablespoons black peppercorns,
   pounded
4 tablespoons chopped fresh coriander
   leaves (cilantro)

1 Soak the mussels in cold water for about 10 minutes to release sand and grit. Using a slotted spoon, remove the mussels from the water. Discard any with cracked or broken shells or any that, if partially open, do not fully close when tapped sharply with a knife. To debeard the mussels, look for threadlike vegetal matter—known as the "beard"—where the two shells meet. Use your fingers to remove the beard, pulling toward the hinge-end of the mussel. Thoroughly clean the mussels by scrubbing the shells under cold running water—this is best done with a wire scourer.

2 Put the mussels in a large saucepan with 1/2 teaspoon of the turmeric and a little salt. Add enough cold water to cover and bring to a boil. Reduce the heat to medium-low and simmer for 2 to 3 minutes, or until the mussels have steamed opened. Discard any that do not open. Quickly drain the mussels by lifting the mussels out of their cooking water with a slotted spoon.

3 Heat the oil in a large skillet over medium heat. Add the cumin, garlic, and onion and fry until the onions are soft, about 5 minutes. Add the remaining 1/2 teaspoon of turmeric, salt and the tomatoes. Cook over low heat, stirring often, for 3 minutes.

4 Add the mussels to the onion mixture and cook, stirring gently, for 2 minutes. Add the lime juice, black pepper and chopped fresh coriander leaves. Stir briefly to combine and remove from the heat and serve immediately.

Spicy Scallops with Grilled Pineapple Chutney

What I love about this dish is the balance between the flavors of the chutney combined with the spices and the textures of the scallops. The addition of the sweet and sour Grilled Pineapple Chutney over the scallops gives the dish a burst of freshness! Scoring the scallops makes for an attractive presentation and allows the flavors to penetrate the scallops. I have used the Indian Grilling and Roasting Rub (page 33) for seasoning for an equally delicious result.

Serves 4
Prep time: 10 minutes
Cook time: 15 minutes

16 large sea scallops (about 1¼ lbs/ 600 g), gently rinsed and blotted dry with paper towels
Extra-virgin olive oil
2 tablespoons Asian chili powder or cayenne pepper
1 tablespoon toasted and ground cumin seeds
1 tablespoon Home-Style Garam Masala (page 35)
1 teaspoon salt
Oil, for oiling grill racks or broiler pan

Grilled Pineapple Chutney
1 small pineapple (about 1½ lbs/ 750 g), peeled and cut crosswise into 1-in (2.5-cm)-thick rounds
1 small red onion (about ¼ lb/125 g), diced
1 small red bell pepper, diced (¾ cup /130 g)
1 fresh green chili pepper, minced
1 tablespoon chopped fresh mint leaves
1 tablespoon chopped fresh coriander leaves (cilantro)
Juice of 1 lime
Salt, to taste

1 To make the Grilled Pineapple Chutney: Preheat the grill to medium-high. If broiling the pineapple, preheat the broiler to high heat and set the oven rack 4 inches (10 cm) below the heat source. To grill, oil the grill plate. Place the pineapple slices on the hot grill and grill for 3 to 4 minutes on each side. To broil, place the pineapple slices on a broiling pan and broil for 4 to 5 minutes on each side.

2 Cube the cooked pineapple rounds, removing the inner core. In a large mixing bowl, mix together the cubed pineapple with the red onion, red bell pepper, green chili pepper, and fresh mint and coriander leaves. Add the lime juice and salt and toss until well coated. Set aside at room temperature.

3 To prepare the scallops: If grilling the scallops, preheat the grill to high heat; if broiling, preheat the broiler to high heat and set the oven rack 4 inches (10 cm) below the heat source.

4 Drizzle a generous amount of olive oil over the scallops—enough to evenly coat them. Combine the Asian chili powder or cayenne pepper, toasted and ground cumin seeds, Home-Style Garam Masala and salt in a bowl. Add the scallop and gently toss them in the spice mixture until they are evenly coated.

5 To grill the scallops: Oil the hot grill grates and grill the scallops over high heat for about 2 minutes on each side.

6 To broil the scallops: Place the scallops on an oiled broiling pan and broil them for 4 to 5 minutes.

7 Serve immediately over the Grilled Pineapple Chutney.

Goan-Style Squid
Goa ki Squid Kari

If there ever was a place in India that no Indian would refuse to go, year after year, decade after decade, just to unwind, relax, party or rejuvenate, it has to be Goa! And the spirit of Goa has traveled far and wide. At any given time, at least 50 percent of the population in this Western coastal area is tourists, and many, if not the majority, are foreigners who've come from around the world to bask in the sounds, sights, and lifestyle Goa has to offer. The best beaches of the country, the greatest seafood, the most affordable holiday lodging, and the cheapest alcohol in the country. So, combined with the simple and good-hearted nature of the locals, it's not surprising that Goa is so popular! My ideal day in Goa would be to slide into a hammock in a beach shack, spend the late afternoon to early evening listening to the sound of the sea and watching the fisherwomen sort the fresh catch of the day, followed by the sights and sounds of chefs preparing my choice of seafood curry and right there on the beach as the sun goes down—painting the horizon like a canvas—and gulping gallons of chilled beer! In Goa, squid is a very popular catch, where it is often cooked as a curry or stir-fried. The fishermen often cook the freshly-caught squid with hot chili peppers, lime and spices, a favorite treat among the locals and tourists. This dish is inspired by a Goan squid dish I've eaten at the source and, though not a traditional Indian ingredient, I've added a touch of soy sauce to provide some zing to the curry. The technique of adding soy sauce is often used by street vendors in India who cook up these mouthwatering treats. Try this with Plain Basmati Rice (page 124), Indian Fried Rice (page 130) or Whole-Wheat Griddle Breads (page 136).

Serves 6
Prep time: 10 minutes
Cook time: 15 minutes

- **1 teaspoon cumin seeds**
- **1 teaspoon coriander seeds**
- **1 teaspoon fennel seeds**
- **2 teaspoons Asian chili powder or cayenne pepper**
- **1 teaspoon ground turmeric**
- **2 lbs (1 kg) fresh or frozen squid, cleaned, bodies cut into rings (see note)**
- **2 teaspoons soy sauce**
- **1 tablespoon chopped green onions (scallions)**
- **2 tablespoons oil**
- **2 onions (about ³/₄ lb/350 g), thinly sliced**
- **10 fresh or dried curry leaves**
- **4 large garlic cloves, crushed with the side of a large knife**
- **2 tablespoons peeled and minced fresh ginger**
- **¹/₂ cup (125 ml) coconut milk, warmed**
- **3 tablespoons lime juice**
- **Salt, to taste**
- **1 recipe Basmati Rice with Whole Spices (page 132), for serving**

1 Dry roast the cumin, coriander and fennel in a small skillet over low heat, until aromatic, about 1 minute. Grind the roasted spices to a fine powder using an electric coffee or spice grinder. Add the Asian chili powder or cayenne pepper and turmeric and pulse the grinder to combine the spices.

2 Toss the squid with the spice mixture, soy sauce and green onions in a large bowl.

3 Heat the oil in a heavy-bottomed skillet over medium-high heat. Add the onions and sauté until lightly browned. Add the curry leaves, garlic, ginger and the squid. Sauté, stirring constantly, for 30 seconds. Add the warm coconut milk and bring to a boil. Stir in the lime juice and salt. Serve with Basmati Rice with Whole Spices.

NOTE For this recipe, I prefer that just the body, cut into rings, be used. However, if you don't have another use for the tentacles, rather than waste them, they can be used as well. If using the tentacles, leave them whole.

Chili Shrimp with Curry Leaves and Coconut

Jhinga Nariyal

Mumbai is the heartbeat of India—the same way Manhattan is for a lot of Americans. It is the city of myriad industries and myriad careers, of the stock exchange, the glitterati, and Bollywood, making it also the tinsel town of India. Like most big cities in India, often the best food is found in quite humble establishments. Street food, lesser known to foreigners, but well known to locals, has its own thrill and flavor. Watching street food vendors at work is like seeing, and hearing, a firework display of sorts—the flaming wok burners, row after row, the tossing of *paratha*, the smell of ghee or Chinese spices and a local pungent chili sauce, the sounds of the plates, cutlery and glasses being turned around in the quickest way possible! This dish is inspired by the food served at these roadside eateries in Mumbai—many open late into the night. Full of fresh flavors, it is inspired by the very popular Indo-Chinese dishes that are based on oriental cooking yet uses local ingredients and spices. And it features one of my favorite flavor combinations—coconut, red chili peppers and curry leaves. Up the chili peppers, if you like heat. Have all the ingredients ready before you heat the wok or the saucepan because this is a quick stir-fry best done over high heat. Beware—the smoke alarm might just go off!! Serve this over Indian Fried Rice (page 130).

Serves 4
Prep time: 10 minutes
Cook time: 10 minutes

1 tablespoon oil
1 teaspoon black mustard seeds
1 tablespoon peeled and chopped fresh ginger
2 tablespoons chopped garlic
1 small red onion (about ¼ lb/ 125 g), minced
10 fresh or dried curry leaves
2 dried red chili peppers, broken in half
20 fresh, large shrimp, peeled and deveined
½ teaspoon ground coriander
½ teaspoon Home-Style Garam Masala (page 35)
¼ cup (25 g) shredded, unsweetened coconut (frozen, reconstituted dried, or freshly grated) (page 24)
1 tablespoon plain yogurt
1 teaspoon Red Masala Paste (page 32)
1 teaspoon soy sauce
Juice of 1 lemon
2 tablespoons minced fresh coriander leaves (cilantro)
Salt, to taste

1 Heat the oil in a wok or very large sauté pan over high heat until hot. Add the mustard seeds, ginger, garlic, onion, curry leaves and red chili peppers and sauté for 1 minute.
2 Add the shrimp and cook just until they start to turn pink, 2 to 3 minutes.
3 Add the coriander, Home-Style Garam Masala, coconut, yogurt, Red Masala Paste, soy sauce, lemon juice and fresh coriander leaves; cook, stirring often, 2 minutes longer. Taste to check for seasoning and sprinkle with some salt if needed.

Stir-Fried Shrimp

Khadai Jhinga

This spicy shrimp dish is flavored with dried red chili peppers, cumin and fresh coriander leaves (cilantro). I always use fresh shrimp but frozen shrimp will also work well. This is one of my favorite and most requested party dishes. Serve this with Fried Puffed Bread (page 138) or Plain Basmati Rice (page 124).

Serves 4
Prep time: 15 minutes
Cook time: 15 minutes

3 tablespoons oil
1 teaspoon cumin seeds
2 dried red chili peppers, broken in half
10 fresh or dried curry leaves
1 red onion (about ⅓ lb/150 g), diced
1 green bell pepper, diced (about 1 cup/175 g)
½ teaspoon ground turmeric
1 teaspoon Asian chili powder or cayenne pepper
2 teaspoons Home-Style Garam Masala (page 35)
1 tablespoon tomato paste
Salt, to taste
16 fresh jumbo shrimp, preferably with tails, peeled with tails left intact
4 tablespoons chopped fresh coriander leaves (cilantro)

1 Heat the oil in a large skillet over medium-low heat. Add the cumin seeds, red chili peppers, curry leaves, onion and green bell pepper, and cook for 3 to 5 minutes, stirring occasionally, until the onion is translucent.
2 Add the turmeric, Asian chili powder or cayenne pepper, Home-Style Garam Masala, tomato paste and salt. Cook for 5 minutes, stirring constantly, until the spices are fragrant.
3 Add the shrimp and cook until they turn pink and are cooked through, about 5 to 6 minutes. Serve sprinkled with the chopped fresh coriander leaves.

Five Spice Blackened Salmon

Bengali Bhuni Macchi

Here's my recipe for perfectly sautéed salmon, which, after much trial and error, does just what I want it to do: maintain the fish's delicate flavor, keep it tender and moist, and, at the same time, create a wonderfully flavorful and crusty exterior. Although salmon is not a traditional Indian fish, I have discovered that aromatic Indian spices suit its richness. The bulk of the spices used in this recipe are inspired by the classic Indian Five Spice Mix (page 31), to which I have added some signature spices used in the classic American "blackening" spice mixture, with one important difference. Usually blackening seasoning has some cayenne pepper to provide heat. If you would like the salmon to be spicy, you could add ¼ teaspoon of Asian chili powder or cayenne pepper. When making this dish, experiment with the blend. I prefer to grind the whole spices to a coarse grind as I like the texture the coarsely ground spices create when the salmon is cooked—though you can certainly grind the spices to a fine powder, if you prefer. I like to serve this dish with Carrot Yogurt Slaw (page 46) and some crisp salad greens for a very flavorful yet light and healthy meal.

Serves 4
Prep time: 10 minutes
Cook time: 10 minutes

4 salmon fillets (about 6-oz/175-g each), skin removed
1 teaspoon cumin seeds
1 teaspoon black mustard seeds
¼ teaspoon fenugreek seeds
1 teaspoon fennel seeds
¼ teaspoon garlic powder
½ teaspoon ginger powder
1 tablespoon paprika
1½ teaspoons salt
½ tablespoon oil
Lemon wedges, for garnish

1 Place the salmon on a tray. Grind all of the whole spices (cumin, mustard, fenugreek and fennel) to a coarse powder in an electric spice or coffee grinder. Mix together the ground whole spices with the garlic, ginger, paprika and salt in a small bowl. Rub the spice mixture on both sides of the salmon fillets and let them marinate for at least 30 minutes. (If marinating longer than 30 minutes, place the fish in the refrigerator. Do not store the marinated fish for more than 12 hours as it will become overpowered by the spices.)
2 Heat the oil in a medium skillet over high heat. Cook the salmon fillets on one side for 2 minutes, without moving them. Flip them over and cook for 2 more minutes, again without moving them. Serve garnished with lemon wedges.

Mangalore Fish Curry

Mangalore Meen Kari

This vibrant and delectable curry comes from Mangalore, a region along the south-west coast of India with a cuisine dominated by fresh seafood, coconuts, dried red chili peppers and spices. The addition of tamarind gives this true southern curry a wonderful sour finish that cuts through the richness of the coconut milk. This curry is an everyday staple and is very common among several communities in the Mangalore region. I have vivid memories of walking with my father through the Saturday morning fish markets of my town with plastic bags looking for the fresh catch of the day to make Mangalore Fish Curry that evening. It is important to remember when preparing this dish to use a gentle hand while stirring as the delicate fish flesh might fall apart if you stir too vigorously. Simply swirl or shake the pan to gently mix everything together. For a complete meal, serve this dish with Plain Basmati Rice (page 124).

> **TIP** The most authentic fish to use for this curry is mackerel, which is very popular in the south-western coastal areas of India. Other medium to full-flavored fish of your choice can be used but do be sure to purchase fish steaks rather than fillets as the bones give a lot of flavor to the curry.

Serves 4
Prep time: 15 minutes
Cook time: 15 minutes

^{1}/$_2$ cup (125 ml) oil
10 fresh or dried curry leaves
1 onion (about ^{1}/$_3$ lb/150 g), sliced
1 tomato (about ^{1}/$_3$ lb/150 g), chopped
2 fresh green chili peppers, slit open lengthwise
2 teaspoons salt
¼ cup (100 g) Red Masala Paste (page 32)
3 cups (750 ml) coconut milk
1 cup (250 ml) water
1^1/$_2$ lbs (750 g) fish steaks (pomfret, cod, kingfish or mackerel), washed and patted dry with paper towels
1 teaspoon tamarind paste

1 Heat the oil in a large skillet over medium heat. Add the curry leaves and onion and sauté until golden brown. Add the tomato, green chili peppers, salt and Red Masala Paste and sauté, stirring constantly, for 2 minutes. Stir in the coconut milk and water and bring to a boil.
2 Add the fish and tamarind paste and reduce the heat to medium-low. Simmer for 8 to 10 minutes, or until the fish is cooked. When done, the flesh of the fish will be tender and easily fall off the bone. Taste and add more salt if needed. Serve hot with rice.

Chapter 7

Poultry and Meat

Not everyone is a vegetarian in India—and several regional specialties made with meat and poultry have become classic dishes, loved by Indians and non Indians alike. Indian cuisine is as rich and diverse as its civilization. There are many regions of India where the cuisine is essentially meat-based. This is especially true in the north of India, in the Kashmir and Delhi regions, where the Mughals have left a deep and lasting influence on the cuisine. In this region, where seafood isn't as readily available as compared to the southern parts, lamb, goat, and chicken form the basis of many popular dishes

Meat dishes are eaten in almost all the regions of India. Whereas meat-eating Hindus and Muslims like lamb and chicken (the cow is sacred to Hindus and Muslims are prohibited from eating pork), Christians prefer pork and beef. Pork is a must for any festive occasion in Goa, an area that was colonized by the pork-eating Portuguese in the sixteenth century. Some tasty beef dishes come from Kerala, a small coastal state in south India which is home to many Christian communities.

I have included some of my favorite traditional dishes in this chapter, along with some nontraditional "Indian-style" dishes, such as Spicy Lamb Burgers (page 117), which are great when grilled and served on a hamburger bun.

All the dishes in this chapter are treated as the main dish in a meal, with the side dishes (appetizers, vegetables and accompaniments) planned around it. Almost always, meat dishes are eaten with breads or rice.

Pepper Chicken

Murg Kali Mirch

The predominant flavors of this simple dish are the freshly crushed black pepper, lemon and fresh coriander leaves (cilantro). I like to make this recipe with double the amount of crushed black pepper. You can adjust according to your taste. Serve this dish with plenty of Baked Garlic Naan (page 134) and a side of Cucumber and Yogurt Raita (page 45) or Avocado and Roasted Cumin Raita (page 44).

Serves 4
Prep time: 15 minutes plus 2 hours for marinating
Cook time: 20 minutes

2 lbs (1 kg) chicken drumsticks, skinned
1/2 cup (125 g) plain yogurt
1 tablespoon plus 1 teaspoon peeled and minced fresh ginger
1 tablespoon plus 1 teaspoon minced garlic
1/2 teaspoon ground turmeric
1 teaspoon Asian chili powder or cayenne pepper
2 teaspoons salt
1/3 cup (80 ml) oil
6 tablespoons black peppercorns, pounded
Juice of 1 lemon
4 tablespoons chopped fresh coriander leaves (cilantro)
2 teaspoons Home-Style Garam Masala (page 35)

1 Mix together the chicken, yogurt, ginger, garlic, turmeric, Asian chili powder or cayenne pepper and salt in a large mixing bowl. Marinate the chicken for at least 2 hours in the refrigerator.
2 Heat the oil in a heavy-bottomed nonstick pan over medium heat. When hot, fry the drumsticks until golden brown, about 10 to 15 minutes.
3 Reduce the heat to low and add the black pepper, lemon juice, fresh coriander leaves and Home-Style Garam Masala. Continue to fry until the chicken is fully cooked, about 5 minutes. Serve hot.

Lemon and Saffron Chicken Kebabs

Murg Zafrani Kebab

This elegant party dish is full of flavor and is very satisfying. Serve this dish with sliced tomatoes, red onions, and cucumber slices seasoned with salt and drizzled with lemon juice. Fold these skewers in whole-wheat wraps or Whole-Wheat Griddle Breads (page 136) to make a perfect grab-and-go meal. Here I broil the skewers, but they can also be cooked on an outdoor grill or in a grill pan on the stovetop.

Serves 6
Prep time: 15 minutes plus 4 hours for marinating
Cook time: 20 minutes

3 lbs (1.5 kg) skinless, boneless chicken breasts, cut into 1-in (2.5-cm) cubes
Twelve 12-in (30-cm) wooden skewers
6 lemon wedges, for garnish

Marinade
1 teaspoon cumin seeds, toasted
1 teaspoon coriander seeds, toasted
1 cup (245 g) plain yogurt
2 tablespoons chopped garlic
2 tablespoons peeled and chopped fresh ginger
2 tablespoons oil
1 tablespoons freshly-squeezed lemon juice
1 teaspoon grated lemon zest
4 tablespoons chopped fresh coriander leaves (cilantro)
Salt, to taste
1/2 teaspoon saffron
1 teaspoon Home-Style Garam Masala (page 35)
1 teaspoon black pepper
1 teaspoon Asian chili powder or cayenne pepper

1 Purée the ingredients for the Marinade in a blender until smooth.
2 Place the chicken and Marinade in a large bowl. Mix well, making sure that the chicken pieces are thoroughly coated with the Marinade. Cover and refrigerate for 4 to 6 hours.
3 Soak the skewers in water for 30 minutes. While the skewers are soaking, bring the chicken to room temperature.
4 Preheat the broiler to high and place the oven rack about 4 inches (10 cm) from the heat source. Brush a broiler pan lightly with oil. Place the chicken cubes on the skewers (5 cubes per skewer), leaving a 1/8-inch (3-mm) space between the cubes, and arrange the skewers on the pan. Broil the chicken, turning the skewers over once, until browned in spots and just cooked through, 10 to 12 minutes total. Serve hot garnished with the lemon wedges.

Chicken Curry in a Hurry

Bhuna Masala Murg

Growing up, in my hometown of Udupi (a temple town near the Mangalorean coast of the state called Karnataka), we had a backyard garden (a *thoota*, as we called it), a cowshed, and always homemade meals made from scratch. Needless to say, the women of the house—my mother, aunts, grandmother—had a tremendously busy daily schedule. I wonder how they managed to beautifully squeeze in everyday's (sometimes mundane!) work with such élan and grace, and always with a smile! This dish is one of my family's favorite dishes, and one of my mother's "quick-fix" meals. When we kids at home were craving a chicken dinner, my mom would cook this curry up in a minute's notice. It is a very simple, easy-to-prepare curry that is almost impossible to mess up! The robust flavors of onions, tomatoes, ginger, garlic and Home-Style Garam Masala goes well with the succulent pieces of tender chicken that are cooked until the meat is falling off the bone. I like the depth of intense flavor that tomato paste gives to the curry, but it can be easily replaced by one medium-size ripe tomato. Serve this dish with some green vegetables like Spicy Coconut Green Beans (page 82) or Stir-Fried Okra (page 87) and Plain Basmati Rice (page 124) on the side.

Serves 4
Prep time: 5 minutes
Cook time: 15 minutes

1 large onion (about $^1/_2$ lb/250 g), peeled and coarsely chopped
2 fresh green chili peppers, coarsely chopped
¼ teaspoon ground turmeric
3 tablespoons coarsely chopped garlic
One 1-in (2.5-cm) piece fresh ginger, peeled and coarsely chopped
1 teaspoon cumin seeds
4 tablespoons oil
$1^1/_4$ to $1^1/_2$ lbs (600 g to 750 g) skinless, boneless chicken thighs and/or breasts, cubed
1 teaspoon salt, plus more if needed
2 tablespoons tomato paste
1 teaspoon Home-Style Garam Masala (page 35)
1 cup (250 ml) water
4 tablespoons chopped fresh coriander leaves (cilantro)

1 Place the onion, green chili peppers, turmeric, garlic, ginger and cumin seeds in a blender and process, adding a few tablespoons of water to make a smooth thick paste.

2 Heat the oil in a large saucepan or wok over medium-high heat. Add the chicken and salt and fry, stirring frequently, for 7 to 10 minutes, or until golden. Using a slotted spoon, remove the chicken from the pan and set aside.

3 To the same pan you used to cook the chicken, add the spice paste and fry over low heat for 2 minutes, until fragrant. Add the chicken, tomato paste, Home-Style Garam Masala and cook gently, stirring well, for 3 to 4 minutes. Add the water, cover the pan, and increase the heat to medium. Simmer gently for 15 minutes, or until the chicken is cooked through and tender. Taste for seasoning, and add more salt if needed. Sprinkle with the fresh coriander leaves and serve hot.

Coconut Chicken Curry *Kori Ghassi*

Curry leaves and coconut give this mild curry, typical fare along the west coast of India, its distinctive flavor and creamy texture. When in India I serve this curry with steamed south Indian red rice, the traditional accompaniment. In the United States, procuring red rice requires a trip to the local Asian or Indian supermarket, so I typically serve Basmati or any long-grain rice, Baked Garlic Naan (page 134) or even a crusty French bread, which is equally delicious. During my childhood, this was (and still is) one of my favorite curries, and when my mother made *dosa* (rice flour pancake) or buttered Western-style white bread to go with it, I would fill up on it and eat nothing else.

Serves 6
Prep time: 15 minutes
Cook time: 20 minutes

1 whole chicken (about 3½ to 4 lbs/1.6 to 1.75 kg), quartered (see "Tips for Cutting Whole Chickens and Chicken Pieces" page 112), or 3½ to 4 lbs/1.6 to 1.75 kg) bone-in chicken pieces of your choice, cut into 2-in (5-cm) pieces
½ cup (125 ml) oil
½ cup (50 g) shredded, unsweetened coconut (frozen, reconstituted dried, or freshly grated) (page 24)
1 tablespoon peeled and minced fresh ginger
1 tablespoon minced garlic
6 fresh green chili peppers, minced
1 teaspoon fennel seeds
1 teaspoon cumin seeds
3 whole cloves
1 whole star anise
One ½-in (1.25-cm) cinnamon stick
10 fresh or dried curry leaves
1 onion (about ⅓ lb/150 g), sliced
1 large tomato (about ½ lb/250 g), chopped
½ cup (125 ml) coconut milk
¼ cup (65 ml) water
4 tablespoons chopped fresh coriander leaves (cilantro)
Salt, to taste

1 Using a cleaver or a large chef's knife, cut the chicken pieces into 2-inch (5-cm) sections. If cutting the legs is too daunting, just leave them whole. Cut the chicken pieces into 2-in (5-cm) pieces.
2 Heat 1 tablespoon plus 1 teaspoon of the oil in a heavy-bottomed skillet over medium-high heat. Add the coconut, ginger, garlic and green chili peppers and sauté, stirring constantly, for 1 minute.
3 Place the sautéed coconut-ginger mixture in a food processor or a blender along with the fennel, cumin and cloves. Process this mixture with a little water to make a smooth paste. Set aside.
4 Heat the remaining oil in a heavy-bottomed skillet over medium-high heat. Add the star anise, cinnamon stick, curry leaves and onion, and fry until the onion slices are light golden brown, about 3 minutes. Add the chicken pieces and cook until browned, about 5 minutes. Add the ground coconut-ginger paste, tomato, coconut milk and water, and reduce the heat to low. Simmer, covered, until the chicken is cooked, about 15 to 20 minutes. Stir in the fresh coriander leaves and salt. Serve hot.

Serves 4
Prep time: 15 minutes plus 2 hours for marinating
Cook time: 20 minutes

⅓ cup (80 ml) thick, Greek-style plain yogurt or sour cream
1 tablespoon plus 1 teaspoon paprika
2 teaspoons ground coriander
3 teaspoons Home-Style Garam Masala (page 35)
1 tablespoon plus 1 teaspoon Ginger-Garlic Paste (page 32)
1¼ to 1½ lbs (600 to 750 g) skinless, boneless chicken pieces, cut into 2-in (5-cm) cubes
Nonstick cooking spray or oil, to grease the grill pan
2 tablespoons oil
1 large red onion (about ½ lb/250 g), minced
1¼ cups (300 ml) tomato purée
2½ tablespoons tomato paste
1 teaspoon salt, plus more if needed
4 tablespoons chopped fresh coriander leaves (cilantro)
2 tablespoons softened butter (optional)

1 Mix together 2 tablespoons of the yogurt or sour cream, 2 teaspoons of the paprika, 1 teaspoon of the ground coriander, 1 teaspoon of Home-Style Garam Masala, and half of the Ginger-Garlic Paste in a large mixing bowl. Add the diced chicken and mix until the chicken pieces are well coated. Let marinate in the refrigerator for 2 hours.
2 Heat a grill pan over medium heat and grease with nonstick cooking spray or a little oil. Place the chicken cubes on the grill pan and cook all sides until well browned, about 4 to 5 minutes per side. Set aside.
3 Heat the oil in a large, heavy-bottomed skillet over medium-high heat. When hot, add the onion and sauté until translucent, about 1 minute. Add the remaining Ginger-Garlic Paste and cook until the mixture turns golden brown, about 1 to 2 minutes. Add the remaining paprika and ground coriander. Mix well and cook for another 30 seconds.
4 Add the tomato purée, tomato paste

Chicken Tikka Masala *Murg Tikka Masala*

This is the most popular dish in Indian restaurants outside India. It was made popular by the curry houses in the UK, and is essentially a restaurant dish and not a home-style dish. I get a lot of requests from my non-Indian friends to make this dish at home. Here is a recipe that is by far the closest that one can get to the restaurant versions of Chicken Tikka Masala—aka CTM. The chicken is cooked two-thirds of the way through and then simmered in the sauce. For an equally tasty version—known as "Butter Chicken" in India—toss cooked and shredded Tandoori Chicken (page 112) into this delectable sauce. I have also used grilled swordfish or halibut with the same recipe with very good results. As with the chicken, the fish is partially grilled and then added to the tomato-onion purée to finish cooking. Cook the fish in the purée for not more than five minutes.

Making the Tikka Masala

and salt, and cook, stirring constantly, until the oil separates from the *masala*, about 2 minutes. This technique is called *bhunao*. Remove from the heat.

5 Transfer the onion-tomato mixture to a food processor or blender and process to a smooth paste. Add a little water if the mixture gets too thick.

6 Pour the tomato-onion purée back into the skillet and set over medium heat. Whisk in the remaining yogurt or sour cream, making sure it is well blended.

7 Add the chicken and reduce the heat to medium-low. Cover the pan and allow the chicken to simmer until it is completely cooked, about 7 to 8 minutes. Stir in the remaining Home-Style Garam Masala, the fresh coriander leaves and butter, if using, and mix well. Taste for seasoning and add more salt if needed. Serve hot.

Tandoori Chicken

Murg Tandoori

Known as the "King of the Kebab," Tandoori Chicken is the best-known Indian delicacy and the tastiest way to barbecue chicken. The chicken should be marinated for at least four hours, but the longer you marinate the chicken, the better. The use of red food coloring, which creates the unique red color for which this dish is known, is optional. I've included instructions for roasting the chicken pieces in the oven or grilling them on a gas or charcoal grill, which will create a more authentic flavor. Traditional accompaniments are Mint Chutney (page 39) and Cucumber and Onion Chaat (page 42). For a complete meal, also serve Basmati Rice with Whole Spices (page 132) and Cucumber and Yogurt Raita (page 45).

Serves 4

Prep time: 20 minutes plus 4 hours for marinating

Cook time: 30 minutes

1 whole chicken, approximately 3¹/₂ to 4 lbs (1.6 to 1.75 kg), skinned, or 3½ to 4 lbs (1.6 to 1.75 kg), bone-in chicken pieces of your choice, skinned

1 teaspoon Asian chili powder or cayenne pepper

1 teaspoon paprika

3 teaspoons salt

Juice of 1 lemon

4 tablespoons malt vinegar

¹/₃ cup (90 g) plain yogurt

¹/₂ cup (125 ml) heavy cream

One 2-in (5-cm) piece fresh ginger, peeled and coarsely chopped

4 tablespoons coarsely chopped garlic

1 fresh green chili pepper, coarsely chopped

1 teaspoon ground cumin

1 teaspoon Home-Style Garam Masala (page 35)

1 teaspoon saffron threads

1 drop red food coloring

1 cup (2 sticks/225 g) melted butter, for basting

4 lime wedges

Mint Chutney (page 39), for serving

1 If using bone-in chicken pieces, jump ahead to Step 2. If using a whole chicken, cut the chicken into four parts, following the tips below.

2 Using a cleaver or a large chef's knife, cut the legs into two pieces (thigh and drumstick) and the breasts into four pieces. If cutting the legs in two is too daunting, just leave them whole. Cut 2-inch (5-cm)-long slits (deep enough to reach the bone) into each side in the leg pieces. Make similar slits on the breast pieces.

3 Mix together the Asian chili powder or cayenne pepper, paprika, salt, lemon juice and vinegar in a small bowl to make a paste. Rub the paste over the chicken pieces evenly and into the slits. Set aside for 15 to 20 minutes.

4 Place the yogurt, cream, ginger, garlic, green chili pepper, cumin, Home-Style Garam Masala, saffron and food coloring in a food processor or blender and process to make a smooth paste. Rub the chicken pieces with the yogurt mixture, making sure the marinade goes into the slits in the chicken. Let marinate in the refrigerator for at least 4 hours or overnight.

5 To roast the chicken: Preheat the oven to its highest setting. Take the chicken out of the marinade and place it on a rack in a rectangular baking pan or roaster. Roast the chicken for 25 to 30 minutes, or until done. This technique is called *bhunnana*. Baste the chicken pieces with the melted butter during the roasting process. Serve garnished with lime wedges.

6 To grill the chicken: Set up the grill for cooking with two heat zones and preheat the grill to high and medium. (Note: The larger pieces of chicken will cook more slowly than the smaller pieces. To have perfectly cooked chicken pieces that are all done at the same time, it is best to cook with two heat zones.) As the smaller pieces become cooked, move them to the low-heat side of the grill to keep them warm while the larger pieces continue to cook. If your grill doesn't have the capability of having multiple heat zones, simply put the large chicken pieces on first, followed by the smaller pieces. Cook the chicken pieces for about 10 to 15 minutes, then turn and cook the other side. Baste the chicken pieces with the melted butter during the grilling process. In about 25 to 30 minutes, the chicken should be cooked. As the chicken cooks, it becomes firmer. To judge doneness, look for good color and firmer meat on the bottom side of the chicken. To be completely sure of doneness, cook until the internal temperature reaches 165°F (74°C).

TIPS FOR CUTTING WHOLE CHICKENS AND CHICKEN PIECES There are different ways to quarter a whole chicken, the easiest and fastest way is starting with the legs. Take a leg in your hand and feel along it until you find the upper joint between the thighbone and leg. This feels like an indentation in the bone. Using a sharp, large knife, cut at the joint. The leg will separate from the breast with ease. Repeat with the other leg. Cut the chicken in half down the center, through the middle of the breast plate. You will now have 4 large pieces. Cutting bone-in chicken pieces—breasts, thighs, legs—into smaller segments isn't difficult. All you need is a large sharp knife. Legs, due to their thicker bone, cause the great challenge, and can be more easily cut with a sturdy cleaver. If cutting the legs in two is too daunting, simply leave them whole.

Madras Chicken

Kozi Varuval

This wonderfully spicy and flavorful dish comes from the south Indian state of Tamil Nadu. The spice combination and abundance of black pepper make this curry very unique, while the addition of yogurt gives it a smooth texture and tangy flavor. It was always a favorite in my family's home in India. Enjoy its fiery flavors and thick texture with Whole-Wheat Griddle Breads (page 136) or Basmati Rice with Whole Spices (page 132).

Serves 4
Prep time: 15 minutes
Cook time: 20 minutes

1/2 cup (125 g) plain yogurt
5 tablespoons black peppercorns,
  pounded
2 tablespoons Ginger-Garlic Paste
  (page 32)
Juice of 1 lemon
2 teaspoons salt, plus more if needed
1 whole chicken, about 3 1/2 to 4 lbs
  (1.6 to 1.75 kg) cut into pieces, or
  3 1/2 to 4 lbs (1.6 to 1.75 kg), bone-in
  chicken pieces of your choice
3 tablespoons oil
1 large onion (about 1/2 lb/250 g),
  chopped
2 tablespoons minced garlic
2 tablespoons peeled and minced fresh
  ginger
2 tomatoes (about 3/4 lb/350 g),
  chopped
1/2 cup (125 ml) water
1 teaspoon Home-Style Garam Masala
  (page 35)
4 tablespoons chopped fresh cilantro
  leaves (cilantro)

1 Whisk the yogurt in a large mixing bowl until smooth. Add the pounded black pepper, Ginger-Garlic Paste, lemon juice and salt to the yogurt and mix well. Add the chicken pieces to the yogurt mixture and marinate for at least 1 hour in the refrigerator.

2 Heat the oil in a large skillet over medium heat. Add the onion and sauté until golden, about 5 minutes. Add the garlic and ginger and fry for another 30 seconds, stirring constantly. Add the tomatoes and sauté for another minute, until soft.

3 Add the chicken pieces with the marinade and increase the heat to high. Cook, stirring frequently, for 4 to 5 minutes. Add the water and cover. Reduce the heat to low and simmer, stirring occasionally, until the chicken is cooked through and tender, about 15 to 20 minutes. Taste and add more salt, if needed. Stir in the Home-Style Garam Masala and fresh coriander leaves and serve hot.

Traditional Lamb Curry

Masala Gosth

I first ate this delicious lamb curry when visiting a friend's home in northern India. My friend's mom added a generous amount of green chili peppers to this dish, a taste I will never forget. Of course I have made this version milder, but feel free to increase the number of chili peppers if you prefer food spicy, like I do. Though this curry originated in the Muslim communities of northern India, it has become the centerpiece of celebration meals in many communities throughout India. I love the aromas of chunks of meat being slowly simmered in spices and yogurt until tender. I sometimes like to cook this recipe with beef or goat as a variation. (If using goat, you will need to cook it about 15 to 20 minutes longer than lamb to become tender.) Any way you make it, this curry is a glorious dish—in fact, it's my "house" curry for parties and for carrying to potluck suppers along with stacks of Whole-Wheat Griddle Breads (page 136).

Serves 6
Prep time: 15 minutes plus 4 hours for
  marinating
Cook time: 30 minutes

3 red onions (about 1 lb/500 g),
  coarsely chopped
1 tablespoon Asian chili powder or
  cayenne pepper
1 tablespoon ground cumin
1/2 tablespoon ground turmeric
1 1/2 cups (370 g) plain yogurt
2 teaspoons Home-Style Garam
  Masala (page 35)
3 teaspoons salt
2 lbs (1kg) boneless leg of lamb, cut
  into 1-in (2.5-cm) cubes
3 tablespoons oil
5 green cardamom pods
3 bay leaves
One 1-in (2.5-cm) cinnamon stick
1 teaspoon cumin seeds
1 tablespoon ground coriander
4 fresh green chili peppers, minced
1 tomato (about 1/3 lb/150 g),
  chopped
2 cups (500 ml) water
4 tablespoons chopped fresh
  coriander leaves (cilantro)

1 Blend together the onions, Asian chili powder or cayenne pepper, cumin, turmeric, 1/2 cup (125 g) of the yogurt, Home-Style Garam Masala and salt in a blender or a food processor until a smooth paste forms.

2 Mix together the yogurt-onion mixture and lamb in a large bowl, making sure all the pieces are well coated with the marinade. Cover with plastic wrap and marinate in the refrigerator, at least 4 to 6 hours, preferably overnight.

3 Heat the oil in a large nonstick saucepan over medium-high heat. Add the cardamom, bay leaves, cinnamon and cumin—the spices should sizzle upon contact with the hot oil. Quickly add the ground coriander and the marinated lamb with the marinade. Stir-fry over high heat for 5 minutes. Reduce the heat to medium-low, cover the pan, and cook until most of the juices are dry, about 15 to 20 minutes. This process is called *bhunao*, which plays an important role in the taste of the finished dish.

4 Add the green chili peppers, tomato, water and the remaining 1 cup (245 g) of yogurt and bring to a boil over high heat. Reduce the heat to medium-low, cover, and simmer until the lamb is tender and the sauce is thick, about 20 to 25 minutes. Serve hot garnished with the chopped fresh coriander leaves.

Kerala Coconut Beef *Eracchi Olathiyathu*

While studying at a hotel school in India I worked with a talented Syrian cook from the northern part of Kerala, who shared this recipe with me. This is one of my dishes most requested by guests and friends. And I can understand why— I could sit and eat a pound of this tender flavorful meat with a chilled glass of summer ale. It's perfect with Whole-Wheat Griddle Breads (page 136) or Baked Garlic Naan (page 134). The beef can be replaced with lamb for an equally delicious dish, but my favorite version is made with bone-in goat meat. If you make this dish with goat, you will need to allow extra time because goat takes about 15 to 20 minutes longer than lamb to cook and become tender.

Serves 4
Prep time: 20 minutes
Cook time: 30 minutes

4 tablespoons oil
1¹/₂ cups (400 g) fresh or frozen thinly sliced coconut meat or shredded, unsweetened coconut (frozen, reconstituted dried, or freshly grated) (page 24)
¹/₂ teaspoon ground turmeric
One 1-in (2.5-cm) piece fresh ginger, peeled
3 tablespoons coarsely chopped garlic
1 onion (about ¹/₃ lb/150 g), coarsely chopped

2 tablespoons coriander seeds
6 dried red chili peppers
4 whole cloves
1¹/₄ to 1¹/₂ lbs (600 g to 750 g) beef round, cubed
One 1-in (2.5-cm) piece cinnamon stick
10 black peppercorns
2 teaspoons salt
15 fresh or dried curry leaves
1¹/₄ cups (300 ml) water
1 teaspoon black mustard seeds
2 fresh green chili peppers, slit open lengthwise

1 Heat 1 tablespoon of the oil in a skillet over medium heat. Add the coconut and turmeric and fry for 1 minute until the coconut is slightly brown and crisp. Set aside.

2 Place the ginger, garlic, onion, coriander, dried red chili peppers and cloves in a food processor or a blender. Process the mixture to a smooth paste. Add a little water if necessary.

3 Mix together the beef with the ground spice paste, cinnamon stick, peppercorns, salt and 5 of the curry leaves in a heavy-bottomed saucepan,. Add the water and bring to a boil. Lower the heat and simmer gently for 30 to 40 minutes, stirring occasionally, or until the beef is tender and cooked.

4 Heat the remaining 3 tablespoons of oil in a large skillet over medium heat. Add the mustard seeds and, when they start to pop, add the remaining 10 curry leaves and the fresh green chili peppers. Stir-fry for 1 minute and then add the cooked meat. Continue cooking, stirring frequently, for about 5 minutes or until the beef mixture is very dry. Garnish with the fried coconut and serve hot.

NOTE ABOUT THE INGREDIENT
The crunch and the texture the sliced coconut meat makes this dish unbelievably delicious. It is worth the effort to get your hands on a fresh coconut and slice the meat into thin slivers because this is the highlight of the dish. Sometimes you get lucky enough to find frozen sliced coconut meat in Asian markets. Alternately, you can simply use grated fresh, frozen or dried coconut.

Spicy Lamb Burgers

These lamb burgers are inspired by the traditional lamb kebabs flavored with spices that I have eaten in Delhi, a capital city in northern India. I love the aromatic smell and complex flavor Indian kebabs and the classic American grilled burger. This is my way of incorporating the two. I often form these burgers into several mini burgers, or "sliders," and serve them open face on store-bought naan bread or homemade Plain Naan (page 134). Whatever size you make them, they are great topped with Mint Chutney (page 39) or Plum Tomato Chutney with Mustard Seeds (page 38) and served with a chilled glass of your favorite beer.

Makes four $^1/_3$-lb (150-g) burgers or sixteen $1^1/_2$-oz (40-g) sliders
Prep time: 15 minutes plus 1 hour to rest the patties
Cook time: 15 minutes

$1^1/_2$ lbs (750 g) ground lamb
3 teaspoons cumin seeds, toasted and pounded
3 teaspoons coriander seeds, toasted and pounded
1 teaspoon Home-Style Garam Masala (page 35)
4 tablespoons minced fresh coriander leaves (cilantro)
2 fresh green chili peppers, minced
2 teaspoon salt
$^1/_2$ teaspoon minced garlic
$^1/_2$ teaspoon peeled and minced fresh ginger
Oil, for brushing the burgers
For sliders: 2 naan breads, homemade or store-bought, or 16 small buns
For burgers: 2 pita breads, cut in half to form 4 pockets, or 4 hamburger buns
Mint Chutney (page 39) or Plum Tomato Chutney with Mustard Seeds (page 38), for serving

TIP Do not press down on the patties with a spatula during cooking—this only squeezes out the juices and dries out the lamb.

1 Place all of the ingredients, except the oil and bread, in a large mixing bowl. Mix together well. With wet hands, mold the mixture into 4 equal-size patties or, to create sliders, 16 equal-size patties. Refrigerate the patties at least for 1 hour.

2 To cook the lamb patties on the stovetop: Preheat a grill pan over medium heat. Lightly brush the pan with oil or a nonstick pan spray. Cook the lamb patties for 3 to 4 minutes on each side for medium doneness, brushing with oil to prevent sticking.

3 To grill the lamb patties: Preheat the grill to high. Lightly oil the grate with oil—pour some oil onto a paper towel, then hold the towel with tongs to wipe the oil onto the grate. Place the lamb patties on the grill directly over the heat. Cook about 2 to 3 minutes per side for medium doneness, brushing with the oil to prevent sticking, turning once.

4 While the meat is cooking, prepare the bread. For sliders, cut each of the naan breads into 6 wedges. Toast the naan wedges on the grill. Serve the sliders on top of the naan or between small buns; serve $^1/_4$-lb (125-g) burgers stuffed into the pita pockets or sandwiched between hamburger buns.

Marinated Roast Leg of Lamb

Raan Masaledar

This spectacular-looking dish involves some time and planning ahead, so I save it for special occasions. Though this recipe involves a few more steps than most, it is actually very easy to prepare. The leg of lamb is scored to the bone with a sharp knife to allow a creamy, aromatic marinade to penetrate deep into the meat. It is then marinated for at least six to eight hours, and preferably overnight. Then a creamy, nutty and flavorful yogurt paste is applied to the skin to form a nice crusty exterior when roasted. Serve the leg of lamb with a side of potatoes and some green vegetables—my favorite side dish accompaniment is a simple combination of fresh sliced red onions, green peppers and tomato wedges tossed with lime juice and seasoned with salt.

Serves 6

Prep time: 20 minutes plus 6 to 8 hours for marinating

Cook time: 1 hour 30 minutes

One 3 to 3½-lb (1.5 to 1.6-kg) leg of lamb, trimmed of all visible fat
1 cup (100 g) blanched almonds, finely chopped
1 tablespoon light brown sugar
½ cup (125 g) plain yogurt

Marinade

1 cup (230 g) thick, Greek-style plain yogurt or sour cream
1 teaspoon ground green cardamom
1 small onion (about ¼ lb/125 g), chopped
4 tablespoons minced garlic
One 1-in (2.5-cm) piece fresh ginger, peeled and minced
3 fresh green chili peppers, minced
1 tablespoon ground cumin
½ teaspoon ground cloves
Salt, to taste
1 tablespoon freshly-squeezed lemon juice

1 Score the leg of lamb with a sharp knife all around so that the marinade will penetrate.

2 Mix together the ingredients for the Marinade in a large bowl.

3 Using your hands, coat the lamb all over with half of the Marinade. Cover the lamb with plastic wrap and marinate in the refrigerator for at least 6 to 8 hours, preferably overnight. Cover the remaining Marinade and refrigerate it.

4 Preheat the oven to 375°F (190°C).

5 Mix the reserved Marinade with the chopped almonds, brown sugar and ½ cup (125 g) plain yogurt.

6 Using your hands, crust the lamb all over with the almond mixture and transfer the lamb to a shallow roasting pan. Cover loosely with oiled aluminum foil and bake for 1 hour. Remove the foil and bake for another 30 minutes, or until the lamb is well cooked and the crust is browned. (When cooked, a thermometer inserted into the meat near to the bone will read 150°F/65°C.) For the best presentation, serve whole on a platter and carve the meat at the table.

Spicy and Fragrant Lamb Curry *Aachari Gosht*

This spicy lamb curry, served breads such as Fried Puffed Bread (page 138) or Whole-Wheat Griddle Breads (page 136), is perfect for cold winter evenings. It is one of a few Indian curries that I enjoy extra fiery; in fact, I usually double the amount of red chili peppers suggested in this recipe. If you don't like curries particularly fiery, discard most of the seeds from the chili peppers; if you enjoy chili heat, use the chili peppers as is, seeds and all. After making the curry the first time you may decide you'd like to use more chili peppers, like I do, but for the first time around, I suggest using the suggested amount. You can either use lamb or goat stewing meat for this dish. Goat takes about 15 to 20 minutes longer than lamb to cook and become tender.

Serves 4
Prep time: 15 minutes
Cook time: 50 minutes

3 tablespoons coarsely chopped garlic
One 1/2-in (1.25-cm) piece fresh ginger, peeled
5 dried red chili peppers
1 teaspoon fennel seeds
2 teaspoons coriander seeds
2 tablespoons oil
2 onions (about 3/4 lb/ 350 g), sliced
2 lbs (1 kg) boneless leg or shoulder of lamb, cut into 1-in (2.5-cm) cubes
1 teaspoon Asian chili powder or cayenne pepper
2 tablespoons ground coriander
2 tablespoons ground cumin
1/4 teaspoon ground turmeric
1/2 teaspoon Home-Style Garam Masala (page 35)
2 cups (500 ml) water
2 teaspoons salt
2 tomatoes (about 3/4 lb/ 350 g), chopped
4 tablespoons chopped fresh coriander leaves (cilantro), for garnish

1 Place the garlic, ginger, dried red chili peppers, fennel seeds and coriander seeds in a blender and process to a paste.
2 Heat the oil in a large skillet over medium-high heat. Add the sliced onions and cook, stirring frequently, until the onions turn golden brown, about 5 to 7 minutes. Sear the meat in the hot skillet while stirring frequently, about 5 minutes.
3 Stir in the spice paste, Asian chili powder or cayenne pepper, ground coriander, cumin, turmeric, and Home-Style Garam Masala and cook for about 1 to 2 minutes over medium heat. Pour the water into the mixture, a little at a time, stirring after each addition, until you have a rich, thick sauce. This process is called *bhunao*, which plays an important role in the taste of the finished dish.
4 Cover the pan and let simmer over low heat for 30 minutes. Add the salt, chopped tomatoes and cook until the lamb is tender, about 10 to 15 minutes more. Serve hot garnished with the chopped fresh coriander leaves.

Pork Tenderloin with Mango Salad

Even though large cuts of meat, such as roasts or tenderloins, are not traditional in Indian cooking, I like to serve them when I want to impress a special someone! Large cuts of meat always make for an elegant and dramatic presentation—something for holidays and special occasions. I like this recipe because the flavor of Indian spices and seasonings marry well with the tender pork, and the fresh mango adds a touch of sweetness to balance the spicy heat. Here I use my favorite combination of spices and herbs to marinate the pork.

Serves 6
Prep time: 15 minutes plus 1 hour for marinating
Cook time: 15 minutes

Two 1-lb (500-g) pork tenderloins, trimmed of fat and skin
4 tablespoons oil
1 tablespoon Asian chili powder or cayenne pepper
2 teaspoons Home-Style Garam Masala (page 35)
2 teaspoons plus 1 pinch of salt
Juice of 2 limes
1 tablespoon minced garlic
1 tablespoon peeled and minced fresh ginger
2 ripe mangoes (about 2 lbs/1 kg total), peeled, pitted and diced
1 small red onion (about 1/4 lb/125 g), chopped
1 fresh green chili pepper, minced
1 tablespoon minced fresh coriander leaves (cilantro)
Fresh coriander sprigs (cilantro), for garnish

1 Preheat the grill to high. Rub the pork tenderloins all over with 3 tablespoons of the oil, and then sprinkle evenly with the Asian chili powder or cayenne pepper, Home-Style Garam Masala and 2 teaspoons of the salt. Rub the tenderloins well with half of the lime juice, the garlic and ginger. Allow the tenderloins to sit, refrigerated, for 45 minutes to 1 hour before cooking.
2 Place the diced mangoes in a medium mixing bowl. Add the red onion, remaining lime juice, a pinch of salt, green chili pepper, and coriander leaves and stir to combine. Set aside.
3 Place the tenderloins on the hottest part of the grill and cook, turning occasionally, until well browned on all sides, about 10 minutes. Reduce the grill temperature to low and continue to cook, turning occasionally, until a thermometer inserted into the center registers 145°F (62°C). Remove the tenderloins from the grill and allow to rest for 5 to 10 minutes before serving.
4 Slice the tenderloins on the diagonal and serve with the mango salad and fresh coriander sprigs.

Pork Vindaloo

The term *vindaloo* derives from the Portuguese dish "Carne de Vinha d' Alhos," a dish of meat, usually pork, prepared with vinegar and garlic. This curry is one of the many tasty HOT pork dishes originally from Goa, where the cooking style combines Portuguese influences, among them the eating of pork, with fiery Indian flavors. What makes this dish unique is the combination of hot spices and vinegar. It tastes better if it is allowed to "pickle" for an entire day. Vindaloo dishes generally require an elaborate cooking process, but they are worth the effort. Though traditional vindaloos do not include potatoes, I have added some in this recipe because I feel the combination works well. I recommend that you ask your butcher to leave some fat from the skin on the meat, which imparts a good flavor into the sauce. When I was in school, I had a friend whose family had roots in Goa and they often made this pork dish—something quite ordinary to them but fascinating to me. Needless to say, I did not decline a single invitation to lunch at my friend's house. Vindaloo is traditionally eaten with steamed rice cakes (*idli*) and rice pancakes (*dosa*), both of which, though delicious, are very time consuming to prepare. I usually don't bother to make them and instead serve Plain Basmati Rice (page 124) or crusty French bread, which is just as tasty.

Serves 4

Prep time: 30 minutes plus at least 6 to 8 hours to marinate the pork

Cook time: 30 minutes

1½ lbs (750 g) leg or shoulder of pork, cut into 1-in (2.5-cm) cubes
2 tablespoons malt vinegar
2 teaspoons black pepper
1 teaspoon sugar
2 teaspoons Aromatic Spice Mix (page 33)
3 fresh green chili peppers, minced
1 teaspoon salt, plus more if needed
¼ cup (65 ml) oil
1 onion (about ⅓ lb/150 g), chopped
1 cup (200 g) Vindaloo Curry Paste (page 34)
¼ cup (65 ml) tomato purée
4 cups (1 liter) water
1 large potato (about ⅔ lb/300 g), peeled and diced
4 tablespoons chopped fresh coriander leaves (cilantro)

1 Place the pork cubes, vinegar, black pepper, sugar, Aromatic Spice Mix, green chili peppers and salt in a large mixing bowl. Let the pork marinate for a minimum of 6 hours in the refrigerator, preferably overnight.

2 Heat the oil in a large heavy-bottomed saucepan. Add the onion and sauté over medium-heat until golden brown, about 5 to 6 minutes. Add the Vindaloo Curry Paste and tomato purée and sauté until the fat separates from the *masala*, about 2 minutes. Add some water to prevent sticking, if needed.

3 Add the pork along with the marinade. Cook, stirring constantly, over high heat for 2 minutes. Add the water and bring to a boil. Add the potato, cover, and reduce the heat to low. Simmer until the pork is tender and the potato is cooked, about 25 to 30 minutes. Check for seasoning and add more salt, if needed. Stir in the chopped fresh coriander leaves and serve hot.

Masala Lamb Chops

Masala Lamb Chops *Bhuni Chaamp*

These chops are always a hit at barbecues. If you are looking for something spectacular that will impress your guests, but don't want to spend a lot of time cooking, this lamb recipe is the perfect choice. The only real time to factor in is the overnight marinate, which makes the chops extremely flavorful. It takes minutes to make this simple marinade. Rub it on the chops and then let the marinade work its magic. Add a salad, potato dish or some corn on the cob and you will have an elegant summer meal in minutes.

Serves 4
Prep time: 5 minutes plus 6 to 12 hours for marinating
Cook time: 10 minutes

8 small lamb or rib chops (about $2^1/_2$ lbs/1.25 kg total), trimmed and cleaned
Salt, to season chops
Lime wedges, for garnish

Marinade
2 fresh green chili peppers
3 tablespoons coarsely chopped garlic
One $^1/_2$-in (1.25-cm) piece fresh ginger, peeled
2 cups (100 g) fresh coriander leaves (cilantro) (from 1 small bunch)
½ cup (15 g) fresh mint leaves (from about 8 to 10 sprigs)
1 teaspoon Home-Style Garam Masala (page 35)
2 teaspoons fennel seeds, toasted and crushed
1 heaping tablespoon thick, Greek-style plain yogurt or sour cream
Juice of 1 lemon

1 Place the ingredients for the Marinade in a food processor or a blender and process to a smooth paste. Rub the paste over the chops, cover, and refrigerate overnight.
2 Heat a grill pan over high heat until almost smoking. Sprinkle the chops with salt and cook on the grill for 2 to 3 minutes per side for medium doneness, or until lightly charred. Serve the chops with the lime wedges.

Chapter 8

Rice and Breads

Served alongside an array of curries and dals, bread and rice are the staples of every Indian meal. Most food is eaten either with bread or rice, or both. Some rice dishes, such as biriyanis (page 125), are hearty enough to be considered the main dish, and served just with a *raita* or salad. Whereas rice is served in a separate bowl alongside curries and dals, Indian breads are used to sop up curries and dals and as wraps for all drier (non-curry) dishes—such as sautéed vegetables, stir-fries or kebabs. But either breads or rice can be served with both curries and dals (dishes with a "gravy" consistency) or drier dishes. When eating rice with curries or dals, many Indians eat the rice and main dish in alternating bites, using the rice to quell the heat of the food. Some spoon some of the curry or *dal* over the rice to flavor it. This is personal preference.

Indian breads are flatbreads, typically unleavened, and most are easy enough to be made fresh daily at every meal. With the exception of a few breads, like naan (page 134), they are made entirely or mostly with whole-grain flours and are great tasting and rich in nutrients. They are usually rolled on a flat surface with a rolling pin and cooked on a hot surface— the exception being *poori* (page 138), which is cooked in hot oil. The cooking skills of an Indian woman are usually judged on the roundness and the softness of the breads she cooks!

Rice is an important part of the Indian meal. For everyday meals, the type of rice used depends on which part of the country you are from. In the south, people prefer the locally available long-grain variety and the medium-grain red variety. The north Indians prefer basmati rice, which is grown in the foothills of the Himalayas. The main rice eating communities are based in the south and in the east of India, but they do serve breads along with rice. The length of the rice grain can be long or short, based on the variety of the rice chosen, but it is generally always white rice. However, brown rice is now making an appearance on Indian tables as a healthy alternative to white rice.

Plain Basmati Rice

Saada Chaaval

This simple yet very flavorful preparation of rice can be served with any Indian meal and is very common in north Indian homes. First the rice, *chaval* in hindi, is soaked and washed to remove the starchy powder on the grains. This helps the grains to remain as separate, individual grains and unsplit when cooked. Because basmati rice has become quite pricey, many Indians now use less expensive long-grain rice and reserve basmati only for festive occasions and parties.

Makes 4^1/$_2$ cups (450 g) cooked rice/Serves 4
Prep time: 5 minutes plus 40 minutes for soaking
Cook time: 15 minutes

1^1/$_2$ cups (315 g) uncooked basmati rice
2^3/$_4$ cups (685 ml) water
1 teaspoon salt

1 Soak the rice for 30 to 40 minutes. Carefully pour out the soaking water and wash the rice in several changes of water, until the water runs clear. Leave it to drain in a fine-meshed strainer for about 15 minutes.

2 Bring the rice, water, and salt to a boil in a heavy-bottomed saucepan over high heat. Cover with a tight-fitting lid, reduce the heat to the lowest setting, cook until the rice is tender, 10 to 12 minutes. Do not stir the rice while it cooks. Lift the lid, mix gently but quickly with a fork, and cover again. Remove from the heat and let the rice rest, covered, for 5 minutes. Serve hot.

Coconut Shrimp Biryani

Coconut Shrimp Biriyani

Goan Jhinga Biriyani

Biriyanis are flavorful one-pot meals loved by all Indians. Created by layering rice and meat or vegetables, they are usually elaborate dishes full of enticing flavors, and a huge part of Indian festivities such as weddings and religious occasions, especially in Muslim communities. Since they are complete meals, they are considered a great traveling food, and are typically served for dinner on trains. Though seafood or fish is not typically used to make biriyanis, here I was inspired to create my own *biriyani* using shrimp—a sort of Indian paella. If you have the patience to peel shrimp, buy them with the shell on. The shells can be used to make a stock for cooking the rice, creating a richer flavor. I find this delicious and hearty rice dish satisfying eaten on its own or with either a simple green salad on the side or with *raita* such as Cucumber and Yogurt Raita (page 45) or Avocado and Roasted Cumin Raita (page 44).

Serves 6
Prep time: 10 minutes plus 40 minutes for soaking rice
Cook time: 15 minutes

1 lb (500 g) fresh, medium-size shrimp (30 to 35), preferably with shells on, peeled, deveined and cleaned (reserve shells)
2 cups (420 g) uncooked basmati rice
2 tablespoons oil
Two 1-in (2.5-cm) cinnamon sticks
4 green cardamom pods
$^1/_2$ teaspoon black peppercorns
1 large onion (about $^1/_2$ lb/250 g), thinly sliced
1 tablespoon peeled and minced fresh ginger
1 tablespoon minced garlic
2 small fresh green chili peppers, chopped
$^1/_4$ teaspoon ground turmeric
2 teaspoons salt
1 small tomato (about 3 oz/85 g), chopped
$^1/_2$ cup (125 ml) coconut milk, warmed
4 tablespoons chopped fresh coriander leaves (cilantro), for garnish

1 If using shrimp with the shells on, place the shrimp shells and 2 cups (500 ml) of cold water in a small pot. Bring the water to a boil and then reduce the heat to medium-low. Let simmer for about 40 minutes. Strain the stock and set aside.

2 Soak the rice for 30 to 40 minutes. Carefully pour out the soaking water and wash the rice in several changes of water, until the water runs clear. Leave it to drain in a fine-meshed strainer for about 15 minutes.

3 Heat the oil in a large nonstick saucepan over medium-high heat. Add the cinnamon, cardamom pods and black peppercorns, and sauté until fragrant, about 1 minute. Add the onion and cook, stirring constantly, until golden, about 5 minutes. Mix in the ginger, garlic, green chili peppers, turmeric and 1 teaspoon of the salt, and cook, stirring constantly, until the ginger and garlic is cooked, about 1 minute. Add the chopped tomato and cook for another minute.

4 Add the shrimp and the remaining 1 teaspoon of salt and stir-fry over medium-high heat for about 1 minute, until the shrimp change color. If using shrimp stock, reheat the stock.

5 Add the drained rice and sauté for 1 minute. Add 1 cup (250 ml) of the hot stock or hot water and warmed coconut milk and bring to a boil over high heat. Reduce the heat to low and simmer, covered, until all of the water has been absorbed and the rice is done, 10 to 15 minutes. Top with fresh coriander leaves and serve hot.

Fragrant Lamb Biriyani

Kheema Biriyani

This tasty rice dish often makes a great one-pot TV dinner at my home. It is excellent on its own or goes great with Pineapple and Beet Raita (page 46) Cucumber and Onion Chaat (page 42).

Serves 4
Prep time: 15 minutes plus 40 minutes for soaking
Cook time: 30 minutes

2 cups (420 g) uncooked basmati rice
8 cups (2 liters) water
2 green cardamom pods
2 whole cloves
1 bay leaf
3 teaspoons salt
2 tablespoons oil or ghee (clarified butter)
1 large onion (about ½ lb/ 250 g), thinly sliced
1 lb (500 g) ground lamb
1 teaspoon Asian chili powder or cayenne pepper
2 tablespoons ground coriander
½ tablespoon peeled and minced fresh ginger
½ tablespoon minced garlic
1 fresh green chili pepper, chopped
¼ cup (60 g) plain yogurt
2 teaspoons Home-Style Garam Masala (page 35)
2 tablespoons chopped toasted cashew nuts or toasted slivered almonds
2 tablespoons golden raisins
Juice of 2 lemons
2 tablespoons finely chopped fresh coriander leaves (cilantro), for garnish

1 Preheat the oven to 350°F (175°C).
2 Soak the rice for 30 to 40 minutes. Carefully pour out the soaking water and wash the rice in several changes of water, until the water runs clear. Leave it to drain in a fine-meshed strainer for about 15 minutes.
3 Bring the water to a boil in a large non-stick saucepan over high heat. Add the whole spices, 2 teaspoons of the salt and the rice. Once the water has returned to a boil, reduce the heat to medium-low and cook, uncovered, until the rice is almost cooked, about 8 to10 minutes. Drain the rice and spices in a fine-meshed strainer. Discard the water.
4 Heat the ghee or oil over medium-high heat in a large nonstick, oven-safe saucepan, Dutch oven, or other type of covered oven-safe baking dish with a tight-fitting lid. Add the onion and cook, stirring constantly, until golden, about 5 minutes. Add the lamb, Asian chili powder or cayenne pepper, ground coriander, ginger, garlic, green chili pepper, yogurt, and the remaining 1 teaspoon of salt. Cook until the lamb is cooked and nicely browned, about 3 minutes, adding a little water if needed to prevent sticking. When the lamb is cooked and dry, stir in the Home-Style Garam Masala.
5 Top this mixture with the cooked rice. Sprinkle on the chopped cashews or almonds and raisins. Drizzle with the lemon juice and seal the pan well with aluminum foil. Then place the lid over the foil. This technique is commonly known as *dum* cooking.
6 Bake for about 10 to 15 minutes. Remove from the oven, fluff the top of the rice lightly with a fork, and add the chopped fresh coriander leaves. Serve hot.

Serves 4
Prep time: 20 minutes plus 5 hours for soaking beans and 40 minutes for rice
Cook time: 40 minutes

1 cup (175 g) black-eyed peas (lobhiya)
1¼ cups (260 g) uncooked basmati rice
3 tablespoons oil
2 onions (about ¾ lb/350 g), thinly sliced
4 cloves garlic, crushed
One 1-in (2.5 cm) piece fresh ginger, peeled and crushed
½ teaspoon ground turmeric
1 teaspoon ground cumin
1 teaspoon ground coriander
1 teaspoon Asian chili powder or cayenne pepper
1 tomato (about ⅓ lb/150 g), chopped
1 teaspoon salt
4 cups (1 liter) water
1 tablespoon ghee (clarified butter) or oil
2 green cardamom pods
4 whole cloves
One 1-in (2.5-cm) cinnamon stick
1 teaspoon Home-Style Garam Masala (page 35)

Black-Eyed Peas and Rice

Lobhiya Pulao

This delicious rice dish is a very nutritious combination of protein and carbohydrates, making it a complete meal if served with a fresh green salad and any *raita*. This rice also makes a good partner for Madras Chicken (page 114) or a vegetable dish, such as Cauliflower with Ginger and Cumin (page 86).

1 Soak the beans in cold water for at least 5 hours or overnight.

2 Soak the rice for 30 to 40 minutes. Carefully pour out the soaking water and wash the rice in several changes of water, until the water runs clear. Leave it to drain in a fine-meshed strainer for about 15 minutes.

3 Heat the oil in a heavy-bottomed pan over medium heat. When hot, add the sliced onions and fry until brown and crisp, stirring frequently. Remove them with a slotted spoon, leaving as much of the oil in the pan as possible, and spread them out on a paper towel to drain. Set aside for garnish.

4 To the same pan that you fried the onions, add the garlic and ginger and sauté for 30 seconds over medium heat. Add the turmeric, cumin, coriander, Asian chili powder or cayenne pepper and tomato and cook until the oil separates from the *masala*, about 1 minute. Add the drained beans, salt, and water and cook, covered, until the beans are tender, about 30 to 40 minutes. Set aside. Do not drain the water.

5 In a heavy-bottomed pan, heat the ghee or oil over medium heat. Add the cardamom, cloves, and cinnamon stick and cook for a few seconds. Add the drained rice and sauté for about 1 minute, stirring gently so as not to break the rice grains.

6 Add the beans and their cooking liquid and bring to a boil. Add the Home-Style Garam Masala and reduce the heat to low. Cook, covered, until the water is evaporated and the rice is cooked, about 5 minutes. Stir once and garnish with the fried onions.

Saffron Chicken Biriyani

Nawabi Murg Biriyani

There is a school of thought that believes the origin of this dish to be somewhere in the Arabian countries where the tribal bedouins would put meat, yogurt, spices and rice into a big pot and then seal and bury it in the warm sands of the desert to slowly cook. The pot was then dug up and unsealed to display a beautifully flavored rice meal. Today, it is almost a festive meal for Indians. This casserole of saffron-scented rice and melt-in-your-mouth chunks of meat or chicken is by far one of my most favorite Indian dishes. I will board a flight impromptu to any destination if someone spills the whereabouts of a good "Biriyani" (the way this dish is known in India)! When served with Cucumber and Yogurt Raita (page 45), nothing more is wanted. If you'd like a centerpiece on your dinner table and a dish to show off your cooking skills, this recipe is the one to make. Be forewarned: it is not something to undertake on a weeknight evening. Though making a perfectly cooked biriyani does take some practice, these tips should help you get near perfect results and with less fuss: **1** Soak the rice for an hour or two (this allows the rice grains to remain separate and fluffy; **2** Use bone-in chicken for the best flavor; **3** Make the Cucumber and Yogurt Raita, if serving, a day ahead to save you time.

Serves 6
Prep time: 45 minutes plus 1 hour for
  soaking rice
Cook time: 1 hour

1¹/₂ cups (315 g) uncooked basmati rice
3 tablespoons chopped garlic
One 3-in (7.5-cm) piece fresh ginger,
  peeled and coarsely chopped
About 10 to 12 fresh mint leaves
¹/₄ cup (10 g) packed fresh coriander
  leaves (cilantro)
2 fresh green chili peppers, stemmed
2 tablespoons freshly-squeezed lime
  juice
2 cups (500 g) plain yogurt, whisked
  until smooth
1 tablespoon Home-Style Garam
  Masala (page 35)
Salt
1 whole chicken, about 3¹/₂ to 4 lbs
  (1.6 to 1.75 kg) skinned and cut into
  serving pieces, or 3¹/₂ to 4 lbs (1.6 to
  1.75 kg), bone-in chicken pieces of
  your choice, skinned
6 cups (1.5 liters) water
5 to 7 green cardamom pods
One 1-in (2.5-cm) cinnamon stick
2 bay leaves
4 whole cloves
3 tablespoons ghee (clarified butter)
  or oil
2 onions (about ³/₄ lb/350 g), thinly
  sliced
4 whole mace blades (optional)
2 teaspoons cumin seeds

2 tablespoons chopped fresh mint
  leaves
4 tablespoons chopped fresh coriander
  leaves (cilantro)
1 teaspoon saffron threads, soaked in
  ¹/₄ cup (65 ml) milk
2 tablespoons almonds, toasted, for
  garnish

1 Preheat the oven to 350°F (175°C).
2 Soak the rice for 1 hour. Carefully pour out the soaking water and wash the rice in several changes of water, until the water runs clear. Leave it to drain in a fine-meshed strainer for about 15 minutes.
3 Process the garlic, ginger, mint leaves, fresh coriander leaves, green chili peppers and lime juice in a food processor or a blender to make a smooth purée. Transfer to a bowl and mix in the yogurt, Home-Style Garam Masala, and a dash of salt. Add the chicken and mix well, making sure all the pieces are well coated with the marinade. Cover and marinate for at least 8 hours, preferably overnight, in the refrigerator.
4 Bring 5 cups (1.25 liters) of the water to a boil in a large nonstick saucepan over high heat. Add 2 of the cardamom pods, the cinnamon stick, 1 of the bay leaves, 2 of the cloves, a pinch of salt and the drained rice. Reduce the heat to medium and cook, uncovered, until the rice is halfway cooked, about 5 minutes. Drain the rice and the whole spices. Discard the water.
5 Heat the ghee or oil over medium-high

heat in a large, nonstick oven-safe saucepan (about 4- to 6-quart-/3.75- to 5.75-liter capacity), a Dutch oven or other type of covered, oven-safe baking dish with a tight fitting lid. When hot, add the sliced onions and fry them for about 8 to 10 minutes, until brown and crisp, stirring frequently. Remove them with a slotted spoon, leaving as much of the oil in the pan as possible, and spread them out on a paper towel to drain. Set aside for garnish.
6 To the same saucepan that you fried the onions, add the remaining whole spices, including the mace and cumin, and fry over medium-high heat, stirring constantly, until fragrant, about 1 minute.
7 Add the marinated chicken and the marinade and sauté, stirring frequently, until lightly browned, about 5 to 10 minutes. Add the remaining 1 cup (250 ml) of water, stir, and bring it to a boil. Lower the heat and simmer until the chicken is almost cooked, about 10 minutes. Remove from the heat.
8 Add the chopped fresh mint and fresh coriander leaves on top of the chicken, and then cover everything well with the partially cooked rice. Drizzle the saffron milk on top of the rice, seal the pan well with aluminum foil, and place the lid over the foil.
9 Bake for about 30 minutes. This cooking technique is called *dum*. Remove from the oven and fluff the top of the rice lightly with a fork. Top with the fried onions and toasted almonds and serve.

Lemon Rice with Peanuts

Huli Anna

Serves 4
Prep time: 10 minutes plus 40 minutes for soaking
Cook time: 15 minutes

2 cups (420 g) uncooked basmati rice
8 cups (2 liters) water
1 teaspoon ground turmeric
1 teaspoon salt
3 tablespoons oil
2 teaspoons black mustard seeds
3 dried red chili peppers
2 teaspoons split yellow peas (chana dal)
6 to 8 fresh or dried curry leaves
1 cup (100 g) unsalted peanuts
Juice of 2 lemons, plus more if needed
Lemon wedges, for serving

With its fresh citrus flavor and fragrance of curry leaves, this dish is one of the most popular of the rice specialties from southern India. In our home, Lemon Rice with Peanuts was prepared for special or festive occasions. This rice dish tastes great even at room temperature, so it is an excellent picnic food. Serve with crisped *pappadum* (page 55) and Green Mango Pickle (page 47) and, for a complete meal, any mild *dal*, such as Delicious Everyday Dal (page 74), or a vegetable dish, such as Stir-Fried Vegetables with Yogurt (page 80).

1 Soak the rice for 30 to 40 minutes. Carefully pour out the soaking water and wash the rice in several changes of water, until the water runs clear. Leave it to drain in a fine-meshed strainer for about 15 minutes.

2 Bring the water with the turmeric, rice and salt to a boil in a heavy-bottomed saucepan. Lower the heat and simmer for 10 to 12 minutes, partially covered, until cooked. Drain the rice thoroughly in a fine-meshed strainer and return the rice to the saucepan. Set the pan aside, off the heat, covered.

3 Heat the oil in a small skillet over medium heat. Add the mustard seeds and, when they start to pop, add the dried red chili peppers, *chana dal*, curry leaves and peanuts. Cook for a minute, stirring constantly or until the chana dal and the nuts are lightly browned. This technique is known as tempering or *tarhka*.

4 Pour the contents of the skillet into a mixing bowl. Add the rice, lemon juice and salt; mix well until incorporated. Taste for lemon and salt, and adjust according to taste. Serve with lemon wedges.

Indian Fried Rice

Bhuni Pulao

The most innovative and best meal ideas often come when your pockets are half empty! And we've all faced this situation while being a student, haven't we?! I still recollect one weekend when I left from Manipal to meet a friend in Mysore. Both of us were students, and in love with food. A student of theater, and used to late nights of rehearsals and shows, my friend knew exactly where to find the quickest, cheapest and the most delicious food at three o'clock in the morning! We went to "Food Street"—a popular strip of pavement with series of stalls serving street food. It is there that I tasted this fried rice. With hunger in our stomachs, perhaps anything that we popped in our mouths that day would have tasted like bliss, but this rice dish was truly delicious. This is my attempt to reproduce that "Food Street" fried rice. Like most fried-rice dishes, this is best made with leftover rice. The array of vegetables, each contributing a different texture, and the piquant flavor of the soy sauce combined with the sharpness of *garam masala* and dried red chili peppers, is delicious. Though most Indian rice recipes use basmati, a generic white long-grain rice is actually better for stir-fries as basmati rice tends to get soft and break apart quite easily when rapidly stirred. Indian Fried Rice makes a good complete meal for vegetarians or a great side dish with seafood dishes like Chili Shrimp with Curry Leaves and Coconut (page 103) or Goan-Style Squid (page 102).

Serves 4
Prep time: 20 minutes
Cook time: 20 minutes

1 1/2 cups (315 g) uncooked long-grain white rice
6 cups (1.5 liters) water
4 tablespoons oil, plus more if needed
2 eggs, beaten
1 tablespoon minced garlic
3 teaspoons peeled and minced fresh ginger
2 small onions (about 1/2 lb/250 g), finely chopped
1 small carrot, peeled and diced (about 1/2 cup/75 g)
8 green beans, trimmed and finely chopped
1 cup (130 g) green peas, fresh or frozen (shelled from 1 lb/500 g fresh pea pods or about half of one 10-oz/300-g package frozen peas)
1/4 head cabbage (about 1/4 lb/125 g) cabbage, chopped
2 green onions (scallions), chopped
2 dried red chili peppers, deseeded and chopped
1 teaspoon soy sauce
1/2 teaspoon Home-Style Garam Masala (page 35)
Salt, to taste
4 tablespoons chopped fresh coriander leaves (cilantro)

1 Wash the rice in several changes of water until the water runs clear. Leave it to drain in a fine-meshed strainer for about 15 minutes.

2 Bring the water to a boil in a large saucepan over high heat and add the rice. Once the water has returned to a boil, reduce the heat to medium-low, and cook, uncovered, until the rice is cooked and tender, about 8 to 12 minutes. Start checking after 8 minutes. Drain the rice and discard the water. It is important to make sure the rice is not over-cooked and just tender.

3 Heat 1 tablespoon of the oil in a large skillet over medium heat. Pour in the beaten eggs and allow to set without stirring. Slide the omelet onto a plate, roll it up, and cut it crosswise into fine strips. Set aside.

4 Heat the remaining 3 tablespoons of oil in a wok or a large skillet over high heat. Add the garlic, ginger, onions, carrot, green beans, peas and cabbage, and stir-fry for about 1 minute, or until the vegetables are tender. Add the green onions, red chili peppers, soy sauce and Home-Style Garam Masala, and sauté for another 30 seconds. Add the rice and some additional oil, if needed, and fry for 1 minute. Check for seasoning and add salt if needed. Stir in the coriander leaves and serve hot.

Indian Fried Rice

Tamarind Rice

Puliogare

This traditional rice dish is very common in the south Indian states of Karnataka and Tamil Nadu. It is made with popular south Indian spices and aromatics like mustard seeds and curry leaves, and tamarind, a locally available souring agent. The addition of peanuts gives the dish a nice crunch, which contrasts nicely with the softness of the cooked rice. This rice dish can be served hot or at room temperature—it will taste great either way. It is lovely by itself and, for a nourishing vegetarian meal, goes well with any *raita*. I like to serve it with crisped *pappadum* (page 55) as well.

Serves 4
Prep time: 15 minutes
Cook time: 15 minutes

2$^1/_2$ **tablespoons tamarind paste**
$^1/_4$ **cup (65 ml) hot water**
3 **tablespoons oil**
3 **teaspoons black mustard seeds**
4 **dried red chili peppers, broken in half**
$^1/_2$ **lb (250 g) shallots (about 15 medium-size shallots), chopped**
2 **fresh green chili peppers, coarsely chopped**
$^1/_4$ **teaspoon ground turmeric**
10 **fresh or dried curry leaves**
1 **recipe Plain Basmati Rice (page 124), chilled or at room temperature**
Salt, to taste
4 **tablespoons chopped fresh coriander leaves (cilantro), for garnish**
2 **tablespoons roasted peanuts, for garnish**

1 Place the tamarind paste and hot water in a small bowl. Use a fork to mix the tamarind paste into the water. Set aside.
2 Heat the oil in a large saucepan over medium-high heat. Add the mustard seeds and cover. After the mustard seeds have sputtered and popped for 10 to15 seconds, add the chopped dried red chili peppers and shallots. Lower the heat to medium and fry for about 1 minute, stirring frequently.
3 Add the green chili peppers and turmeric and fry over medium heat, stirring frequently, until the chili peppers begin to soften, about 2 minutes. Toss in the curry leaves and give them a stir.
4 Add the cooked rice to the mixture and stir in the salt. Increase the heat to high and fry for 3 to 4 minutes, while stirring constantly. Add the tamarind liquid and fry for a few minutes, tossing the mixture to avoid lumps of rice. Serve hot, garnished with fresh coriander leaves and roasted peanuts.

Basmati Rice with Whole Spices

Saada Pulao

There are many variations and methods of preparing and cooking basmati rice, but the goal is always the same—when cooked, every grain should be separate and whole. In this method, known as a *pulao*, or pilaf in the West, the rice is sautéed in hot oil or ghee and then cooked in a seasoned liquid with spices. A minimum amount of water is used and, once absorbed and the rice tender, the pan is taken off the heat to allow the rice to rest. It is very important to keep a watchful eye because once you take the rice off the heat it continues to cook in its own steam. For best results, basmati rice should be soaked for about 30 to 40 minutes and washed in several changes of water before it is cooked. This is one of the most common, finest and flavorful rice dishes, and it can be served with any Indian meal or dishes.

Serves 4
Prep time: 5 minutes plus 40 minutes for soaking
Cook time: 15 minutes

$1^1/_2$ cups (315 g) uncooked basmati rice
$1^1/_2$ teaspoons cumin seeds
1 teaspoon whole cloves
$^1/_2$ teaspoon black peppercorns
5 to 7 green cardamom pods
1 tablespoon ghee (clarified butter) or oil
$2^3/_4$ cups (685 ml) water
1 teaspoon salt
1 tablespoon chopped fresh mint leaves

1 Soak the rice for 30 to 40 minutes. Carefully pour out the soaking water and wash the rice in several changes of water, until the water runs clear. Leave it to drain in a fine-meshed strainer for about 15 minutes.
2 Place the cumin, cloves, black peppercorns and cardamom in a medium saucepan and roast, while shaking the pan, over medium-high heat until highly fragrant, about 1 minute. Add the drained rice and ghee or oil and sauté for 1 to 3 minutes, stirring gently with a wooden spoon—be careful not to break the grains of the rice.
3 Add the water and salt, and bring to a boil over high heat. Reduce the heat to the lowest setting, cover the pan, and cook until the rice is done, 10 to 12 minutes. Do not stir the rice while it cooks. Remove from the heat and let the rice rest, covered, for 5 minutes. Transfer to a serving platter, garnish with the fresh mint leaves, and serve.

Basmati Rice with Whole Spices

Mint Rice with Potatoes and Toasted Cumin *Aloo Pudina Pulao*

This rice dish is mildly flavored with cumin seeds and mint leaves, making it suitable for almost any kind of meal. I particularly like to serve this with Masala Lamb Chops (page 121).

Serves 6

Prep time: 15 minutes plus 40 minutes for soaking

Cook time: 15 minutes

1¼ cups (260 g) uncooked basmati rice
2 tablespoons oil
1 onion (about ⅓ lb/150 g), thinly sliced
1 potato (about ½ lb/250 g), peeled and cut into ½-in (1.25-cm) dice
2 tablespoons peeled and minced fresh ginger
1 small fresh green chili pepper, minced
3 tablespoons chopped fresh mint leaves
2¼ cups (565 ml) water
Salt, to taste
1 tablespoon cumin seeds, toasted and coarsely crushed

1 Soak the rice for 30 to 40 minutes. Carefully pour out the soaking water and wash the rice in several changes of water, until the water runs clear. Leave it to drain in a fine-meshed strainer for about 15 minutes.

2 Heat the oil in a large saucepan over medium-high heat and sauté the onion until brown, about 5 to 7 minutes. Add the potato, ginger, green chili pepper and half of the mint leaves. Cook, stirring constantly, until fragrant, about 2 minutes.

3 Add the rice and sauté for 3 minutes. Add the water and salt and bring to a boil over high heat. Reduce the heat to the lowest setting, cover the pan, and cook until the rice is done, 10 to 12 minutes. Do not stir the rice while it cooks. Remove from the heat and let the rice rest, covered, for about 5 minutes. Transfer to a serving platter, sprinkle on the roasted cumin and the remaining mint leaves, and serve.

Baked Garlic Naan *Lasooni Naan*

This is the most popular breads served in Indian restaurants. Naan is eaten in all parts of India but is more popular in the north. Traditionally naan is made with all-purpose flour and is cooked in a hot clay oven, or *tandoor*, which gives it a very special taste. Though it is almost impossible to reproduce the smoky flavors of breads cooked in a tandoor, this recipe, adapted for a conventional oven, creates results surprisingly close to the authentic tandoori naan. Every home oven acts differently, so cooking time usually varies from 5 to 10 minutes. Sometimes I bake nann on a cookie sheet under the broiler of a conventional oven until the top is slightly browned. A pizza stone is the best choice when using the broiler method because once heated, the stone radiates heat and the naan can bake simultaneously from the top and bottom.

Makes 8 naan
Prep time: 15 minutes plus 1 hour for
  resting
Bake time: 7 to 10 minutes

1¼ cups (300 ml) milk, warmed (about
  110°F/43°C)
2 teaspoons sugar
¼ ounce (1 envelope) active dry yeast
**4 cups (480 g) all-purpose flour, plus
  extra to dust work surface**
½ teaspoon baking powder
½ teaspoon salt
½ cup (100 g) chopped garlic (1 to 2
  heads garlic)
1 egg, lightly beaten
2 tablespoons oil
¾ cup (180 g) plain yogurt, lightly
  beaten

1 Combine the milk, sugar and yeast in a small bowl. Stir to mix. Set aside for 15 to 20 minutes.

2 Sift the flour and baking powder in a large bowl. Make a well in the center and add the salt, half of the garlic, the egg, oil, yogurt and yeast mixture. Mix to form a soft dough. If the dough seems dry, add a little more milk. Turn onto a floured work surface and knead the dough by pressing your knuckles lightly into the dough, spreading the dough outward, gathering the ends towards the center with your fingers, and pressing the center down. Repeat for about 3 to 5 minutes, or until you have soft, pliable dough that does not stick to your fingers. Place in an oiled bowl. Cover with a damp cloth or a plastic wrap and let rest in a warm place to double in size, about 1 to 2 hours.

3 Preheat the oven, with the oven rack in the highest position, to 400°F (200°C) or to the highest temperature.

4 Punch down the dough, knead it briefly, and divide it into 8 portions. Roll out the dough either into circles 6 to 7 inches (15 to 17.5 cm) in diameter or into tear shapes. Sprinkle the dough circles or tear shapes with the remaining garlic. Gently press the garlic into the dough.

5 Arrange the rolled breads on a greased cookie sheet or a preheated pizza stone. Bake on the top oven rack for 5 to 10 minutes, or until slightly brown on the edges. Serve hot.

Variation:

Plain Naan and Flavored Naan

To make plain naan, simply omit the garlic. The basic recipe for all naan is the same. Variations can be done by adding different flavors from herbs, spices and other aromatics. These flavors can be added to the dough while making the dough, before rolling, or they can be pressed onto the surface of the dough after rolling, or a combination, as was done when making Baked Garlic Naan.

Whole Wheat Griddle Breads

Chapati

Chapati, also called *roti* or *phulka*, is made with whole-wheat flour, salt and water. This simple unleavened flatbread is the most common type of bread made in Indian homes. They are made fresh at every meal, and are best eaten hot as they are cooked. (Typically, chapatis are rolled out and cooked in small batches while people are eating so that everyone enjoys them fresh.) They are served at just about every meal and go well with vegetables, meats or just pickles. Chapati is typically made on a *tava*—a round, slightly concave, cast-iron griddle that looks like an omelet pan without a lip and with a slight curve to the bottom. If you want to buy one, look for tava griddles in Indian markets. You can use a cast-iron or nonstick griddle, or even a large cast-iron skillet, with equally good results. A perfect chapati comes with practice. I can never match the skill, speed and perfection of chapati-making achieved by my mom and the other women in my family. I have learned some tips over the years from the experts that will help you master this great, everyday bread. Tip 1: Chapati dough has to be quite soft. The amount of water added to the flour can be tricky—it depends on the brand of flour and humidity in the air. So, it is important to add the water in small quantities. Note that the amount of water suggested in the recipe is a guideline only—you may need to add more or less water. Tip 2: When rolling out the individual chapatis, do not worry if they do not come out in a perfect round. Your chapati will become more perfect looking with practice.

Makes about 10 chapatis
Prep time: 10 minutes plus 1 hr for resting
Cook time: 10 minutes

2 cups (250 g) whole-wheat flour, plus extra to dust work surface
¹/₂ teaspoon salt
About 1 cup (250 ml) water
¹/₂ cup (125 ml) oil or melted ghee (clarified butter), for brushing

REHEATING TIPS Though chapatis are best eaten hot off the griddle, they can also be refrigerated or frozen for later use. They can be kept in the refrigerator for up to 5 to 6 days, and frozen for as long as 2 months. To store the breads, make sure the breads are cooled completely. Then stack them one on top of the other and tightly wrap in plastic wrap. Then wrap them with aluminum foil or place them in freezer bags. They can be reheated in a 450°F (230°C) toaster oven wrapped in aluminum foil; on a hot tava, griddle or skillet, under the broiler or in a single layer on an ungreased broiler-safe tray, 4 to 5 inches (10 to 12.5 cm) from the heat source.

1 Sift the whole-wheat flour and salt into a bowl. Make a well in the center. Slowly add the water in small quantities, while mixing, until a soft dough has formed. Turn onto a floured work surface and knead the dough by pressing your knuckles lightly into the dough, spreading the dough outward, gathering the ends towards the center with your fingers, and pressing the center down. Repeat for about 3 to 5 minutes, or until you have soft, pliable dough that does not stick to your fingers. Place in an oiled bowl. Cover with a damp cloth or a plastic wrap and let rest for about an hour. (This allows the gluten to develop). If keeping for longer periods, refrigerate the dough.

2 Heat a *tava*, griddle or a large cast-iron skillet over medium heat. Divide the dough into 8 to 10 equal portions. Work with one portion at a time, keeping the rest covered with a damp cloth. On a lightly floured surface, roll out each portion to a circle about 6 to 7 inches (15 to 17.5 cm) in diameter. Carefully shake the excess surface flour off prior to cooking.

3 Place each rolled bread on the tava, griddle or skillet and cook for about 7 to 10 seconds, until brown. Turn the bread over to brown the other side, about 12 to 15 seconds. Turn it over and lightly smear the hot bread with the oil or ghee. Serve hot.

Fried Puffed Bread *Poori*

Makes 16 poori
Prep time: 10 minutes plus 30 minutes
    for resting the dough
Cook time: 15 minutes

Poori, or "puffed bread," have a magical and delicate appearance. When freshly made, they fill with steam and puff up. And, though deep-fried, this whole-wheat bread is light and almost melts in your mouth. It is one of the many pleasures of Indian cuisine. Pooris can be served with all meals but they are most popular in India as a breakfast or a brunch staple. Most often, poori is served with potatoes or chickpeas. Serve with Mangalore Spiced Potatoes (page 91), Bengali Potatoes with Spices (page 81) or Northern Chickpea Curry (page 69) and any flavored lassi (page 152)

1 cup (120 g) whole-wheat flour
1 cup (120 g) all-purpose flour, plus
    extra to dust work surface
1/2 teaspoon salt
3 tablespoons oil
6 to 8 tablespoons water
Oil, for deep-frying

1 Sift both the flours in a bowl. Mix in the salt. Drizzle the oil into the flour mixture. Rub it into the flour with your fingers. Slowly add the water to form a medium-soft ball of dough. Turn onto a floured work surface and knead the dough by pressing your knuckles lightly into the dough, spreading the dough outward, gathering the ends towards the center with your fingers, and pressing the center down. Repeat for about 3 to 5 minutes, or until you have soft, pliable dough that does not stick to your fingers. Form a smooth ball, rub it with a little oil, and place it in a mixing bowl, covered with a plastic wrap. Set aside for 15 to 30 minutes.

2 Heat 2 inches of oil in a *kadhai*, small wok or large saucepan over medium heat to 325°F (160°C) on a deep-fry or candy thermometer. To gauge the temperature of the oil without a thermometer, drop a piece of bread about 1-inch (2.5-cm) square into the oil, turning the piece of bread often as the oil heats up. When the oil reaches 325°F (160°C), the bread will begin to brown quickly and turn golden brown all over—like a crouton—in about 40 seconds.

3 As the oil heats up divide the dough into 12 balls. Roll each ball into a 5-inch (12.5-cm) round disc. Keep the rolled pooris covered with plastic wrap until ready to fry. When the oil is hot, carefully lay each poori on the hot oil without letting it fold up. It should sizzle immediately. Using the back of a slotted spoon, gently push the poori into the oil with quick strokes. It should puff up in seconds. Turn the poori over and cook for a few seconds, until slightly brown. Drain on paper towels. Serve immediately.

Flaky Paratha Breads Stuffed with Potatoes

Aloo Paratha

This flaky, pan-fried bread is very popular in north Indian homes. Traditionally served for breakfast or as a late afternoon snack, it is loaded with melted butter and is served with homemade pickle and *raita*. I just love this golden brown and crispy bread. I can eat more than a few *paratha* if someone is frying them and serving them hot off the griddle. Parathas are a popular item in school and office lunch boxes and, when filled with a vegetable, like this version, make a delicious light lunch. For a wholesome light meal, serve this bread with any raita (pages 44–46) or plain yogurt and a salad of your choice.

Makes 14 aloo paratha
Prep time: 15 minutes plus 1 hour for resting
Cook time: 20 minutes

4 cups (500 g) all-purpose flour, plus extra
   to dust work surface
1 teaspoon salt
2 tablespoons oil, plus more for oiling
   griddle
1¼ cups (300 ml) water
½ cup (115 g) melted ghee (clarified
   butter) or butter, for brushing cooked
   breads

Potato Filling
2 tablespoons oil
¼ teaspoon cumin seeds
1 small onion (about ¼ lb/125 g),
   chopped
1 fresh green chili pepper, minced
1 potato (about ½ lb/250 g), boiled,
   peeled and mashed
Salt, to taste

1 Sift the flour and salt into a bowl. Make a well in the center. Add the oil and 1 cup (250 ml) of the water and mix into soft dough. If the dough is not soft and pliable, mix in up to ¼ cup (65 ml) more water, 1 tablespoon at a time. Turn onto a floured work surface and knead the dough by pressing your knuckles lightly into the dough, spreading the dough outward, gathering the ends towards the center with your fingers, and pressing the center down. Repeat for about 3 to 5 minutes, or until you have soft, pliable dough that does not stick to your fingers. Place in an oiled bowl. Cover with a damp cloth or a plastic wrap and let rest for about an hour. (This allows the gluten to develop.) If keeping for longer periods, refrigerate the dough.

2 To make the Potato Filling: Heat the oil in a saucepan over medium heat. Add the cumin seeds and let them pop. Add the onion and fry for 1 minute. Stir in the green chili pepper and potato and cook over low heat for 5 minutes, stirring constantly. Season the potato mixture with salt and let cool completely.

3 To form the paratha: Divide the dough into 14 portions and roll each into a 4-inch (10-cm) circle. Spread 1 tablespoon of the Potato Filling in the center of each circle. Bring the edges together, pinch and seal them, and then shape into a ball once again. With well-floured hands, flatten the stuffed ball of dough. Place on a well-floured surface and roll into a 7-inch (17.5-cm) circle of even thickness. As you roll, keep turning and dusting the dough with flour; otherwise, it may stick to the rolling surface. If holes develop as they stretch, seal the holes by putting a little dry flour over them or pinching them together.

4 Heat an oiled griddle over medium heat. Gently remove the excess flour from each bread and place on the hot griddle. Cook each bread for 2 to 3 minutes, or until slightly brown. Turn the breads over and cook until golden brown and crispy, lightly brushing with the ghee or butter. Serve warm.

Chapter 9

Desserts and Drinks

An Indian meal is not complete without its distinctive sweets and drinks. In the classic Indian style, sweet dishes may often be served right along with the main dishes. However, desserts are also served after the meal. They help set a stage for celebrations, holidays, weddings and family meals. Indian desserts feature unique flavors such as saffron, rosewater and cardamom, to name a few. When in season, mangoes are a very popular ingredient in Indian desserts. This chapter features a range of desserts, from the traditional Creamy Rice Pudding (page 149), known as *kheer* in Hindi, to contemporary creations like Chai Crème Brûlée (page 147). Some Indian sweets, such Almond Butter Cookies (page 148) and Pistachio Biscotti (page 146) may form a part of the early evening or late afternoon "tea time" menu.

The drinks that are served in India are quite different from those in any other part of the world, each having its special Indian touch. They range from ginger-infused lemonades, hot tea and milk laced with cardamom, or frothy yogurt blended with ice and freshly crushed cumin seeds. Traditional drink recipes, like Ginger Cardamom Chai (page 153) are included, as well as new inventions like Watermelon Lemonade (page 154) and Mumbai Fruit Punch (page 150). The drinks in this chapter can be served with any meal and go well with all Indian foods.

Watermelon Mint Ice

Tarbuj ki Baraf

This recipe is inspired by the flavored shaved ice *golas* that are served by the street vendors and ice cream trucks in India. Whereas the Indian golas use artificial flavors and coloring, this natural version combines the flavor and color of fresh watermelon and rosewater (*khewda*). In many Indian households, fresh watermelon is served at the end of the meal as a salad or sliced on a platter with fresh mint. In keeping with that tradition, I like to serve this very refreshing dessert after a heavy meal.

Serves 4
Prep time: 15 minutes plus 2 hours for freezing

- **6 tablespoons sugar**
- **7 tablespoons water**
- **3 to 4 large fresh mint sprigs**
- **3 tablespoons rosewater**
- **4 cups (500 g) chunked, seedless watermelon (about $1/3$ of a 3 to 4-lb (1.5 to 1.75-kg) baby seedless watermelon)**
- **Fresh mint leaves, for garnish**

1 Place the sugar, water and fresh mint sprigs in a small saucepan. Heat gently over medium-low heat until the sugar dissolves, stirring occasionally. Pour the sugar water through a fine-meshed strainer set over a bowl. Discard the mint sprigs and set the sugar water aside to cool.

2 Purée the watermelon in a food processor and mix it into the sugar syrup. Chill the mixture for 3 to 4 hours. Stir in the rosewater.

3 Place the mixture in an ice cream maker and churn until it is firm enough to scoop.

4 Alternatively, you may pour the mixture into a flat container and place it in the freezer for 2 hours. Remove from the freezer and beat with a fork to break up the ice crystals. Return the mixture to the freezer and let freeze 2 hours more, beating the mixture at half-hour intervals. Freeze until firm.

5 Serve the frozen ice in sundae cups garnished with mint leaves.

Sweet Mangoes in a Creamy Custard *Aam Ki Baraf Malai*

The Alphonso mango, one of the sweetest in the world, is the mango of choice for this dessert. If you can't find Alphonso mangos, simply use the ripest, sweetest mangos you can find. This is a very popular but simple Indian dessert combination and is one of my all-time favorite desserts.

TIP If time is an issue, use one of my favorite short-cuts for a creamy mango-based dessert: Fold the diced mango into 1 pint (463 ml) of softened premium-quality vanilla ice cream. You now have a delicious dessert, created on the spur of the moment, worthy of culminating any Indian meal.

NOTE The custard can be made in advance and kept in the refrigerator for a couple of days before adding the mango.

Serves 4
Prep time: 15 minutes plus 6 hours
   for chilling
Cook time: 10 minutes

2 cups (500 ml) milk
4 egg yolks
7 tablespoons sugar
2 teaspoons pure vanilla extract
2 large, ripe mangoes (about 2 lbs/
   1 kg), peeled and diced
1 cup (500 ml) whipped cream

1 Bring the milk to a boil in a heavy-bottomed saucepan over medium heat. While the milk is heating, whisk the egg yolks in a mixing bowl until smooth. Add the sugar to the egg yolks and continue to beat until the mixture is pale and thick. While constantly beating the egg mixture, slowly pour the hot milk into the bowl.
2 Pour the egg and milk mixture back into the saucepan and set over medium-low heat. Cook until the mixture is thickened, stirring constantly, about 5 to 7 minutes. Do not let the mixture come to a boil since this will cause it to curdle.
3 Once thickened, immediately pour the mixture into a clean large bowl. Stir in the vanilla extract. Cover and refrigerate for at least 6 hours or until ready to serve.
4 When ready to serve, add the diced mangoes to the bowl with the custard. Mix together and divide among 4 individual serving bowls. Serve topped with a dollop of whipped cream.

Sweetened Yogurt with Saffron and Pistachios *Shrikhand*

This creamy, pale-hued dessert made with fresh yogurt is a favorite in the western Indian state of Maharashtra. Made with aromatic and upscale ingredients, like rosewater and saffron, it is often reserved for special occasions, especially traditional weddings, and is sometimes paired with *poori*, a deep-fried Indian bread (page 138). When entertaining, and I really want to impress my guests, I serve this dessert as a sundae or as a parfait layered with berries or any seasonal fruits in tall glasses. This dessert can be made two days ahead of time, which makes it a great option when entertaining.

Serves 6

Prep time: 10 minutes plus 3 hours for draining

- **4 cups (1 kg) whole-milk plain yogurt**
- **¹/₂ teaspoon saffron threads, soaked in ¹/₃ cup (80 ml) warm milk for 15 minutes**
- **¹/₃ cup (75 g) sugar, preferably superfine**
- **¹/₂ teaspoon ground cardamom, preferably freshly ground green cardamom seeds (from about 6 green cardamom pods) (see tip, page 145)**
- **¹/₂ teaspoon rosewater**
- **2 tablespoons chopped pistachios, for garnish**

1 Line a sieve or colander with a double layer of muslin or cheese cloth and place it over a bowl. Pour the yogurt into the sieve and let it drain in the refrigerator for about 2 to 3 hours. Most of the liquid should have drained out of the yogurt and the consistency of the yogurt should be of a thick pudding.

2 Mix together the drained yogurt, saffron milk, sugar, cardamom and rosewater in a large bowl. Taste and adjust the sugar and flavorings to taste if necessary. Cover and refrigerate for a minimum of 2 hours and up to 2 days.

3 Divide the yogurt among 6 small dessert bowls. Top with the chopped pistachios and serve.

1 Whisk the cream, milk and rice flour in a heavy-bottomed saucepan until smooth. Bring it to a slow boil on medium low heat, stirring continuously to avoid scorching the milk. (Scorched milk adds an unpleasant taste and unattractive color to kulfi.) Once the milk has come to a boil, reduce the heat to low. Continue to cook for 30 to 40 minutes, until the mixture thickens. Stir regularly, scraping the sides of the pot and not the bottom to avoid mixing any scorched bits into the milk.

2 Turn off the heat. Stir in the sugar and cardamom. The consistency should resemble that of whipped cream. Set aside and cool for 20 minutes. Stir in the mango pulp and pistachios.

3 Evenly pour the mixture into eight 4 to 6-ounce (125 to 185-ml) individual serving containers or ramekins. Cover each of them tightly with plastic wrap and freeze for at least 8 hours or overnight. Remove the kulfi from the freezer about 5 minutes before serving. If you are serving the kulfi out of the molds, place each one under warm running water for 15 to 20 seconds. Hold the containers from underneath so that if the kulfi starts to slip you can catch it. You might need to give the mold a firm tap on the top or sides to release a stubborn one. Transfer the kulfi to individual dessert plates and serve.

NOTE The rice flour used in this recipe is made from finely ground rice. It can be found in Indian grocery stores or online. Brown rice flour, available in many health foods stores, should not be used as a substitute.

Pistachio Mango Ice Cream

Pista Aaam Ki Kulfi

This dessert is a favorite among Indians, and is always a crowd-pleaser at my parties. *Kulfi*, literally "Indian ice cream," can be made with any flavor of your choice, and is easier to make than American ice cream. In India, street vendors sell kulfi on a stick—like a popsicle. Since good fresh mangoes are not available year-round, I recommend using the canned Alfonzo mango purée available in Indian grocery stores. The purée is refreshingly and tasty. Some purées are sweetened, so adjust the sugar according to your taste. I prefer to use rice flour as a thickening agent in this recipe because the resulting texture is creamier as compared to when cornstarch is used.

Serves 8
Prep time: 10 minutes plus 8 hours for cooling
Cook time: 30 minutes

1 cup (250 ml) heavy cream
6 cups (1.5 liters) whole milk
1 tablespoon white rice flour or corn starch
5 tablespoons sugar
$\frac{1}{2}$ teaspoon ground cardamom, preferably freshly ground green cardamom seeds (from about 6 green cardamom pods) (see tip)
1 cup (250 ml) unsweetened, canned mango pulp or purée (or puréed flesh of 2 ripe, preferably Alfonzo, mangos)
$\frac{1}{2}$ cup (55 g) pistachios, chopped

TIP To extract cardamom seeds from the pod, place the cardamom pods in a mortar and lightly pound the pods with the pestle. Or place the pods in a small ziplock bag and roll over them with a rolling pin on a flat surface. The pods will burst open and the seeds will come out. **To grind the extracted cardamom seeds,** remove the pods from the mortar or bag. If using the ground cardamom to flavor desserts and beverages, mix the seeds with a teaspoon of sugar. (The sugar acts as an abrasive and allows you to grind the seeds to a finer powder more easily, but can only be used for sweet dishes and beverages.) If using the mortar and pestle, pulverize the seeds with the pestle until they are finely ground. If using the bag and rolling pin method, crush the seeds with a rolling pin, moving the pin back and forth over the seeds, applying a fair amount of pressure, until they are finely ground.

Makes 30 to 40 cookies
Prep time: 20 minutes
Bake time: 30 minutes

1 cup (120 g) all-purpose flour, plus
    extra for dusting work surface
1/2 cup (115 g) sugar
1 teaspoon baking powder
1 cup (110 g) shelled pistachios
2 teaspoons grated orange zest
2 eggs, beaten

1 Preheat the oven to 350°F (175°C).
2 Mix the flour, sugar, baking powder, pistachios and orange zest together in a large bowl. Make a well in the center. Place the eggs in the well and then fold them into the flour mixture to make a sticky dough.
3 Turn the dough out onto a clean floured surface. Divide the dough into two sections and, using your hands, roll each portion into a log approximately 1 1/2 inches (3.75 cm) in diameter. Place the logs on a large cookie sheet lined with parchment, leaving approximately 3 inches (7.5 cm) between each log to allow for spreading.
4 Bake for 30 minutes. Remove and allow to cool. Reduce the oven temperature to 275°F (135°C).
5 Remove the cookie logs from the cookie sheets and, with a sharp bread knife, cut each of the loaves into slices approximately 1/4-inch (6-mm) wide. Lay the cookies on the cookie sheet, cut-side down, and return them to the oven. Bake for 20 minutes, turning the cookies once until slightly brown on the edges. Remove from the oven and cool the cookies on wire racks.

Pistachio Biscotti

In preparation, texture and shape, these cookies are similar to Italian biscotti, and, like the Italian cookies, they are great for dunking into a hot beverage. In India, these nutty, tasty treats are served as an afternoon snack with chai (Indian tea) or coffee. One word of advice: Don't skip the freshly grated orange zest—you won't believe the difference it makes. These cookies keep well at room temperature for at least 3 to 4 weeks if stored in an airtight jar.

Chai Crème Brûlée

In India, teas take their names from the regions in which they are grown, hence the names Darjeeling, Assam, and Nilgiri, all referring to places in India, and most have their own distinct and delicate flavor. Though teas, in India, are not typically used for making desserts, the idea of combining spiced tea with crème brûlée, a delectable, all-time favorite custard, struck me as an interesting idea. As a perpetual student of food, nothing excites me more than bringing a smile to my family and friends with a new creation, especially a sweet treat. Serve this with seasonal berries or fresh fruits.

Serves 4

Prep time: 10 minutes plus 6 to 8 hours for chilling

Cook time: 15 minutes

2 cups (500 ml) heavy cream
1 cup (20 g) black tea leaves or 6 to 8 black tea bags, preferably Assam, Nilgiri or Darjeeling tea
1 vanilla bean, split open
4 green cardamom pods
One 2-in (5-cm) stick cinnamon
1 teaspoon black peppercorns
1 teaspoon whole cloves
4 egg yolks
$\frac{1}{2}$ cup (100 g) sugar
1 tablespoon unsalted butter, chilled and cut into small pieces

1 Place the cream, tea leaves or tea bags, vanilla bean, cardamom, cinnamon, black peppercorns and cloves in a heavy saucepan and bring to a boil. Reduce the heat and simmer for 5 minutes, stirring occasionally. Set aside for 10 minutes to infuse. Strain and set aside. Discard the tea leaves/bags and spices.
2 Whisk the egg yolks and 4 tablespoons of the sugar in the top of a double boiler over gently simmering water until pale and thick. Do not overcook. Add the reduced tea extract, whisking constantly. Cook slowly, stirring occasionally, until the mixture thickens and coats the back of a spoon, approximately 10 to 12 minutes. Remove from the heat and whisk in the butter a little at a time, until thoroughly combined.
3 Pour the custard mixture into 4 individual 4-ounce (125-ml) ramekins and chill thoroughly, preferably overnight.
4 Just before serving, evenly sprinkle the custard with the remaining sugar. To evenly distribute the sugar, pour 1 tablespoon of the sugar in the middle of each custard. Then tilt the ramekins and gently tap the sides, letting gravity move the sugar across the surface of the custard until they are evenly covered. Take a kitchen butane torch or propane blow torch and, holding it about 1 to 2 inches (2.5 to 5 cm) from the top of the custard, heat the sugar until it bubbles and changes color. Take your time and don't move from one area of the custard to another until the spot you've been working on has achieved a nice golden brown color. With a typical kitchen torch, this takes a little less than a minute for each crème brûlée. Don't worry about heating up the custard underneath; you can refrigerate the crème brulee for a bit before serving. To avoid catching your kitchen counter on fire, place the ramekins on an aluminum foil lined cookie sheet or sheet pan.

Almond Butter Cookies

I just love these cookies. These sweet bites are easy to make. The flavor of cardamom, honey and almonds makes them so special. Cardamom is a commonly used spice in Indian cooking in both sweet and savory dishes. I have used almond flour in this recipe, which can be made at home simply by pulsing blanched whole almonds to a fine powder in a blender or a food processor. (To make 1½ cups almond flour, you will need 3 cups (450 g) whole almonds. You can substitute store-bought almond flour, which is sold in specialty food stores.) Serve these cookies with Ginger Cardamom Chai (page 153).

Makes about 30 to 35 cookies
Prep time: 15 minutes
Bake time: 20 minutes

1½ cups (3 sticks/335 g) unsalted butter
1¼ cups (245 g) sugar
½ cup (125 ml) honey
2 cups (240 g) all-purpose flour
2 teaspoons baking powder
1½ cups (240 g) almond flour
1 tablespoon ground cardamom, preferably freshly ground
   green cardamom seeds (from about 10 green cardamom
   pods) (see tip, page 145)
Almond slices, for decoration (optional)
Confectioners' sugar, for dusting

1 Preheat the oven to 325°F (160°C).
2 Melt the butter, sugar and honey in a small saucepan over medium heat, stirring until the sugar dissolves.
3 Sift the all-purpose flour and baking powder in a large bowl. Stir in the almond flour and cardamom. Add the butter mixture and stir until just combined. Do not over mix.
4 Line two cookie sheets with parchment. Place tablespoons of the dough, 2 inches (5 cm) apart, on the prepared cookie sheets. Flatten each portion of dough slightly to form a flat disc. Lightly press an almond slice in the center of each cookie and bake for 15 to 18 minutes, until lightly brown. Let rest for 5 minutes on the cookie sheets. Transfer to wire racks to cool completely. Dust lightly with the confectioners' sugar and serve. These cookies should be stored in an airtight jar at room temperature.

Almond Butter Cookies

Creamy Rice Pudding

Kheer

This creamy cardamom-spiced rice pudding, known as *kheer*, can be enjoyed hot or cold, and is probably the most popular pudding in India. It is often served during Indian festivals. When I was growing up, my mother would make it for the occasional elaborate Sunday meal. The whole milk and cream can be substituted with nonfat milk for a lower fat version. I have used basmati rice as I feel it makes the most flavorful Indian rice pudding. Kheer made with basmati is a north Indian or a Punjabi specialty. In the south, they make a similar version using long-grain white rice and, in Bengal, they make a version using Bengali short-grain rice. I've included a contemporary twist on the traditional kheer using apples. When making Cardamom Apple Kheer, I like to use tart firm apples like Granny Smith.

Serves 4
Prep time: 10 minutes plus 2 hours for cooling
Cook time: 40 minutes

$\frac{1}{3}$ cup (70 g) uncooked basmati rice
$5\frac{1}{2}$ cups (1.3 liters) whole milk
$\frac{1}{2}$ teaspoon ground cardamom (see tip, page 145)
2 cups (500 ml) heavy cream, plus more if needed
$\frac{1}{3}$ cup (55 g) golden raisins
$\frac{1}{4}$ cup (50 g) sugar
1 tablespoon slivered almonds, toasted, for garnish

1 Combine the rice and milk in a heavy-bottomed saucepan. Bring the milk to a gentle boil over medium-high heat. Once the milk has come to a boil, lower the heat and gently simmer for 35 to 40 minutes, uncovered, until most of the milk has been absorbed. Stir frequently while the rice is cooking to avoid scalding, which will add a burnt flavor to the pudding. (If you think the milk is beginning to burn, lower the heat and avoid scraping the bottom of the pan.) Stir in the ground cardamom, cream and golden raisins.
2 Remove from the heat and stir in the sugar. Let cool, stirring occasionally to prevent a skin from forming. This pudding will be thick and creamy. Stir in additional cream if the pudding is too thick. Refrigerate until cold. Serve in individual serving bowls garnished with the toasted slivered almonds.

Variation:

Cardamom Apple Kheer

Peel and dice 2 apples. Heat 2 tablespoons of unsalted butter in a skillet over medium heat. Add the apples and sauté until soft. Add a pinch of ground cardamom and sugar to taste. Cook for 2 to 3 minutes, until the apples are caramelized lightly. Let the apples cool. Fold half of the apples into the cooked and cooled kheer and use the rest as a topping.

Mumbai Fruit Punch

Mumbai Thandai

Summer holidays while growing up meant trips to Mumbai to spend time with cousins and taste delicacies made by my favorite Shanta Aunty! This fruit punch brings back very fond memories of me and my cousins getting together for a fun-filled school vacation—running around the neighborhood, playing cricket in the sweltering sun, breaking glass windows with a swing of the ball, and then running away from a beating . . . as far as the eye can see. What can be more refreshing than a glass of chilled homemade fruit punch, post such notorious behavior! This punch is an ode to my unforgettable childhood days. I make it with sparkling wine, but it can be made without any alcohol—simply replace the wine with ginger ale or lemon soda.

Serves 10 to 12
Prep time: 20 minutes

2 cups (500 ml) freshly-squeezed orange juice (from 5 to 6 oranges)
$1/4$ cup (65 ml) freshly-squeezed lime juice (from 2 to 3 limes)
1 cup (250 ml) freshly-squeezed ruby red grapefruit juice (from 1 large grapefruit)
3 cups (750 ml) pineapple juice
2 cups (300 g) diced watermelon
2 cups (250 g) diced, fresh pineapple
1 orange, cut into wedges
1 apple, cored and diced
1 cup (150 g) seedless grapes, cut in half
1 lemon, sliced
2 limes, sliced
$1^1/2$ cups (375 ml) dry sparkling wine (2 splits or one-half 750-ml bottle)
Crushed ice

1 Mix everything together, except the sparkling wine and ice, in a large bowl or jar. Let the mixture sit for 30 minutes.
2 Fill 8-ounce (250-ml) glasses with ice and fill three-quarters of the way with the punch. Add a splash of the sparkling wine just before serving.

Mumbai Fruit Punch

Mint Lime Cooler

Pudina Limbu Sharbat

This barely sweetened drink is a delightful thirst quencher on hot summer afternoons. I enjoy this drink with an extra kick of ginger. Adjust the ingredients according to your taste. Add some white rum to transform this cooler into a great mixed drink.

Serves 4
Prep time: 10 minutes

One 3-in (7.5-cm) piece fresh ginger, peeled
4 tablespoons coarsely chopped fresh mint
   leaves
$^1/_2$ cup (125 ml) freshly-squeezed lime
   juice (from about 4 limes)
6 cups (1.5 liters) sparkling water or club
   soda

6 teaspoons sugar
1 teaspoon salt
$^1/_4$ teaspoon ground black pepper
   (optional)
5 to 6 ice cubes

1 Blend together all the ingredients, except the ice, in a blender.
2 Strain and pour into four, tall 6-ounce (185-ml) glasses filled with ice.

Sweet Mango Yogurt Lassi

Aaam ki Lassi

Lassi, pronounced *luh–see*, is a very common cold yogurt drink made throughout India. There are many variations—some with fruits, spices or herbs depending on the season and geographic location. Mango lassi is probably the most popular of them all. If fresh mangoes are not available, you can buy mango pulp in cans from many supermarkets and most Asian stores. You can also make this recipe with fresh strawberries, bananas or peaches.

Serves 4
Prep time: 5 minutes if using canned mango purée, 15 minutes if using fresh mangoes

4 cups (1 kg) plain yogurt
2 tablespoons sugar, or to taste
3 ripe mangoes (about 3 lbs/1.5 kg), peeled and cut into chunks, or 3 cups (750 ml) canned mango pulp or purée
$1/_2$ teaspoon ground cardamom, preferably freshly ground green cardamom seeds (from about 6 green cardamom pods) (see tip, page 145)
1 cup (135 g) crushed ice

Blend the ingredients in an electric blender until the yogurt is frothy. Pour into four 8-ounce (250-ml) glasses and serve.

Variations:

Salted Lassi

Compared to Sweet Mango Yogurt Lassi, this is a thinner version. Just combine 4 cups (1 kg) of plain yogurt, 2 cups (500 ml) of water, 1 cup (250 ml) of crushed ice, 2 teaspoons of salt, 1 teaspoon of toasted cumin seeds and 1 tablespoon of chopped fresh mint leaves in an electric blender and blend. Pour into four 8-ounce (250-ml) glasses and serve.

Masala Spiced Lassi

This spicy and refreshing drink is perfect for a hot summer day. Just combine 4 cups (1 kg) of plain yogurt, 6 tablespoons of chopped fresh coriander leaves (cilantro), about 20 fresh mint leaves, 1 small fresh green chili pepper, 1 teaspoon of salt, 1 teaspoon of toasted cumin seeds and 1 cup (135 g) of crushed ice in an electric blender and blend until smooth and frothy. Pour into four 8-ounce (250-ml) glasses and serve.

Pistachio Lassi

This lassi, which is served at roadside cafés and restaurants in India, is said to help the body digest hot and spicy food. As a variation, fruit purées can be added to this recipe. Just combine 2 cups (500 g) of plain yogurt, 4 teaspoons of sugar, 2 cups (500 ml) of water, 1 teaspoon of ground cardamom, 1 cup (135 g) of crushed ice and 6 tablespoons of crushed pistachios in an electric blender and blend until smooth and frothy. Pour into four 8-ounce (250-ml) glasses and serve.

Sweet Mango Yogurt Lassi

Ginger Cardamom Chai

Adrak Masala Chai

Chai is a generic term for tea in India. The popularity of *masala chai* (spiced tea) has spread around the world. Sipping on a hot cup of this chai is a perfect way to unwind after a long day of work or finish a good meal. For me, chai is the first drink of the morning. In fact, for most of the Indians I know, having a cup of tea in the morning is like religion. We probably got this habit as a gift from the British, who ruled India for almost 100 years from the mid-1800s to the mid-1900s. I like to use whole milk in my tea, but nonfat milk works well too. Typically Indians add sugar to the chai while boiling the milk, but in this recipe I suggest adding it later as per the tastes of your guests. I prefer to use English breakfast tea to make this recipe. Serve this spiced beverage with Pistachio Biscotti (page 146) or Almond Butter Cookies (page 153).

Serves 2
Prep time: 5 minutes
Cook time: 10 minutes

2 cups (500 ml) water
$1/4$ teaspoon fennel seeds
One 1-in (2.5-cm) piece peeled fresh ginger, lightly
  crushed
6 green cardamom pods, crushed
$1/2$ cup (125 ml) milk
2 teaspoons loose black tea leaves or 1 black tea
  bag, preferably English breakfast
Sugar, for serving

1 Bring the water, fennel seeds, ginger and cardamom to a boil in a medium saucepan over high heat. Lower the heat to medium and continue to boil another minute to extract maximum flavor.
2 Add the milk and bring to a boil once again. Add the tea leaves and remove from the heat. Cover the pan and set aside to steep for about 3 minutes.
3 Pour the mixture through a strainer into 2 teacups. Discard the spices. Serve hot with sugar on the side.

Indian Lemonade

Desi Limbu Pani

This refreshing summer drink is a common beverage of choice in most parts of India. In addition to the classic Indian lemonade, I've included three variations: raspberry, watermelon and ginger.

Serves 4
Prep time: 10 minutes

2 cups (500 ml) water
2 cups (500 ml) sparkling water or club soda
1¹⁄₂ cups (300 g) sugar
1 cup (250 ml) freshly-squeezed lime or lemon juice (from about 8 limes or 4 to 6 lemons)

Combine all the ingredients in a large container or pitcher with a lid and shake or stir to combine, until the sugar is dissolved. Chill and serve in four, tall 8-ounce (250-ml) glasses filled with ice.

CLOCKWISE FROM LEFT:
Indian Lemonade, Raspberry and Watermelon

Raspberry

This is a perfect summer drink that complements most Indian meals. Just combine 4 cups (1 liter) of water, ¹⁄₂ cup (100 g) of sugar, or to taste, the juice of 3 lemons, and 2 cups (150 g) of raspberries in a blender. Blend until smooth. Serve in four, tall 8-ounce (250-ml) glasses filled with ice. Garnish with fresh raspberries and lemon slices. *Note*: this recipe can be made with strawberries too.

Watermelon

Just blend together 6 cups (900 g) of seeded and cubed watermelon, ¹⁄₂ cup (100 g) of sugar, or to taste, the juice of 3 lemons and few fresh mint sprigs in a food processor. Strain and chill. Serve cold in 2 tall 8-ounce (250-ml) glasses filled with ice. Garnish this drink with thin slices of watermelon and lemon and a sprig of mint.

Ginger

This drink is ideal as a chaser at a cocktail party, and it is a perfect after dinner drink as ginger is considered a digestive. To make, combine one 6-inch (15-cm) piece of peeled and coarsely chopped fresh ginger and ¹⁄₂ cup (125 ml) of water in a blender and process to a make a ginger juice. Pass it through a strainer. Set aside the juice. In a large pitcher. Combine the ingredients for Indian Lemonade and the fresh ginger juice and mix until the sugar is dissolved. Chill and serve cold in four tall 8-ounce (250-ml) glasses filled with ice.

Shopping Guide

Indian markets can seem intimidating at first, but a trip to one is well worth it, and may also encourage you to be adventurous and experiment with new ingredients. I always appreciate the range of fresh produce, spices and dry foods, such as rice and Indian lentils, available at such markets, and which tend to be more economically priced than at regular supermarkets. Here are few of my favorite stores for Indian food and spices. Many of these stores also sell Indian clothes, specialized Indian cookware, and Indian music and Bollywood movie CDS.

Bharat Bazaar
11510 West Washington Boulevard
Los Angeles, CA 90066
(310) 398-6766

Bombay Spice House
1036 University Avenue
Berkeley, CA 94702
(510) 845-5200

Bombay Bazaar
548 Valencia Street
San Francisco, CA 94100
(415) 621-1717

Coconut Hill Indian Market Place
554 South Murphy Avenue
Sunnyvale, CA 94086
(408)737-8803
http://coconuthill.com/
(Three store locations, plus a
South Indian eatery called Tiffin)

Foods of India
121 Lexington Avenue
New York, NY 10016
(212) 683-4419

Kalustyan's
123 Lexington Avenue
New York, NY 10016
(212) 685-3451, (800) 352-3451
www.kalustyans.com

Patel Brothers
2600 West Devon Avenue
Chicago, IL 60631
(773) 262-7777, (773) 764-1857
www.patelbros.com

(The above location in Chicago is their
flagship store, they have stores all over
the U.S.—see website for locations.)

Asia Imports, Inc.
1840 Central Avenue NE
Minneapolis, MN 55418
(612) 788-4571
www.asiaimportsinc.com

**SOME GOOD ONLINE RE-
SOURCES FOR INDIAN INGRE-
DIENTS ARE:**

Vanns Spices, Ltd.
www.vannsspices.com
In addition to the website, their
spices are available at gourmet
food stores throughout the country
(check website for locations).

Penzeys Spices
www.penzeys.com
In addition to the website, their
spices are available at gourmet
food stores throughout the country
(check website for locations).

Morton and Bassett Spices
www.mortonbassett.com

Shop Indian
www.ishopindian.com

Spice Sage
www.myspicesage.com

Ethnic Grocer
www.theethnicgrocer.com

Indian Blend
www.indianblend.com

Indian Foods Company
www.indianfoodsco.com

To locate any Indian grocery store and a
good resource for anything Indian go to:
http://thokalath.com/

Acknowledgments

I enjoyed the process of making *My Indian Kitchen*, and I could not and would not have finished it without the significant influence and inspiration of many people.

Thanks to my mom and dad, who gave me the gift of taste, my talent and passion for cooking and, most of all, the freedom to follow my passion for good food. And to my wonderful, loving family, who support and motivate me to pursue my dreams and realize my passion and love for cooking.

And to all the wonderful and talented people who helped put this cookbook together, including everyone at Tuttle Publishing, especially Holly Jennings, my editor, for her stellar advice and longstanding support, and Eric Oey, who guided me and the vision for this book. A big thank you to Jaden Hair, blogger and author of *The Steamy Kitchen Cookbook*, who connected me to Holly, which lead to making my vision a reality. I'd like to thank Sambrita Basu, a dear friend and a gifted writer who was always there a phone call away to help me voice some of my thoughts into words that are in the book today.

The talented photographer Jack Turkel, who skillfully made my vision for the food and settings come alive in the photographs, and for making the food look luscious.

The teachers and mentors at the hotel management school in Manipal, India, and also at the Culinary Institute of America, for teaching me the discipline and fundamentals of cooking.

There are many more people, friends and mentors that I would like to thank, but can't possibly fit on this page. To them I offer big thanks for their continuous support and belief in me.

Index

A

Aachari Gosht 119
Aam Ki Baraf Malai 143
Adrak Masala Chai 153
Adraki Gobhi 86
ajwain seeds 35
Almond Butter Cookies 148
almond flour 148
almonds 42, 57, 118, 126, 128, 148, 149
Akhroth aur Hara Phool Gobi ka Soop 66
Aloo aur Anardana ki Chaat 56
Aloo aur Makki ki Tikki 52
Aloo Paratha 139
Aloo Pudina Pulao 133
amchoor 35
apple 57, 150
Aromatic Spice Mix 33
Asafetida 23, 35, 67, 91
Asian chili powder or cayenne pepper 23, 34, 35, 41, 42, 43, 46, 47, 51, 52, 53, 58, 61, 68, 69, 70, 73, 74, 75, 79, 80, 85, 86, 87, 88, 97, 98, 101, 102, 103, 108, 112, 115, 119, 126
Avocado and Roasted Cumin Raita 44
avocadoes 44

B

Baingan Bharta 84
Baingan ki Chutney 54
Baked Garlic Naan 134
baking powder 61, 134, 146, 148
Basmati Rice with Whole Spices 132
bay leaves 23, 35, 53, 66, 67, 115, 126, 128
Beans Poriyal 82
beef 53, 116
beet 46
bell pepper 57, 81, 85, 90, 101, 103
Bengali Aloo 81
Bengali Bhuni Macchi 104
Bengali Potatoes with Spices 81
Bhindi Subzi 87
Bhuna Masala 33
Bhuna Masala Murg 109
Bhuni Lamb Chops 121
Bhuni Masala Macchli 97
Bhuni Pulao 130
Bhutta 79
Black-Eyed Peas and Rice 127
Black-Eyed Peas with Mushrooms 72
bread, naan, pita 117
broccoli florets 66, 80
Broccoli Soup with Walnuts 66
butter 41, 66, 70, 75, 110, 112, 139, 147, 148

C

cabbage 130
cashew 126
Cardamom Apple Kheer 149
cardamom pods 23, 33, 34, 35, 41, 42, 53, 66, 115, 118, 125, 126, 128, 132, 147, 153
ground cardamom 144, 145, 148, 149, 152
Carrot Yogurt Slaw 46
carrots 46, 78, 80, 130
cauliflower 86
florets 80
Cauliflower with Ginger and Cumin 86
celery seeds 31
Chai Crème Brûlée 147
Chaat Masala 35
Chapati 136
chicken breasts 108
chicken drumsticks 108
chicken thighs 109
chicken, boneless pieces 110
chicken, whole 110, 112, 115, 128
Chicken Curry in a Hurry 109
Chicken Tikka Masala 111
Chili Shrimp with Curry Leaves and Coconut 103
Chukandar aur Annanas Raita 46
Chana Masala 69
chili peppers 23
fresh green chili peppers 23, 35, 39, 40, 43, 45, 46, 50, 52, 53, 54, 55, 57, 58, 60, 61, 62, 67, 68, 69, 70, 73, 74, 75, 78, 80, 84, 85, 90, 91, 98, 101, 105, 109, 110, 112, 115, 116, 117, 118, 120, 121, 125, 126, 128, 131, 133, 139
dried red chili peppers 23, 32, 34, 38, 40, 43, 47, 67, 69, 74, 80, 82, 84, 90, 98, 103, 116, 119, 129, 130, 131
dried red pepper flakes 23, 56
cinnamon 24, 32, 33, 34, 35, 41, 53, 66, 72, 84, 110, 115, 116, 125, 126, 128, 147
cloves 33, 34, 35, 50, 66, 110, 126, 128, 132, 147
ground cloves 118
coconut
coconut milk 24, 71, 78, 102, 105, 110, 125
coconut meat 24
shredded coconut 24, 32, 34, 40, 62, 78, 82, 84, 98, 103, 110, 116
Coconut Chicken Curry 110
Coconut Shrimp Biriyani 125
coriander leaves 24, 35, 40, 42, 44, 45, 46, 50, 52, 53, 54, 55, 57, 58, 60, 61, 62, 67, 68, 69, 71, 72, 73, 74, 75, 78, 80, 84, 86, 89, 90, 91, 94, 98, 99, 100, 101, 103, 108, 109, 110, 115, 117, 120, 121, 125, 126, 128, 130, 131
coriander seeds 24, 32, 33, 34, 35, 38, 52, 53, 58, 61, 69, 72, 73, 86, 90, 95, 102, 108, 116, 117
ground coriander 51, 72, 73, 74, 75, 78, 82, 84, 86, 87, 88, 89, 103, 110, 115, 119, 126
corn 79

corn kernels 52, 85
cornstarch 88, 145
crabs 98
cream 66, 88
cream, heavy 112, 145, 147, 149
cream, sour 118, 121
cream, whipped 143
Creamy Rice Pudding 149
Crispy Masala Fish Fingers 51
Crunchy Potato and Corn Croquettes 52
Cucumber and Onion Chaat 42
Cucumber and Yogurt Raita 45
cucumbers 24, 42, 45, 62, 94
cumin seeds 25, 31, 32, 33, 34, 35, 38, 42, 43, 44, 46, 51, 52, 53, 56, 58, 61, 67, 69, 70, 73, 74, 75, 82, 84, 86, 87, 89, 90, 97, 100, 101, 102, 103, 104, 108, 109, 110, 115, 117, 128, 132, 133, 139
ground cumin 72, 78, 87, 89, 112, 115, 118, 119, 126
curry leaves 25, 34, 39, 40, 43, 46, 47, 50, 60, 67, 74, 78, 82, 84, 91, 98, 102, 103, 105, 110, 116, 129, 131

D

Dal kae Pakorae 60
Dal Palak 71
Dal Shorba 68
Delicious Everyday Dal 74
Desi Limbu Pani 154
Dhaba Dal 70
Dhaba Masala 34
Dhaba Spice 34
dried apricots 42
dried bread crumbs 52, 53, 95
dried green mango powder (amchoor) 35
dried legumes 25
dried chickpeas (kabuli chana) 69
dried red kidney beans (rajmah) 75
dried split lentils 74
mung beans (moong dal) 62, 68
split black gram (urad dal) 70, 73
split green lentils (moong dal) 73
split pigeon peas (toor dal) 67, 71, 73, 89
split red lentils (masoor dal) 68, 73
split yellow peas (chana dal) 56, 60, 68, 73, 129
dried black-eyed peas (lobhiya) 72, 126

E

egg 53, 130, 134, 146
egg yolks 143, 147
eggplants 54, 84
Eracchi Olathiyathu 116

F

fennel seeds 26, 34, 41, 43, 47, 53, 86, 97, 104, 110, 119, 121, 153
fenugreek leaves 26, 69, 80, 88, 90

fenugreek seeds 26, 31, 32, 33, 35, 43, 47, 102, 104
Fiery South Indian Tomato Soup 67
fish steaks (pomfret, cod, kingfish or mackerel) 105
Fish Tikka 94
Five Spice Blackened Salmon 104
Flaky Paratha Breads Stuffed with Potatoes 139
flour
    all-purpose flour 51, 53, 58, 67, 134, 138, 139, 146, 148
    chickpea flour (besan) 61
    rice flour 145
    whole-wheat flour 136, 138
food coloring, red 112
Fragrant Lamb Biriyani 126
Fried Puffed Bread 138
Fruit Chaat 63

G
Gaajar Pachadi 46
Garam Masala 35
garlic 32, 34, 35, 38, 39, 43, 51, 52, 57, 58, 66, 67, 68, 70, 71, 72, 73, 74, 78, 80, 82, 88, 89, 90, 100, 102, 103, 108, 109, 110, 112, 115, 116, 117, 118, 119, 121, 125, 126, 128, 130, 134
garlic powder 33, 34, 104
Garlic and Peanut Chutney 39
ghee (clarified butter) 26, 67, 73, 84, 126, 128, 132, 136, 139
ginger 26, 32, 34, 35, 40, 42, 51, 52, 60, 61, 66, 67, 68, 69, 70, 73, 74, 78, 80, 82, 84, 86, 90, 102, 103, 108, 109, 110, 112, 115, 116, 117, 118, 119, 121, 125, 126, 128, 130, 133, 151, 153
Ginger Cardamom Chai 153
Ginger Lemonade 154
ginger powder 33, 35, 46, 71, 104
Ginger-Garlic Paste 32
Goa ki Squid Kari 102
Goan Jhinga Biriyani 125
Goan-Style Squid 102
golden raisins 42, 126, 149
grapefruit juice 150
grapes 150
    green grapes 63
    red grapes 63
green beans 78, 80, 82, 130
Green Chili Masala 35
Green Mango Pickle 47
green onions (scallions) 46, 80, 102, 130
green peas 58, 78, 91, 130

H
Hara Mirch Masala 35
Harae Aam ki Chutney 47
Home-Style Garam Masala 35
honey 56, 148
Huli Anna 129
Hyderabadi hara Subzi 78
Hyderabadi Mixed Vegetables 78

I
Indian Five Spice Mix 31
Indian Fried Rice 130
Indian Grilling and Roasting Rub 33
Indian ingredients 22
    Storage tips 22
Indian Lemonade 154
Indian-Style Lentil Soup 68

J
Jhinga ka salaad 57
Jhinga Kebab 99
Jhinga Nariyal 103

K
Kaddu Narialwalla 84
Kadhai Anda 90
Kadhai Paneer 90
Kallumakai Varuthathu 100
Kerala Coconut Beef 116
Khadai Jhinga 103
Kheema Biriyani 126
Kheer 149
Kheera aur Mung Dal ka Salaad 62
Kheera Pyaz ka Chaat 42
Kheera Raita 45
Khubani Chutney 42
Kori Ghassi 110
Kozi Varuval 114

L
Lal Mirch Masala 32
lamb 53, 58, 115, 117, 118, 119, 121, 126
Lasooni Naan 134
Lemon and Saffron Chicken Kebabs 108
Lemon Rice with Peanuts 129
lemons 57, 62, 82, 87, 94, 104, 108, 112, 129, 150
lemon juice 50, 51, 56, 57, 69, 70, 83, 103, 108, 118, 121, 126, 129
lemon zest 108
lettuce 99
limes 55, 112, 121, 150
lime juice 35, 39, 42, 44, 46, 63, 96, 97, 99, 100, 101, 102, 119, 128, 151, 154
lime zest 96
Lobhiya Khumb Masala 72
Lobhiya Pulao 127

M
Macchi Kae Pakorae 50
Macchi ke Tikke 94
mace 27, 34, 128
Madras Chicken 114
mahi mahi steaks 94
Makhanphal aur Bhuna Jeera Raita 44
Makki Khumb Masala 85
Malabar Crab Curry 98
Malabari Kekda Kari 98
Mangalore Aloo Masala 91
Mangalore Fish Curry 105
Mangalore Meen Kari 105
Mangalore Spiced Potatoes 91
mango juice 63
mango pulp or purée 145

mangoes 27, 41, 47, 63, 119, 143, 152
Marinated Roast Leg of Lamb 118
Masala-Baked Red Snapper 96
Masala-Crusted Tilapia 97
Masala Lamb Chops 121
Masala Pappadums 55
Masala Spiced Lassi 152
Masala Zucchini aur Dal ki Subzi 89
Masaladar dal Lahsooni 74
Masaladar Oven ki Macchi 96
mint leaves 27, 33, 39, 42, 45, 46, 51, 56, 63, 101, 121, 128, 132, 133, 142, 151
Mint Lime Cooler 151
milk, low-fat or whole milk 83, 134, 143, 145, 149, 153
Mint Chutney 39
Mint Rice with Potatoes and Toasted Cumin 133
Mitha Aam Chutney 41
Moong-Phalli aur Lahssun ki Chutney 39
Mumbai Fruit Punch 150
Mumbai Thandai 150
Mung Dal and Cucumber Salad 62
Murg Kali Mirch 108
Murg Tandoori 112
Murg Tikka Masala 110
Murg Zafrani Kebab 108
mushrooms 85
    button mushrooms 72
Mushrooms and Corn in a Spicy Curry 85
mussels 100
mustard seeds 27, 34, 58
    black mustard seeds 31, 38, 39, 40, 43, 46, 47, 50, 62, 67, 71, 82, 91, 98, 103, 104, 116, 129, 131

N
Nariyal ki Chutney 40
Nawabi Mugh Biriyani 128
nigella seeds 31
Northern Chickpea Curry 69

O
olive oil, extra-virgin 50, 56, 101
oil and fats 27
okra 87
onion 42, 43, 54, 58, 61, 66, 68, 69, 70, 73, 81, 84, 85, 86, 87, 89, 98, 102, 105, 109, 110, 115, 116, 118, 120, 125, 126, 128, 130, 133, 139
    red onion 38, 55, 56, 57, 60, 71, 72, 75, 78, 84, 94, 100, 101, 103, 110, 115, 119
orange juice 150
orange zest, grated 146
oranges 63, 99, 150

P
Palak ka Soop 67
Palak Paneer Kofta 88
Panch Phoran 31
Pancharatni Dal Fry 73
paneer cheese 52
Paneer Cheese 83
    Flavored Paneer Cheese 83
Panner Kae Kebab 52

pappadums 54
paprika 28, 38, 72, 84, 89, 104, 110, 112
peanuts 39, 55, 129, 131
Pepper Chicken 108
pepper, black 108, 120, 151
pepper, white 67, 88
peppercorns 28
peppercorns, black 32, 33, 34, 35, 38, 42, 44, 46, 66, 67, 100, 108, 115, 116, 125, 132, 147
pineapple 46, 63, 101, 150
pineapple juice 150
Pineapple and Beet Raita 46
Pissa Adrak Lahsoon 32
Pista Aaam Ki Kulfi 145
Pistachio Biscotti 146
Pistachio Lassi 152
Pistachio Mango Ice Cream 145
pistachios 144, 145, 146
Phal ki Chaat 63
Plain Basmati Rice 124
Plain Naan and Flavored Naan 134
Plum Tomato Chutney with Mustard Seeds 38
Pomegranate and Mint Potato Salad 56
pomegranate seeds 56, 63
Poondu Kolumbu 43
Poori 138
pork, leg or shoulder 120
pork, tenderloins 119
Pork Vindaloo 120
Potato and Onion Fritters 61
potatoes 52, 56, 58, 61, 78, 80, 81, 88, 91, 120, 133, 139
Pudina Limbu Sharbat 153
Pudine ki Chutney
Puliogare 131
pumpkin 84
Pumpkin with Coconut 84
Puréed Spinach with Cheese Balls 88

R

Raan Masaledar 118
Rajmah Masala 75
Rasam 67
Raspberry Lemonade 154
Red Kidney Bean Curry 75
Red Masala Paste 32
rice 28
    basmati rice 124, 125, 126, 128, 129, 132, 133, 149
    long-grain white rice 130
rosewater 28, 142, 144

S

Saada Chaaval 124
Saada Pulao 132
saffron 28, 35, 108, 112, 128, 144
Saffron Chicken Biriyani 128
salmon fillets 95, 104
Salmon Kebabs 95
salt 29, 33, 34, 38, 39, 40, 41, 42, 44, 45, 46, 47, 51, 52, 54, 55, 56, 57, 58, 60, 61, 62, 66, 67, 68, 70, 71, 72, 73, 74, 78, 79, 80, 81, 82, 84, 85, 86, 87, 88, 89, 90, 91, 94, 96, 97, 98,

99, 100, 101, 102, 103, 104, 105, 108, 109, 110, 112, 115, 116, 117, 118, 120, 121, 124, 125, 126, 128, 129, 130, 131, 132, 133, 134, 136, 138, 139
    black salt 29
    sea salt 35, 79
Salted Lassi 152
Samosas Three Ways 58
scallops 101
sesame seeds 29, 39, 46,
sesame seeds, black 71
shallots 50, 78, 131
shrimp 50, 57, 99, 103, 125
Shrimp and Apple Salad 57
Shrimp Bruschetta 50
Shrikhand 144
Smoky Eggplant Dip 54
Smoky Fire-Roasted Eggplant 84
snapper, red 96
South Indian Coconut Chutney 40
soy sauce 102, 103, 130
sparkling water or club soda 151, 154
Spicy and Fragrant Lamb Curry 119
Spiced Garlic 43
Spiced Meatballs 53
Spicy Apricot Chutney 42
Spicy Coconut Green Beans 82
Spicy Lamb Burgers 117
Spicy Mixed Beans and Lentils 73
Spicy Paneer Cheese Kebabs 52
Spicy Scallops with Grilled Pineapple Chutney 101
Spicy Urad Beans 70
spinach 58, 60, 61, 67, 68, 71, 88
Spinach Soup 67
Split Pea Fritters 60
squid 102
star anise 29, 33, 110
Stir-Fried Okra 87
Stir-Fried Paneer Cheese with Bell Peppers 90
Stir-Fried Shrimp 103
Stir-Fried Telicherry Mussels 100
Stir-Fried Vegetables with Yogurt 80
Street-Style Grilled Corn on the Cob 79
Subz Jhalfrazie 80
sugar 34, 35, 39, 41, 42, 94, 120, 134, 142, 143, 144, 145, 146, 147, 148, 149, 151, 152, 153, 154
    confectioners' sugar 148
    light brown sugar 33, 41, 84, 118
Sukka Kofta 53
Sweet Mango Chutney 41
Sweet Mango Yogurt Lassi 152
Sweet Mangoes in a Creamy Custard 143
Sweetened Yogurt with Saffron and Pistachios 144
swordfish 94

T

tamarind 29, 32, 39, 40, 43, 67
Tamarind Rice 131
tamarind paste 105, 131
Tamatar Sarso ki Chutney 38
Tandoori Chicken 112

tandoori seasoning, store-bought 99
Tandoori Skewered Shrimp 99
Tarbuj ki Baraf 142
tea leaves/bags, black 147, 153
Techniques
    Simple Techniques 16
    Browning 19
    Deep-frying (Talna) 17
    Roasting (Bhunnana) 18
    Roasting and Grinding of Spices 16
    Sautéing (Bhunao) 17
    Steaming (Dum) 19
    Tempering (Tarkhka) 18
tilapia 97
tomatoes 42, 43, 45, 54, 55, 57, 67, 68, 69, 70, 71, 72, 73, 75, 80, 81, 84, 85, 86, 98, 100, 105, 110, 115, 119, 125, 126
    plum tomatoes 38
    red cherry tomatoes 56
tomato paste 38, 58, 70, 103, 109, 110
tomato purée 53, 57, 70, 88, 90, 110, 120
Tools
    Some Helpful Tools 20
    Cast-iron skillets and griddles 20
    Electric blender 20
    Electric food processor 21
    Electric spice grinder or coffee grinder 21
    Kadhai, kadai, kadahi, karhai or karahi 21
    Mortar and pestle 21
turmeric 29, 32
    ground turmeric 34, 43, 46, 47, 50, 58, 67, 70, 72, 73, 74, 78, 80, 82, 86, 87, 88, 89, 91, 98, 100, 102, 103, 108, 109, 115, 116, 119, 125, 126, 129, 131

V

vanilla bean 147
vanilla extract, pure 143
Vindaloo Curry Paste 34
Vindaloo Masala 34
vinegar
    malt vinegar 41, 112, 120
    red wine vinegar 34
    white vinegar 38

W

walnuts 66
watermelon 99, 142, 150
Watermelon Lemonade 154
Watermelon Mint Ice 142
Whole Wheat Griddle Breads 136
wine, dry sparkling 150

Y

yeast, active dry 134
Yellow Mung Beans with Spinach 71
yogurt 29, 44, 45, 46, 52, 53, 54, 62, 80, 103, 108, 110, 112, 115, 118, 121, 126, 128, 134, 144, 152

Z

Zucchini 80, 89
Zucchini with Lentils and Roasted Garlic 89